WASHINGTON'S DARK SECRET

WASHINGTON'S DARK SECRET

THE REAL TRUTH ABOUT TERRORISM AND ISLAMIC EXTREMISM

JOHN MASZKA

POTOMAC BOOKS
An imprint of the University of Nebraska Press

Chapter 7, "From Bin Laden to Baghdadi,"
appears as chapter 2 in *Al-Shabaab and
Boko Haram: Strategic Terrorism or Guerrilla
Insurgency?* (Hackensack NJ: World Scientific,
2018). Used with permission from World
Scientific Publishing Co. Pte. Ltd.

Library of Congress Cataloging-in-Publication Data
Names: Maszka, John, 1963– author.
Title: Washington's dark secret: the real truth about
terrorism and Islamic extremism / John Maszka.
Description: Lincoln: Potomac Books, an imprint
of the University of Nebraska Press, [2018] |
Includes bibliographical references and index.
Identifiers: LCCN 2017060419
ISBN 9781640120242 (cloth: alkaline paper)
ISBN 9781640121096 (epub)
ISBN 9781640121102 (mobi)
ISBN 9781640121119 (pdf)
Subjects: LCSH: Terrorism. | Islamic
fundamentalism. | Natural resources—Political
aspects. | United States—Politics and government.
Classification: LCC HV6431 .M3785 2018 | DDC
363.325—dc23 LC record available at
https://lccn.loc.gov/2017060419

Set in Charis by E. Cuddy.
Designed by N. Putens.

*For my little boys Rohi and Taavi and
my amazing wife (and best friend), May.
I thank God for you every day.*

CONTENTS

PREFACE

This book is written for intelligent, socially conscious people who refuse to accept everything they're told at face value. Regardless of your profession, your level of education, your race, your ethnicity, or your religion, if you're a critical thinker, then this book is written for you.

Books in general—and particularly books on terrorism or Islamic extremism—tend to fall within a certain predetermined style or genre. The author's approach is often singular, following a well-trodden path that is easy to navigate. Books such as these tend to require less imagination from either the writer or the reader, so it shouldn't be all that surprising that many of these books also tend to be, well, let's just say, unimaginative.

Rather than follow the well-trodden path, I've chosen to blaze a new trail. In the pages that follow, I pursue a fairly ambitious agenda. As a terrorism scholar, I'm all too aware of the shortcomings of my discipline—and I detail several of them in this book. I also reveal many of the myths surrounding Islamic extremism and particularly the misnomer "Islamic terrorism." However, this book is more than a mere exposé of the field of terrorism studies.

Much of the book's content deals with two of the world's most infamous Islamic militant organizations—al-Qaeda and the Islamic State—as well as the state and corporate powers that brought them into being. As I'll demonstrate, both groups are acting strategically toward the reestablishment of a global caliphate. Yet the strategies these groups employ are polar opposites of each another.

As we progress through the chapters, we'll explore both the similarities and the differences of these two groups. As we do so, it will become apparent that neither of these organizations exist in a vacuum—each one has grown out of a complex cultural and historical context. It will also become clear that in order to comprehend these groups and their strategic objectives, one needs to have a working knowledge of the economic and political circumstances in which they've emerged—as well as the cultural lens through which they interpret those conditions.

As a terrorism scholar, I employ strategic theory to better understand the goal(s) of those I study. Strategic theory, in turn, requires an in-depth understanding of the individuals or groups under examination. One side of this coin consists of objective fact such as the historical and political context in which the violence occurs as well as the perpetrator's socioeconomic position within that context. Objective fact paints only half of the picture, however.

Often it's possible to glean enough information from the historical and political context to determine what an actor's strategic goal is, but one is still left guessing about other important considerations. The opposite side of the coin is subjective in nature, requiring insight concerning how actors view themselves and those around them. For example, al-Qaeda and the Islamic State share the same strategic goal of establishing an Islamic caliphate, yet they employ very different tactics in pursuit of this goal. They also target different victims. Why?

The answer to this question requires subjective information that sheds light in the shadows. Only by attempting to view these actors and the world through their eyes rather than our own can we begin to see a more complete picture.

A component of this analysis is the theory of perception of the other. Strategy is the use of one's resources toward the attainment of one's goals. Therefore, how an actor perceives its own resources vis-à-vis the resources of another plays as large a role as the strategic goal itself. Perception also plays a huge role both in the decision to engage in violence and in the way targets and victims respond.

Anyone even remotely familiar with the Holocaust has been confronted with the disturbing compliance demonstrated by both those who collaborated with the Nazis and their victims. Fear of punishment (along with at least some sense of racial superiority) explains much of the former behavior, but how do we explain the passive acceptance displayed by millions of Jews as they faced their own extermination? Objective fact alone provides few answers to such questions.

An equally disturbing question has arisen in more recent years. Why do groups such as the Islamic State and others target fellow Muslims? Even more puzzling is why startling numbers of Westerners have accepted the call to join them. Perception of the other affords us a measure of insight into these challenging realities and is therefore indispensable for understanding how to interpret each group's actions as a means for obtaining their respective goals.

Because everyone shares the disadvantage of viewing the world through a unique cultural lens (however difficult that may be to identify), the larger message of this book is one of reform. Reform of what? Reform of the way people look at themselves, at one another, and also at the world around them.

Throughout history the human race has been graced (and cursed) by the legacy of a myriad of ideas and reforms. On the systemic level, we have religion and philosophy. From the Hindu caste system and Buddhism's oneness with the universe to capitalism, Marxism, and even anarchism, a variety of abstractions have informed how people order society. Beyond these other distinctions such as polytheism, monotheism, collectivism, and individualism all serve to shape and define the great civilizations of the earth.

Which is right and which is wrong? Humans have spilled oceans of blood over these very questions. Millions have fought and died in the war of us versus them. This epic struggle is arguably the world's first and oldest conflict, pitting brother against brother, father against son, and nation against nation. While battles have been won and lost, the quest for answers continues because, for the most part, we're asking the wrong questions.

For all of humanity's "nasty, brutish and short" span of history, a plethora of artists, musicians, writers, and thinkers has attempted to enlighten our path.[1] André Breton founded surrealism, which—in addition to inspiring the genius of Salvador Dali, Frida Kahlo, and Pablo Picasso—revolutionized the way we celebrate the human experience. Likewise, Renaissance composers challenged the expressive austerity of the medieval period, while Baroque composers such as Bach, Handel, and Vivaldi captured the very essence of life, joy, and pain with astonishing textual clarity.

In the world of literature, romanticism broke the shackles of aristocratic hegemony. Later, transcendentalists such as Emerson and Thoreau exercised this freedom by venturing beyond the walls of society into the realm of nature to explore the limits of imagination and the power of ideas.

The list goes on and on. The Greeks gave us democracy, Franklin gave us electricity, and Luther gave us his ninety-five theses. While I don't claim to offer any reality-shattering new discovery, I do hope to shatter some aspects of our current reality—particularly the illusion of us versus them.

This book is an eclectic mixture of exposé, political and social commentary, forensics, and strategic analysis. It's an ambitious interdisciplinary project that attempts both to address the origins of Islamic extremism and terrorism and to understand these very separate issues in all their complexity—while at the same time offering a parsimonious approach to distinguishing one from the other. It also contains autobiographical accounts of my experiences in the field along with a few of the lessons I've learned along the way. Much of this book was written between 2016 and 2017 when the Islamic State was at its height. Nevertheless, the observations that I've applied are still applicable to terrorism studies in general, even though the group itself has waned considerably since the time of this writing.

I don't think it necessary to write like an academic to produce an important piece of scholarship. Therefore, my use of contractions and anecdotal digressions are intentional literary devices. I'm reminded of a conversation I once had with a colleague from Purdue University. We were discussing Jessica Stern over a late-evening dinner at Panda Express. I greatly admire Dr. Stern as both a scholar and a writer; however, this particular colleague kept insisting that her writing was "weird."

Interjected between mouthfuls of noodles and walnut shrimp, his words were as pointed as his chopsticks. "She writes like a novelist," he snorted sarcastically, chewing his breath with his food. "Who cares what color people's eyes are?"

I can only hope that this book will merit an equally caustic review.

INTRODUCTION

THE NOTORIOUS D. J. TRUMP

Never believe anything until it has been officially denied.

—Anonymous

Donald Trump is an anomaly—a man who claims to say what everyone is thinking but doesn't seem to care what anyone thinks. From his blatant degradation of women to his infamously unpopular position on minorities, immigration, and even global warming—the temperature goes up, it goes down, it goes up . . . it's called weather!—the world loves to hate Donald Trump.

While this book isn't about Donald Trump, it is about the political and economic forces that led to his triumph. No, not the dysfunctional Electoral College, illegal immigrants, wiretapping, the Kremlin, or fake news—the *real* forces behind his success. As we'll discover, the election victory of a billionaire Washington outsider signifies much more than the media is willing to tell us. Why? Because the powers that be—the true puppet masters who own the media outlets, the oil companies, the banks, and everything else—don't want people to know that they've committed the crime of the century.

But the curtain has finally fallen, and the truth is revealed: the American two-party system is broken. The Democratic and the Republican Parties have converged to the point that what little difference exists between them is nominal at best. Multinational corporations have taken over, and Washington insiders are finally exposed as the hired guns that they are. Mega-conglomerates use international laws and organizations to create cartels and monopolies, but when need be, they're not above good old-fashioned colonialism. And Washington is always there with its mercenary military force—ready and willing to fight on behalf of the highest bidder.

The international community is terrified. Will Trump enact real change? How could he possibly? The neocolonial corporate powers that run the world would never allow it. And let's not forget that Trump is a billionaire himself, so he doesn't exactly have an incentive to change the neoliberal world order. He's putting on a great show, but if he begins to take himself too seriously he's likely to suffer the same fate as those who refused to play the game before him—Mossadegh, Allende, Hussein, Gaddafi, and all the others—eliminated by that gang of corporate hit men known as the CIA.

What does neoliberalism have to do with the Global War on Terrorism (GWOT)? How did Islamic extremism become Washington's greatest threat? What brought about this sad state of affairs, and what will it take to change it? These are the questions this book attempts to address.

ABBREVIATIONS

AEI	American Enterprise Institute
AIOC	Anglo-Iranian Oil Company
APOC	Anglo-Persian Oil Company
AQI	al-Qaeda in Iraq
ARAMCO	Arabian-American Oil Company
DPG	Defense Policy Guidance
GATT	General Agreement on Tariffs and Trade
GDP	gross domestic product
GNP	gross national product
GWOT	Global War on Terrorism
IMF	International Monetary Fund
IRA	Irish Republican Army
IS	Islamic State
ISI	Islamic State of Iraq
ISIL	Islamic State of Iraq and the Levant
ISIS	Islamic State of Iraq and al-Sham
JN	Jabhat al-Nusra

JTJ	Jamāʿat al-Tawḥīd wa-al-Jihād
MNC	multinational corporation
MP	military police
MSM	Majlis Shura al-Mujahedin (Mujahidin Shura Council)
NAFTA	North American Free Trade Agreement
NATO	North Atlantic Treaty Organization
NGO	nongovernmental organization
NIE	National Intelligence Estimate
NIU	Northern Illinois University
NSC	National Security Council
NSS	*National Security Strategy*
OPEC	Organization of the Petroleum Exporting Countries
PLO	Palestinian Liberation Organization
TPP	Trans-Pacific Partnership
UN	United Nations
UNITAF	Unified Taskforce
WB	World Bank
WMD	weapons of mass destruction
WTO	World Trade Organization

WASHINGTON'S DARK SECRET

CHAPTER ONE

WHO'S THE ENEMY?

I see God in every human being.

—Mother Teresa

The Tree of Life

The famous Persian poet Rumi once told the story of a king who sent his servant to find the tree of life and bring him back some of its fruit. The servant searched for months throughout every corner of the king's realm, but never found the tree of life. Exhausted and ashamed, the servant decided to give up and return to the king empty-handed.

On his way back, he saw a hill and remembered that a wise man lived at the top. The servant climbed the hill and inquired about the tree of life.

"What you are looking for exists," the wise man assured him. "Your mistake was to try to find a form with a name."

Smiling, he gently placed his hand on the servant's shoulder. "Go back and tell the king that he need not worry about finding the fruit from some magic tree. Rather, instruct him to be fair and just to his people. If he does this, no one will ever forget him."

In many ways the current understanding of sensational violence is like the search for the tree of life. People see coverage on the news and just accept that it is what the mainstream media and politicians tell them it is—never once considering that it may be something else entirely.

People have a certain idea in their heads, so they see the Islamic State behind every attack. Meanwhile, rather than governing with justice and integrity, policy makers appropriate billions to fight an enemy that doesn't even exist—at least not in the form that's been popularized by the mainstream media. In the process they victimize the world's most vulnerable, trample on human rights, and then wonder why they're held in contempt. The situation is so ridiculous that it would actually be comical if it weren't so dire.

The Boston Marathon Bombings

When the Boston Marathon bombings occurred in April 2013, I was the director of international relations at a university in Tokmok, Kyrgyzstan. Like many things in this world, Tokmok is both beautiful and harsh at the same time. The city is landlocked by sharp, exquisite mountain ranges, so living there is hard and life itself is a miracle. The people are warm and proud and strong. They love foreigners, yet they're always a little suspicious of strangers.

In Kyrgyz the word *tokmok* means punishment. At one time Stalin exiled political dissidents to this place (the fortunate ones, anyway). In fact Stalin displaced the entire Chechen population after Hitler invaded the Soviet Union in a desperate bid for oil.[1] Suspecting the Chechens of collaborating with the Nazis, Uncle Joe deported them en masse to Central Asia. The Tsarnaev family was among them.

Chechnya has a long history of resistance against its Russian occupiers.[2] The region that today is known as the Caucasus had been in dispute between the Persian and the Russian empires since 1796, changing hands in a series of territorial conflicts. Chechnya was eventually ceded to Russia in 1813, but the Chechens didn't take too kindly to the new arrangement. Their story has since been one of suffering and a bloody struggle against foreign occupation.[3]

The Chechens were allowed to return to their homeland in the 1950s under Khrushchev's de-Stalinization program, but oil remained a contentious issue. To this day Chechnya is a major front in Russia's war on terror.[4] Following the two devastating Chechen wars, the region continues to be a tinderbox as East and West vie for access and control of its vital resource.[5]

The two Tsarnaev brothers who were accused of committing the Boston Marathon bombings had gone to elementary school at a madrassa right down the road from my office. *Madrassa,* of course, is simply the Arabic word for school (in Russian, *schkola*). However, after 9/11 the word has taken on a diabolical connotation as a breeding center for Islamic terrorists.

For the first few weeks after the attacks, the community expressed genuine fear that the United States would retaliate with a drone strike. In the people's eyes America was the real threat, not the two Tsarnaev boys, whom most still remembered as children who grew up among them. To this day many insist that the two brothers were framed.

One of my students at the university had a sister who worked for a nongovernmental organization (NGO) in Afghanistan. He had grown accustomed to checking in on her frequently and was all too familiar with the reality (and frequency) of U.S. drone strikes against civilian targets.

That very same month, the Islamic State of Iraq (ISI) entered Syria, claimed control of vast oil fields, and changed its name to the Islamic State of Iraq and al-Sham (ISIS). ISIS changed its name again to the Islamic State of Iraq and the Levant (ISIL), and on June 29, 2014, the group officially became the Islamic State (IS) after announcing the establishment of a new caliphate.[6]

Given these events the world largely forgot about the Boston Marathon bombings, but I never forgot the feeling of living and working so close to ground zero of a potential U.S. target. Every day as I walked past Schkola no. 1 before and after work, the school-age children would run up to me, laughing and wanting to practice their English. My wife and I knew many of them personally as we used to give free English lessons at the library every Saturday. I tried not to think about the fact that the entire school and the surrounding blocks could be eliminated—in the blink of an eye—by someone sitting behind a simulator with a cup of coffee seven thousand miles away. But I knew better.

David Koresh and the Branch Davidians

The single most common question I'm asked is "Why do you study terrorism?" I guess the best response is that I don't study terrorism—I study people. After all, it isn't the violence per se that's interesting (although violence certainly attracts the media); it's the people behind the violence that fascinate me.

I had originally thought that I wanted to study literature. After enrolling in a PhD program, I quickly realized that reading about other people's experiences would never be enough—I needed my own adventures. You know what they say though . . . be careful what you wish for.

Studying people is a lot like walking on the beach—you never know what's going to wash up. I learned this lesson during my first ethnographic study when I lived with David Koresh and the Branch Davidians.

Two friends of mine had joined the sect a few months earlier. Moved by Koresh's charisma, they exclaimed, "We've found the Messiah! David Koresh from Waco, Texas."

"Can any good thing come from Waco?" I replied skeptically.

"Come and see!"

The next thing I knew, I was on a plane. At that time the Branch Davidians had three compounds: one in Waco, one in Los Angeles, and one in Honolulu. My two friends invited me to come and stay with them in Honolulu. Little did I realize that they had over a dozen roommates (and another dozen or so sect members lived in the apartment next door).

At first the sect seemed like a tight-knit group—all true believers and fiercely loyal to Koresh. But things are not always as they seem. It turned out that one of the "members" was only staying there for the cheap rent. He wasn't at all convinced by Koresh and his message concerning the soon-approaching apocalypse. Still, this particular individual was remarkably well-informed regarding Koresh's plans.

He revealed to me that the groups in LA and Honolulu were planning to move to Waco, where the sect would prepare for the end. The Branch Davidians believed that, like the Levites in the days of Moses, God was about to command them to slay the wicked—beginning with the members of the Christian churches. He also told me that I should get out of there before I got killed: "Some of these nutcases are just itching to start killing."

I decided to take his advice seriously, but there was someone I needed to take with me. Another member—a Samoan woman in her late teens who had recently joined the group. She confided in me that she had been trying to contact her father because she was frightened and wanted to go home. The newer members were all monitored very closely, however, and no one was allowed to leave.

We plotted our escape, and the next day we simply ran away. Several sect members chased us, but we were able to dodge them in the crowded streets. Ducking inside a busy pizza parlor, we ordered a pie and called her father. The group packed up and moved to Waco soon afterward, and the rest is history. To the best of my knowledge, everyone in the Honolulu group died except the two members mentioned above. It still makes me sad.

Were they terrorists? No. They had no political aspirations. They weren't attempting to obtain concessions from the government or provoke a reaction. They simply believed that they were "wave sheaves"—first fruits of God—and that they would be instrumental in ushering in the apocalypse. They were no more terrorists than the school shooter at Northern Illinois University (NIU) who killed himself along with five others and wounded twenty-one more.

The Saint Valentine's Day Massacre

Most people don't remember the NIU shooting because, let's be honest, there have been so many it's hard to keep track of them all. I remember it though. I was on campus that day. It was the fourteenth of February 2008—Valentine's Day. The air was filled with the expectation of gifts and love and romance. But no one expected a jaded ex-boyfriend to seek revenge by opening fire on an auditorium full of students.

The scene was surreal. First the gunshots, then the screaming and the blood . . . and then the helicopters arrived. For some reason the sound of the helicopters hovering above us stuck in my mind. Like the shutter on a camera, their propellers sliced the frenzied motion on the ground below into still-life mementos—isolating each second one from the next. They were like a swarm of locusts feeding on the story, and we were the main course.

When you go into shock, your mind shuts down. You're still conscious, but every moment occurs in a vacuum. Nothing seems connected to anything else. The tinted glasses through which you normally view reality are torn from your eyes, and for a brief moment you experience every sensation in its purest form. The clarity is beyond description, and yet you don't feel anything at all.

I recall students running and screaming—and others lying perfectly still. Before I was able to wrap my mind around what had happened, it was over. The entire campus was on lockdown for over a week—held under siege by a battalion of police investigators and news helicopters. I found out later that one of my interns was killed in the attack.

The shooter wasn't a terrorist. Whatever he wanted, it wasn't political concessions. If it was attention he craved, he certainly received it. It's truly unfortunate that the media is so willing to make such people into instant celebrities. Some of our young people are literally dying for attention.

The June 2016 shooting at a nightclub in Orlando, Florida, is a case in point. Because it was the worst mass shooting in U.S. history, the media milked all the hype it could get out of the story (which in today's currency is headlines for a few days). This wasn't a terrorist attack, however. What concessions were demanded? Besides, no true IS operative calls 911 and confesses to be a member *during* an attack. This was clearly a case of a disturbed young man seeking his five minutes of fame. Again, the media was more than happy to oblige.

Friends from Afar

I grew up in a small midwestern town in the United States—just about as far from Africa as one can imagine (in every conceivable way). Oddly enough I met Daʿuud (David), my first Somali friend, right there in that same small town. I was a freshman at the university, working the overnight shift at a local Kinko's copy shop, trying to make ends meet. The fall semester had barely just begun.

In the wee hours of the morning, a dark, thin man with bloodshot eyes entered the lobby and moved slowly toward the counter. Articulate and soft-spoken with a flat affect, Daʿuud appeared to be in his midforties. He handed me a thick packet and inquired about sending a fax.

I opened the envelope routinely and began to flip through the pages. "You want to fax *all* of this?" I questioned, glancing up as I passed him a cover sheet.

"Yes," he replied quietly. "I need to fax it to this number here."

The number Daʿuud gave me belonged to the U.S. Embassy in Kenya. The document contained over 150 pages of names, dates, and photos of charred corpses and bodies that had been hacked to pieces. At first I was afraid to ask, but the fax was taking so long that the silence began to feel awkward.

"What happened?" I mumbled under my breath, not realizing that he could hear me.

The pain in his eyes spoke volumes. In a thick Somali accent, he explained that his family had been attacked in their home while they were sleeping. The attackers raped his sisters and brutally hacked several of his brothers to death. Those who managed to escape were scattered and fled on foot to Kenya. One by one the survivors found one another in the huge refugee camp that would become their home for nearly a year.

This had all happened while Da'uud was attending university in the States. Forced to drop out of school, he'd been working three jobs for the past six months: one job to provide for his wife and two children in America; a second job to support his parents and surviving siblings and their children in Kenya; and a third job to pay for the daily faxes.

Da'uud had been applying for refugee status for his family so that they could come to the U.S. and live with him. But the red tape was such that after faxing the documents every day for six months, he'd gotten nowhere.

When the fax finally transmitted, Da'uud reached for his wallet. "$78.50?" he confirmed with the confidence of someone who'd done this many times before.

"No, please," I insisted, pretending to have an employee discount. "Let me take care of it."

An expression that faintly resembled a smile appeared on his face. "You would do that?"

I tried to answer, but the words got stuck in my throat. So I just nodded in the affirmative. Offering a reciprocal nod, he turned to leave. Suddenly a wave of compassion mixed with outrage washed over me.

"W-why don't I just fax the document every night when I come in to work?" The words didn't come out as smoothly as I would have liked, but at least this time I managed to say something.

Da'uud looked stunned. He didn't say a word. I didn't know him, and he didn't know me, but at that very moment we became brothers, and we both knew it. Feeling the need to lighten the mood, I quipped, "Besides, you need to start saving your money for airline tickets."

"Yes," he exhaled, and I finally saw him smile.

Hope is an amazingly powerful force. For the next six months, I actually looked forward to going to work. During that time I poured over the report of his family, staring at their photos and reading the details of their lives until I felt as though I knew them personally.

The attack took place under the cover of an undeclared war—launched by the U.S. against the army of General Muhammad Farah Aideed, a warlord who had been instrumental in toppling the Barre regime.

An alliance of clan militias armed with American and Soviet military-grade weapons drove Barre from power. With Barre out of the way, fighting broke out between the militias themselves as they spewed their venom on each other.[7] Egypt cosponsored a conference in Djibouti in which an interim government was set up, and Ali Mahdi Muhammad (a wealthy hotel proprietor) was named as interim president. Aideed rejected the agreement and took control of the southern part of Mogadishu. Meanwhile, Ali Mahdi retained control of the northern districts. A green line initially divided the two camps, but the civil war disintegrated even further into all-out clan warfare as clans and subclans fought for control over scarce resources.[8]

The civil war posed a serious threat to extensive ongoing oil prospecting operations in Somalia by Conoco, Amoco, Phillips, and Chevron. These American corporations had invested a considerable amount of time and money in Somalia, but the political instability in the region forced three of them to cut their losses and pull out. Only Conoco remained.

The Conoco compound effectively served as the U.S. embassy. Not only did Conoco provide intelligence for the American military; the company also assisted in planning the logistics for the U.S. Marine landing in December 1992.[9] Coincidentally, longtime Washington insider Richard Armitage (former assistant secretary of defense, former deputy secretary of state) also serves on Conoco's board of directors.

While the U.S. originally backed Aideed, it switched sides after one of Aideed's key allies, Omar Jess, lost control of Kismayo. In return Mahdi offered Conoco exclusive oil rights after the war. Thus, the intervention of twenty-eight thousand (mostly American) forces largely turned into a bilateral war between the United States and Aideed's coalition.[10]

The presence of U.S. troops in Somalia attracted al-Qaeda's attention, and the group dispatched operatives to train Somali militants and fight beside them.[11] Al-Qaeda operatives fought in the Battle of Mogadishu (and the infamous Black Hawk Down incident) of October 3, 1993, in which Somali militants killed eighteen U.S. soldiers and paraded their corpses in triumph through the streets of the city.[12] Contrary to popular belief, the infamous Black Hawk Down incident didn't happen because U.S. troops were protecting UN food deliveries. Although the United Task Force (UNITAF, also called Operation Restore Hope) received a UN mandate to establish a safe zone for humanitarian intervention, it wasn't a humanitarian mission at all. Rather it was a botched attempt to safeguard private oil interests. Daʿuud's family just happened to be in the wrong place at the wrong time.

On a particularly cold February morning around 3:00 a.m., an entourage of eight colorfully dressed Somalis passed in front of the Kinko's store window. As they approached the entrance, a strangely familiar young man in his midtwenties emerged through the door.

"Daʿuud?" The words had hardly escaped my lips when his father and mother entered behind him followed by six others. Daʿuud's father stepped toward me. Grasping both of my arms, he squeezed them as tightly as he could.

"*Mahadsanid . . .*" He spoke warmly in a voice that sounded like it was coming from somewhere else. I had never seen a human being so thin and frail, and yet so dignified, in all my life.

These eight people had somehow managed to survive one of the worst humanitarian crises in modern history—something my sheltered American mind couldn't even begin to comprehend. They were survivors. But others wouldn't be so fortunate.

Tombstones

On May 12, 2003, a suicide bomber entered an American military compound in Riyadh and exploded his vehicle near a huge gas tank before going on to paradise. In his wake he left behind a graveyard of sand and ashes. For more than a decade, huge chunks of concrete block served as tombstones—silently standing watch around the perimeter of the blast.

As I approached the site, the midday sun was scorching hot. Like a laser it penetrated the desert sky and created a glare so bright that I could barely keep my eyes open. My retinas literally felt like they were melting. I had entered a restricted area. Like the chocolate factory in

Willie Wonka, no one ever went in, and no one ever came out. But on that particular day, I decided that this would change.

The scene evoked images of a fierce future slaughter in which ancient hatreds would clash with apocalyptic fury. Faithful blades of rebar impaled the enemies of Allah. Like ten thousand arrows in the quiver of al-Qaadir (the All-Powerful One), they had all found their mark. Carnage and obliteration had defeated the forces of the enemy. Together they had laid siege to the former haunt of the Great Satan, now a mere skeleton of warped metal, dust, and shattered glass.

The sight reminded me of endless Saturday mornings I'd spent at catechism in the church basement. And now the dark fears that had haunted me as a boy—purgatory, everlasting punishment, hellfire and brimstone—all returned with a vengeance.

My eyes watered and stung as I squinted in the sandy wind. I hunted for something that might have survived the intense heat—anything . . . a watch, a coin, a set of keys—but there was nothing. Then an eerie realization crept up my spine . . . that was the point.

I once interviewed Richard Behal, a former member of the Irish Republican Army (IRA) who had become somewhat of a local celebrity after escaping from Limerick Prison in 1966. Behal had been imprisoned for attacking a British naval vessel (the HMS *Brave Borderer*) in Waterford in 1965. Originally authorized to use a bazooka in the attack, he used an antitank rifle instead so as not to hurt anyone. As someone who took pride in fighting for Ireland's freedom, Behal insisted that his intent was to coerce the British government to change its Ireland policy—*never* to hurt anyone. He was emphatic about this point throughout the entire three-hour interview.

Four decades later and some seven thousand kilometers to the east, collateral damage was no longer a problem. If this were an isolated incident, one could consider it a hate crime or the realization of a sick fantasy played out by a deranged lunatic (like the many school shootings we've encountered). However, attacks such as these have become commonplace, routine, almost clockwork.

If these atrocities were all perpetrated by a unitary actor (or even a coalition of actors) with an identifiable goal, then like the Bush administration, one could call them an act of war. But if this is a war, who's the enemy? The Global War on Terrorism implies that terrorism itself is the enemy. But how can terrorism be the enemy? It's merely a tactic that can be employed by virtually anyone.

So who's the enemy? Is it the militants who attacked Daʿuud's family? Is it the IRA or the British government? Is it al-Qaeda or the American servicemen who regularly consume alcohol, pork, and pornography in the land of the two holy mosques? Is it the Tsarnaev brothers or the children from Schkola no. 1?

The short answer is there are many enemies. There are literally dozens of conflicts raging at any given moment with both sides routinely denouncing each other as "terrorists."

The long answer?

As a graduate student, I was taught to view terrorism as an abstract phenomenon. Inside the classroom terrorism is explained via theories and models and causal variables. Students are taught not to be too descriptive in their approach and not to base their conclusions on single case study analyses because they're not generalizable enough.

But there I was, standing on the unmarked graves of the people who had once lived and worked there. Their memories, their hopes, and their dreams—their plans for the future—everything was gone. For them, and for their loved ones (indeed for the suicide bomber and his loved ones as well), there was nothing abstract about it.

I realized that in order to truly understand terrorist violence, I needed a more *realistic* conceptual framework through which to view it. I set off on a quest for illumination. My journey has taken me to more than a dozen countries around the world—to hotspots and cold (both literally and figuratively)—and this book is largely the result.

Three Themes

Three themes run throughout this book. Since all three themes are both interconnected and interdependent, it's very difficult to discuss them individually. Therefore, readers may notice a bit of repetition here and there as the themes overlap at times. I apologize for that in advance. I've done my best to parse them out as efficiently as possible.

The most important theme is that the Global War on Terrorism—like every major conflict since the turn of the twentieth century—is a war for resources. Access and control of the Middle East have long been a coveted prize.[13] Terrorism has nothing to do with it. Closely related to this theme is the fact that the religion of Islam is not an inherently violent religion. Islamic extremists constitute a miniscule percentage of the total Muslim population, and they interpret Islam's sacred writings in a way that justifies violence. Such behavior is not a strictly Muslim phenomenon, nor is it a strictly modern one. One can find examples of violence in the sacred writings of most world religions, and one can also find examples of people throughout history who used those texts to justify committing acts of violence. I discuss several examples in this book.

However, this is not the message that the average consumer of the news receives. The media not only promotes nearly every act of violence as terrorism; it also automatically assumes that the perpetrator was an Islamic extremist (neither of which is always true). It then manufactures the "truth" to reflect this "reality." I call this the media-terrorism industrial complex. The media distorts the facts and makes the threat of Islamic extremism appear to be much more serious than it actually is.[14]

Shark attacks are a comparable phenomenon. Popularized by the movie *Jaws* and other films and kept alive by urban legends and folk tales, the common consensus is that sharks are far more dangerous to humans than they really are. New Smyrna Beach in Florida is known as the shark attack capital of the world.[15] However, in the United States only one in 11.5 million people are attacked by sharks annually, and fewer than one in 265 million are killed. In fact in New York alone people are bitten by other people ten times as often as people worldwide are bitten by sharks each year.[16]

Likewise, foreign-born terrorists have killed only one American per year since 9/11—certainly nowhere near the top of the list of the most deadly threats to humanity.[17] Still the threat of terrorism (and particularly Islamic terrorism) continues to be greatly exaggerated by both the media and the politicians who use fearmongering as a political tool.

First of all, the term "Islamic terrorism" is misleading as it assumes a relationship between Islam and the violence itself. However, violence results from a wide variety of factors (and regardless of what you may have heard, terrorism isn't "caused" by anything)—not to mention that extremists of any stripe rarely represent their mainstream counterparts. Despite the amount of violence taking place in Muslim countries, it is extremely difficult to demonstrate a positive correlation between the religion of Islam and violence.

Those who attempt to correlate the two base their argument on the fact that a significant amount of violence today involves Islamic extremists. But as I'll clearly demonstrate, much of this violence takes place in the context of civil war and has been initiated by Western armies on behalf of corporate interests and the quest for oil.

Many of the so-called Islamic terrorists in Iraq, Afghanistan, Libya, Syria, Yemen, and other countries are simply trying to defend their country against a foreign invader/occupier. If Americans acted the same way under similar circumstances, they would be considered freedom fighters and celebrated as heroes. But since the United States is typically the occupying force, American news outlets rarely articulate the facts in their entirety.

Since September 11, 2001, there's been a surge of interest in Islam's alleged relationship to violence and terrorism.[18] One suggestion is that perhaps the Muslim world is more prone to terrorism than other regions of the world because of the great disappointment it has experienced in falling so far behind the Western world.[19] Ironically, the infrastructure in most Western cities is crumbling. Meanwhile, cities such as Dubai and Abu Dhabi host some of the most innovative architecture in the world.

Others assert that as far back as the sixteenth century, Muslims faced two choices: either embrace those aspects of the West that made it so successful or return to the pure faith of the past.[20] In more contemporary times, the twentieth century witnessed the rise of secular nationalism and the neofundamentalist ideology that opposed it.[21] Adherents of the two respective alternatives have supposedly been at odds ever since. Of course, each of these assessments is a gross oversimplification at best.

Several Christian Moral Majority leaders advance a misguided view of Islam by asserting that it's inherently evil and therefore the source of modern-day jihadist violence. Still others insist that violence is a central element in Islam and has been for over a thousand years. Unfortunately, assertions such as these are made even by academics and scholars.[22]

Attempting to attribute violence to the religion of Islam (or any religion for that matter) is as misguided as claiming that the cock's crow causes the sun to rise. One often accompanies the other. If one didn't know any better, one might think that there's a causal relationship between the two. Fortunately, we do know better. Or at least we should.

The second theme running throughout this book is the need for a standardized understanding of terrorism, not for better academic debates but because the subjectivity of our current approach has led to blatant politicization and abuse of the term. Any act of violence can now be labeled terrorism if one so wishes. And of course every state and nonstate actor on the planet labels its enemies as "terrorists" but claims that its own violence is legitimate and necessary—and therefore justified. In truth much of the violence that's now being touted as terrorism is not terrorism at all. It's just politically beneficial for someone to label it as such. This is particularly true of Islamic extremism.

The U.S. National Strategy for Combating Terrorism officially declared the 9/11 attacks an act of war against the United States and made both counterterrorism and antiterrorism national security priorities. The Bush administration insisted that the war on terror be brought to the perpetrators wherever they may be. The war was to be global. Therefore, America's counterterrorism efforts needed to be global as well. In addition to G. W. Bush's famous one-liners, the 9/11 attacks also resulted in the passage of a number of United Nations Security Council resolutions. Calling upon all UN member states to join the fight, the U.S. insisted that they pass legislation criminalizing terrorism. The official U.S. stance on the war made the very narrow assumption that anyone not with us was with the terrorists. It just isn't possible to get any more us versus them than that.

The problem with such a black-and-white position is that it makes the war on terror very political. Any violence with which the U.S. or its allies doesn't agree is labeled terrorism—and as such, it needs to be punished.

Socrates taught us to question our assumptions, and one of the biggest assumptions this book challenges is the idea that terrorism is an "enemy." Each chapter in this book makes its own individual contribution to the overriding argument that there's no such thing as a "terrorist." Terrorism isn't an enemy to be fought, nor is it an ideology in and of itself. It's a tactic—a means to an end and nothing more. As such any actor can commit acts of terror. Still, there's an immense amount of confusion regarding what terrorism actually is.

As I'll establish, the word "terrorist" is not a noun. It's an adjective, but it doesn't describe any particular person or organization. It doesn't even describe a certain type of violence. Any violence can constitute an act of terrorism. What defines terrorism is not the type of violence employed but the strategic objective behind the violence. Furthermore, terrorism can be employed by virtually anyone against a variety of actors.

The third theme running throughout this book is the observation that the current practice of publicizing every violent attack is radicalizing more people than al-Qaeda or IS combined. Young people don't have to be radicalized by religious extremism; the simple lure of fame is often enough. There wouldn't be nearly as many violent incidents if the media and its consumers simply stopped rewarding the perpetrators. This celebration of violence creates two problems.

The first is that we now live in a society where anyone can become an instant celebrity by simply killing a lot of people. The constant diet of savage violence leads to even more bloodshed as viewers who may be young and impressionable, unstable, disgruntled, depressed, mentally ill, or just desperate for attention decide to go on their own killing rampage. In the process they become famous—and in turn, they inspire others.

The second problem is that the majority of these incidents are automatically assumed to be "terror" attacks, and the perpetrator is assumed to have either been connected to or radicalized by Islamic State.

After constant exposure to this type of reporting, the public begins to conflate Islamic extremism with mainstream Islam, which opens the door for widespread Islamophobia. Bigotry and fear, in turn, create an environment of hostility toward Muslims and breed tolerance for social and political policies that are both unjust and inhumane.

Us versus Them

As should be clear, we're confronted with the classic chicken-or-the-egg dilemma. What comes first? Is it Islamophobia, which creates the tendency to assume that all violent attacks are caused by Islamic extremists? Or is it the tendency to assume that all violent attacks are caused by Islamic extremists, which leads to Islamophobia? Furthermore, is it simply a fundamental lack of understanding regarding the true nature of terrorism that causes us to assume that all forms of violence are terrorism? Or is it the assumption that all forms of violence are terrorism that drives our ignorance?

Oscar Wilde once claimed that "irony is wasted on the stupid." I could add that enlightenment is wasted on the willfully blind. If ignorance were the only enemy, much of the present confusion could be cleared up rather easily. Unfortunately, other demons appear to be lurking in the shadows.

I believe that much of the confusion regarding Islamic extremism and terrorism results from the reliance on simple black-and-white explanations. Humans have an intrinsic tendency to separate the world into good and evil (or good and "bad" to quote George Bush Sr.). This tendency was played out during the Cold War. In much of the West, communists were the enemy of the people—scapegoats for everything—as were capitalists in much of the East.

But of course, not all communism is the same. Nor is all capitalism the same. There are huge differences between Marxism and Leninism, just as neoliberalism differs from the Keynesian approach. I won't even get into China, which (at least in theory) combines capitalism and communism—something that was largely assumed impossible during most of the Cold War.

The same tendency to artificially break the world down into mere caricatures of reality is evident in popular television shows and movies. From the Lone Ranger and Batman to the Austin Powers films (to name just a few examples), good and evil exist as archenemies. Tactics and strategic objectives are conflated within the characters themselves. The good guys are always good, and the bad guys are always bad—that's just what they do.

This overly simplistic worldview is alive and kicking today in the ten-second sound bite. The "crusader" West versus "Islamic terrorism" is a popular sequel to capitalism versus communism and the most common scenario in which nearly all violent attacks are framed today.

The Christian West (which is itself an oversimplification) allegedly blames everything unholy and evil on Islamic terrorism—a ridiculous and misguided term that's applied to everything from random acts of violence to civil wars and Islam itself. Meanwhile, the 1.6 billion Muslims in the world are often considered guilty by association. Alternatively, the Muslim world (also a ridiculously huge oversimplification for a number of reasons) is presumed to blame everything decadent and immoral on the West.[23]

The problem is not necessarily that everyone believes this cartoonish rendition of the facts (not yet anyway) but rather that it permits no space for alternative explanations. Therefore, when push comes to shove and violence occurs, the knee-jerk reaction is to assume that it must have been perpetrated by ISIS.

We've seen the results of this knee-jerk reaction many times before in modern history. From the Nazi concentration camps to the American internment camps for Japanese Americans in World War II—and from the communist purges of the 1950s to the more recent war on terror—the temptation to blame everything from unemployment to famine on a single scapegoat has consistently proved too strong to resist. However, as I emphasize throughout this book, the Islamic State is not a "terrorist" organization, and a good many of the attacks attributed to it were likely orchestrated by somebody else.

So what's the answer? While I'm certain I don't know, it just seems common sense that if one wants to avoid the persecution of an entire group of people, the first step would involve the elimination of scapegoats. And since that can only happen by dispelling the myth of us versus them, that's where we should focus our efforts. Collective action is tricky but not impossible. Remember how boycotts helped eradicate apartheid in South Africa? As consumers of the news, we can also put an end to the sensationalizing of violence. The onus is on us.

As an American who lives in the Middle East, I can testify that not all Westerners are Islamophobes and not all Muslims hate America. To even imply that all Muslims hate America is to suggest that they're all somehow the same. This, of course, is utterly ridiculous. But many people nonetheless allow themselves to be boxed into this closed kind of mind-set.

Furthermore, not all Muslims are Islamic extremists (on the contrary, *very* few are). Additionally, there are varying degrees of Islamic extremism, and not all Islamists engage in terrorism. In fact most are nonviolent, while the majority of those who are violent (called jihadists) are insurgents, not "terrorists" (we'll discuss this distinction in more detail in chapter 2).

To put it another way, only a very tiny number of Muslims are Islamists. Beyond that an even smaller number of Islamists are violent—and an even smaller number of these are terrorists.[24]

So what's the difference between Islamic extremism, violent jihadism, and terrorism? And how can we tell one from the other? In the pages that follow, I'll explore the various facets of Islamic extremism as well as various degrees of Islamism. I'll analyze the most deadly Islamic extremist organizations in existence today in an effort to understand whether they are indeed "terrorist" organizations or something else entirely. Finally, I'll deconstruct dozens of so-called terrorist attacks to determine if they were in fact acts of terrorism or some other form of violence. Let's start with a definition of terrorism.

The Essence of Terrorism

Terrorism is the use of violence to coerce political concessions. One could add that it can be committed by anyone (both states and non-state actors), as well as perpetrated against any actor with the ability to grant political concessions. Shorter is generally sweeter, though, so I'll stick with this definition for now.

There are literally hundreds of definitions of terrorism (some better than others), but nearly all are completely focused on the actor, the deed itself, or the ideology of the actor rather than the strategic objective of the actor. This focus poses a huge problem considering that the one and only thing that distinguishes terrorism from other acts of violence is the strategic objective behind the violence.

Of course, people are entitled to choose any definition they like (or elect not to define terrorism at all for that matter). Regardless of what they ultimately decide, certain fundamental realities exist nonetheless. And it's these realities that matter, not some pedantic argument over semantics.

According to this simple definition, any violence intended to coerce political concessions can be considered terrorism. Since no single act or set of actions constitute terrorist violence per se, we cannot categorically differentiate it from other acts of political violence except by the strategic goals of those who engage in it.

By strategic goal I don't mean motive. A strategic goal is *what* an actor wishes to accomplish. Motive is *why* the actor wishes to accomplish it. It may seem as if I'm splitting hairs, but the distinction is an important one. It can be very difficult to establish motive with any degree of certainty. However, most violent actors tend to publicize their strategic goals.

The strategic goal of overthrowing a government is quite different from the strategic goal of attempting to exact political concessions or impose political changes within the framework of an existing regime. The first wants to replace the government. The second wants to coerce the government to either do something, stop doing something, or grant some type of concession. The difference is not just a matter of degree.

In other words actors who engage in terrorism aren't just insurgents who lack the ability to overthrow the existing order and therefore opt for political concessions as a second-best option. No doubt, this is the case with some actors such as al-Qaeda (see below). However, not all actors want to govern. For instance, al-Shabaab began as an insurgent group that sought to overthrow the corrupt Transitional Federal Government and end the Ethiopian occupation. However, the group no longer seems to be interested in governing Somalia. Therefore, overthrowing the existing regime no longer appears to be its strategic objective.[25]

The decision to employ terrorism is a strategic decision, one that an actor deliberately chooses as the best way to coerce political concessions given the circumstances and the resources available. For example, al-Qaeda is strategically sophisticated enough to realize that it must approach its strategic goal in stages.[26] If al-Qaeda believed that it could have overthrown all the American-backed puppet regimes (and indeed the West itself) and set up an Islamic caliphate with the resources at its disposal, it most likely would have set this as its strategic goal. But it pursued a much sounder strategy of attempting to coerce the Western powers (particularly the U.S.) to pull their militaries out of the Muslim world first. With the West out of the picture, the puppet regimes would then be weak enough for al-Qaeda to overthrow them.

Al-Qaeda's strategy is often referred to as attacking the far enemy.[27] By recognizing that it has to set its eyes on smaller prizes first, al-Qaeda hopes to realize its ultimate goal in the more distant future. In this respect al-Qaeda can be viewed as an insurgent group in waiting—one whose time just hasn't yet come. In the meantime it's employing acts of terror in order to inch itself closer to the goal post.

This strategy works for al-Qaeda because it's in line with the group's overall philosophy of how the caliphate should be established. I'll discuss this in more detail in chapter 3. For my purposes here, suffice it to say that al-Qaeda adheres to the more benign idea that the *ummah* (the Muslim community) needs to be taught by the *ulama* (Muslim scholars) regarding the true way of Islam. According to al-Qaeda, the true way is Salafism, which stresses a strict interpretation of the Quran and demands much more rigid outward conformity to Islamic precepts. Salafist teaching often rejects Western culture and advocates both the purification of Islam and the establishment of an Islamic caliphate.[28]

Because of this benign approach, which it adopted from Hassan al-Banna, al-Qaeda is much more tolerant toward individual Muslims who do not practice Salafism than *takfiri* groups tend to be. Takfiri groups such as the Islamic State, al-Shabaab, and Boko Haram take a different approach. These groups adhere to the belief that a strict version of Salafism must be imposed from the top down. Rather than patiently teaching the ummah regarding the true way of Islam, these groups punish violators and kill Muslims whom they view as apostate. Takfiri groups believe that they are the only ones that will be saved on judgment day. They base this belief on various hadiths, and one in particular: "My Ummah will split into 73 sects: one will enter Paradise and 72 will enter Hell."[29]

This second approach is known as the takfiri doctrine, which we'll also discuss in greater length in chapter 2. According to the takfiri doctrine, there's no place in the caliphate for apostates, so eliminating them is an end in itself.[30] In other words takfiri groups don't kill apostate Muslims in order to achieve some other strategic goal. Eliminating apostate Muslims is a major part of their strategic goal.

Why is this distinction so important? As stated above, political violence is a tactic (however one labels it). As such it can be employed by virtually any actor, whether individual, organizational, or state, because it's defined by the actor's strategic objective, not by the violence itself (or the actor, or the actor's ideology). And this is where the media, most policy makers, and even the majority of terrorism scholars get it wrong.

Hence, the term "terrorist," as it's used today, is a misleading one. So who cares? What difference could it possibly make what we call it? People are still dying, right? Yes, people are still dying. However, what we call the violence makes all the difference in how we respond to it.

First, if we believe (as many people do) that the spate of attacks in France, Belgium, Turkey, Iraq, Saudi Arabia, Bangladesh, Germany, Afghanistan, Israel, Britain, and so on were all terror attacks committed by the Islamic State because it was losing ground, as the media tells us, then what are our options?[31] We can refuse to negotiate because we don't negotiate with "terrorists." Alternatively, we could attempt to bargain with IS, as Neville Chamberlain did with Hitler. Finally, we could either focus all our resources on hardening our assets in every conceivable location on the planet (antiterrorism), or we could significantly escalate our military responses to include greater and deadlier counterterrorism efforts.

To blatantly refuse to negotiate would be to assume that the Islamic State is a terrorist organization and to completely ignore any and all other possible alternatives. To pursue a strategy of antiterrorism would only give Baghdadi time to strengthen his position and the freedom to strike somewhere else, while counterterrorism often backfires by killing more civilians than militants.[32] Bargaining could be problematic if—like Chamberlain—we failed to consider the Islamic State's strategic objective(s).

However, if we were to consider Baghdadi's strategic objective(s), we would quickly realize that many of these attacks have little or no strategic value for IS in the first place. How does an attack in Bangladesh aid Baghdadi in achieving his objective of defending the caliphate? Did the army of Bangladesh drive IS out of Fallujah? Analysis of these and many other attacks suggests that IS very likely had nothing to do with many of them.

Radical Islamist groups such as the Algerian Armed Islamic Group and others moved to Europe after they were forced out of their own countries.[33] While IS was probably behind the attacks that specifically targeted Shia, it also seems reasonable that at least some of the violence in Europe was the work of a number of these other nationalist militant groups continuing to press their demands from exile.[34] The remaining attacks were most likely perpetrated by copycats or highly disturbed individuals.

So what's the best way to respond? First and foremost, each attack should be considered and dealt with as a separate incident. Until a clear connection to the Islamic State is established (*if* a connection is ever established), we should stop automatically assuming that IS (or whatever group happens to be notorions at the time) was behind every attack.

Second, no attempt should ever be made to appease Baghdadi because he's not after political concessions. Killing Shia is part of the Islamic State's strategic objective. The entire idea that Baghdadi is lashing out because he's losing territory is ludicrous. The theory is entirely grounded in motive, not strategy (just as the fact that Saddam Hussein once tried to kill George Bush Sr. had nothing to do with the strategic objective for invading Iraq).

Politics

Closely related to the widespread confusion over the essence of terrorism is the endeavor to come to terms with how we've arrived at such a state of confusion in the first place. Again, the short answer is politics.

Harold Lasswell famously defined politics as "who gets what, when and how."[35] There's no doubt that since the beginning of the twentieth century, the vast majority of politicking has been over oil. As I'll demonstrate in this book, World War I, World War II, and the Cold War were all fought over oil, as were most of the many wars that followed. While the alleged enemies have changed (e.g., Nazis, communists, terrorists), the prize has always been the same. Demonizing others who stand in the way of that prize simply makes it easier to justify killing them—and using taxpayers' money to do it. Terrorism is just the latest and greatest enemy in the ongoing war of us versus them, which in its simplest form, is a competition for resources.

As is often true with many things, we can become so absorbed in the details that we miss the larger picture. This is called missing the forest for the trees. In my case the trees were all the many models and theories and various levels of analysis I was taught in graduate school. In terrorism studies students are trained to employ these tools to try to discover the various "causes" of terrorism. But as I've already pointed out, there are no causes—only uses. Terrorism is a tactic, a tool (what's the "cause" of a screwdriver?). The forest, of course, is politics.

Since all people approve and disapprove of different things (at different times and places, under different circumstances and for different reasons), many who analyze the same data arrive at wildly different conclusions. In other words the concept of terrorism (and therefore the discipline of terrorism studies itself) is highly subjective.

Once I was finally able to see the bigger picture, I began to realize why the Foucauldian battle for truth raging within terrorism studies has been so unfruitful. The only agreement among most scholars today is that terrorism consists of "violence of which we do not approve."[36]

Consider Nelson Mandela, Menachem Begin, Yasser Arafat, and Sean McBride. Each one was previously denounced as a terrorist. But now they're all celebrated as Nobel Peace Prize winners. A similar point can be made concerning the Afghan *mujahidin* who were widely described as freedom fighters in the 1980s but later became known as Islamic terrorists.[37] Clearly, no group considers itself a terrorist organization, which is perhaps the best example of the subjectivity of the term. In the words of Eqbal Ahmad, "The terrorist of yesterday is the hero of today, and the hero of yesterday becomes the terrorist of today."[38] Barack Obama is a perfect example.

Given that some of the greatest minds in the discipline have endeavored to gain an objective understanding of the phenomenon, one has to wonder what's preventing them from finding it. The biggest challenge to establishing a universal definition of terrorism has been the subjective nature of the term and the us-versus-them framework in which all violence is presented.

No actor views his own actions as terrorism. The subjective nature of the label, in turn, has allowed for such blatant politicization of violence that everyone labels his own violence heroic and his enemy's as terrorism. Like fish in water, our understanding of terrorism has been immersed in this subjectivity on a global scale—and it permeates society right down to the individual level.

Given the right conditions, such as the current Global War on Terrorism, labeling your enemy as a "terrorist" is likely to afford you substantial financial and military support (if you're a state). However, if you're an academic or a journalist, blowing the whistle on the United States or one of its allies could trigger serious repercussions ranging from a lack of funding to the loss of your job—perhaps even the loss of freedom (e.g., Julian Assange, Edward Snowden).

In my case it nearly cost me my education. In graduate school I was labeled a radical because I was always asking the politically incorrect questions. Day after day I was bombarded with comments like, "I hate Noam Chomsky!" Clearly, I did *not* fit in. Nor did I want to.

In fact after completing my MA, I was nearly denied admission into the PhD program—not because of my grades or academic ability—but because of my personal and political views. One day not long after I applied, the program chair called me into his office. He explained that the department was *very* conservative and suggested that I apply somewhere else.

The department was indeed very conservative. It was a haven for young, hawkish types who still lived with their moms and had never missed a meal in their lives. Yet they loved to make confident assertions about the world and places they had never visited, people they had never met, and circumstances they couldn't possibly begin to understand. In a sense they were the perfect candidates to go into terrorism studies— they could blindly apply their cherished theories regardless of the facts.

Glibly repeating trite clichés such as, "If you want to make an omelet . . . ," the vast majority openly expressed enthusiasm for the GWOT and fully supported unlawful detention practices, torture, and drone strikes against civilian targets, claiming they were "reasonable and necessary under the circumstances." I disagreed. Needless to say, the department fast-tracked these types, and they have long since become part of the problem.

But I digress. The reason that the discipline of terrorism studies is in such a state of chaos is politics. All this politicking serves as a gate-keeping function that protects the status quo. If I'm starting to sound like a critical theorist, I apologize.

While I agree with much of the critical position, I'm fundamentally opposed to using words that most people can't pronounce. Talk about hegemony of discourse! Isn't the whole point to try to connect with your audience? Seriously though, as I enjoy the peace and security of my office in the Middle East, I'm reminded that it's afforded me by men and women who put their lives on the line every day. Using abstruse words doesn't make you appear more intelligent than everyone else. It just means that you don't have anything better to do than look up obscure synonyms that no one else cares about (it also probably means that you don't have any friends).

But again I digress. If we were to eliminate all the politics, we could arrive at a greater position of clarity. How do we do this? In the words of Sherlock Holmes, "Elementary, My Dear Watson!" We simply go back to where we got off track in the first place, and we fix it. So where did we get off track? That part isn't so simple.

Bread and Circus

Construction of the Flavian Amphitheater in Rome was started by the Emperor Vespasian in AD 70. Although Vespasian died just one year before its completion, his son Titus finished it in his father's honor. On the opening day, tens of thousands of Roman citizens flooded through the numerous arched gateways. Excitement and great expectation hung in the air as something truly spectacular was about to take place. To commemorate the inaugural event, Titus ordered two of Rome's most famous gladiators, Verus and Priscus, to fight each other to the death.

Although gladiators were often slaves or even condemned prisoners, they were also immensely popular, and many became celebrities. Facing each other before huge bloodthirsty crowds, they were expected to fight with honor and die with dignity.

The gladiator fights were ancient Rome's equivalent of blockbuster movies. The "games," as they were called, were sponsored by wealthy politicians to entertain the masses and distract them from less popular realities (sound familiar?). These spectacles involved as many as twenty or more pairs of gladiators fighting both each other and even wild beasts. Inevitably, some would die while others lived to try and cheat death another day. The longer a contestant managed to stay alive, the more popular he became and the more valuable he was to his owner. Others, if they really pleased the emperor, were awarded their freedom.[39]

It would seem that people have always loved to watch violence. Things are not so different today. From violent movies to violent video games and even violent cartoons, the average child has viewed more than two hundred thousand acts of brutality and over eight thousand murders by the time she enters sixth grade.[40] And that's just the beginning.

Our adult lives are inundated with scenes of violence, and most of it is for entertainment. Much of this entertainment is called "news." With each new outbreak of violence in the world, scores of television cameras and reporters flock to the scene, while billions of spectators eagerly watch, their eyes glued to the screen as images of savage misery break the monotony of their otherwise uneventful lives.

This observation isn't intended as a scathing rebuke of the media per se. After all the media celebrates violence only because it attracts viewers. Of course, viewers attract corporate advertising, which is how everyone gets paid. However, it isn't just that the media capitalizes on the public's obsession with violence; it's the generic us-versus-them framework in which it's presented that demonizes one group while canonizing another. Again, the media didn't create this framework—it's been around for a very long time, and it will most likely continue to be around until consumers demand something more intelligent. So consumers bear the greater burden.

If the coverage were at least balanced or neutral, it might not be so bad. However, so-called experts are invariably brought in to interpret the violence for us. Most simply read a script that has been prepared for them in advance (watch their eyes). With both the questions and the answers scripted to reflect the position of the media outlet, there's no room for dissenting opinions. Either the relevant questions never get asked, or they're dismissed out of hand with oversimplified "facts" that have little or nothing to do with the issue.

For example, nearly every act of extremist violence today is immediately attributed to the Islamic State until proven otherwise. Even terror suspects are "suspected" of being IS affiliates—as is the case with the ten who were arrested in Rio in July 2016. Although no proof of any connection with IS existed, the headlines still read, "Rio Olympics: ISIS Terror Cell Arrested over Plot to Launch Large Scale Attack at Games."[41]

The same happened with the shooting in Munich on July 22, 2016. Before any details had been confirmed whatsoever, and while the shooting was still in progress, headlines claimed that the gunman had shouted, "Allahu Akbar!"[42] As it turns out, this claim is highly unlikely because the audio of the shooting—which was released after the incident—records the shooter yelling epithets about Muslim immigrants. But it made great headlines.

According to news reports, the Munich shooter lured young people to a specific McDonalds by promising free food in a post on Facebook. What was the shooter's strategic objective? Reportedly it was to kill people of Turkish and Arab descent. His motive? The shooter wanted revenge for being bullied.

If there's any doubt that this was a hate crime and not a terror attack, the shooting occurred on the fifth anniversary of the Breivik massacre in Norway, when Anders Breivik murdered seventy-seven people. (I would have refused to mention his name so as not to reward him with further publicity, but they named the massacre after him so what can you do?) Coincidence? Maybe. Maybe not. But this wasn't terrorism.

As often happens when a massacre is named after someone, Breivik has become an icon among far-right militants in both Europe and America. The young Munich shooter was likely one of Breivik's many fans.[43]

Scores of studies have been undertaken concerning how to stop the radicalization process. Yet few consider that by broadcasting violence on a daily basis, the media is doing more to radicalize young people than al-Qaeda or IS combined. Young people don't have to be radicalized by an ideology; the simple lure of fame has led many to extreme behavior. Jason Burke makes a similar point when he argues that al-Qaeda is more dangerous as an ideology than it is as an organization, and much of its power comes from society itself.[44]

While the media has both the right and the responsibility to broadcast the news, consumers also have the right and the responsibility to insist that international headlines don't make instant celebrities out of killers. Society idolizes the rich and the famous with millions of adoring fans who want to be just like them. If Michael Jackson can inspire thousands of people to wear just one glove, then mass murderers are bound to have an effect on their own followers as well. Yet we reward the most violent people with fame and then shake our heads in defeat, wondering why the violence keeps happening.

Foucault maintains that "each society has its regime of truth . . . the types of discourse which it accepts and makes function as true."[45] In other words societies don't just have beliefs, they *enforce* them. In the modern world, where the mainstream media enjoys global reach and a platform that influences billions of people, "truth" is both manufactured and distributed en masse.

The news is literally saturated with incidents involving Islamic extremism but very little, if anything at all, on Islam itself. The reason for this imbalance is that the steady diet of ten-second sound bites requires that everything be oversimplified into easily digestible half-truths. Such disproportionate (and sensationalist) coverage has led many to conflate Islamic extremism with mainstream Islam.

As a result the average viewer is led to believe that the threat from Islamic extremism is far greater than it actually is. This perception creates fear, and fear leads to toleration of and even demand for policies that are both oppressive and discriminatory. The Holocaust is a perfect example, but there are contemporary instances as well.

The "Rape Epidemic"

While there's absolutely no excusing the rape of another human being under any circumstances, when the media uses phrases like "rape epidemic" and "rape crisis" and then blames it on Muslim migrants, it is not only manufacturing the "truth" but also distributing it on a global scale.[46] But how much truth is there really?

Let's look at Sweden, for example. Of the ten countries that experienced the highest number of reported rapes per capita in 2015, Sweden listed sixth.[47] A number of media reports have linked the rise in reported rape cases in Sweden to Muslim migrants. However, rape is a very complex phenomenon, and statistically it isn't mono-causal. Therefore, to link national rape statistics to any single factor (such as an influx of Muslim migrants) may make sensational headlines, but it isn't likely a reasonable assessment of the problem.

No doubt some Muslims were involved in these cases. This shouldn't be surprising as Muslims are people just like anyone else. While most obey the law, some don't, as is the case in any society. A popular online video depicts a white woman allegedly being gang-raped by "Muslims."[48] Even though the video does not show the act itself, it strongly suggests that the woman is about to be gang raped by a group of Muslim men (I guess because they have brown skin they're Muslim). If this is truly the case, which is questionable based solely on the video footage, then we should all be outraged. However, where's the outrage over the Muslim women who are raped (or any woman who is raped for that matter)? Are we simply choosing to be blind to the larger truth?

Sweden is also among the most liberal countries in the world regarding sexuality, nudity, and drug use. Again, this in no way justifies rape under any circumstances. However, from a sociological perspective it's conceivable that Sweden's liberal standards may have a role to play in the number of rapes occurring in the country.

Many Muslim migrants to Sweden come from conservative societies. Culturally, definitions of public decency vary considerably. For example, in several Muslim states it's considered indecent for a woman to appear in public with her hair uncovered (in Saudi Arabia it's actually illegal).

Contrast such conservatism with Sweden's more liberal attitudes, and it's understandable that conservative migrants (of any religion) would experience a certain level of culture shock when confronted with nude beaches, topless swimming pools, and legalized prostitution—things that would make even most conservative Westerners blush.

Combine these cultural differences with the fact that many migrants are also young men, and you have a recipe for sexual temptation. Any young man, whether Muslim or not, is going to be tempted by sexual stimuli (as the billion-dollar porn industry attests). As with anything, what constitutes sexual stimuli is different for everyone. For someone accustomed to women who are fully covered from head to toe, something as everyday as shorts and a tank top can be a temptation. The fact that a few individuals gave in to that temptation in an illegal and violent way does not (and should not) incriminate the rest.

Now, I'm going to be very careful here so that no one can twist my words. I'm not referring to Swedish women as sexual stimuli, and I'm certainly not referring to the rape victims as sexual stimuli—nor am I attempting to justify the perpetrators. I am, however, attempting to distinguish between criminals and noncriminals because that's the issue, not the religion of the perpetrators. I'm also suggesting that as consumers we insist on more-intelligent reporting of the facts. Is rape really an "epidemic" in Europe?

Of the ten countries that experienced the most reported incidents of rape per capita in 2015, South Africa recorded 132.9 rapes per 100,000 people; Botswana 92.9; Lesotho 82.7; Swaziland 77.5, and Bermuda 67.3. All five of these states experienced higher reported rapes per capita than Sweden (63.5 rapes per 100,000 people).[49] Yet of those five states, four have a Muslim population of less than 1 percent. Only Lesotho's Muslim population is higher (a whopping 5 percent!). Clearly, Islam doesn't offer a very compelling explanation for rape (any more than Catholicism offers an explanation for child molestation). But the truth is often the first casualty in the war of us versus them.

All Lives Matter

The race riots in the United States are a comparable issue. The year 2016 turned out to be particularly dark for race relations in the U.S., and it's an incredibly sad indictment of our humanity. However, those who immediately draw the race card to explain the spate of police shootings largely ignore other facts.

It's absolutely true that African Americans constitute only 12–13 percent of the population, yet they represent 24 percent of the total number of Americans who are fatally shot and killed by police.[50] It's also true that non-Hispanic black males represent 34–37 percent of the total U.S. correctional population.[51]

Is this because a disproportionate percentage of African Americans are criminals? I seriously doubt it. Obviously other issues are involved. Yet even if this assertion were true, criminals have a right to a trial in America. So why are so many American citizens being shot and killed by police every year? This is an important question that needs to be addressed.

Is the problem a racial one? No doubt, some police officers are racist just the same as in any demographic. However, police shoot and kill a substantially larger number of white Americans every year than they do black Americans. Complicating the matter is the race of the police officers involved in the shootings. Surely at least some of them are black. Therefore, racism can't be the *only* explanation.

And so it is with Islamic extremism. With the help of the mass media and those who benefit from the politicization of violence, many conflate mainstream Islam with Islamic extremism. But how logical can such a conclusion be? Just as the majority of victims in police shootings in America continue to be white, the majority of victims in Islamic extremist attacks continue to be Muslim. Does this mean that Islam is a religion of both homicide and suicide? Certainly we, as a society, are capable of a more intelligent conclusion than that, aren't we? Unfortunately, logic has less to do with public perception than anger and fear.

I recently watched a debate concerning whether Muslim citizens of the EU should be allowed to remain in Europe or whether they should be forced out. It wasn't a debate about migrants, mind you; it was about citizens. More frightening still, it wasn't hosted by some crackpot ultraconservative talk-show host. It was aired on a fairly balanced mainstream news outlet. The fact that a significant number of people within the general population are even willing to consider such a question smacks of Jewish ghettos and the Red Scare.

To paraphrase John Locke's *Letter concerning Toleration*, no one should be denied civil rights because of his or her religion. Locke wrote that back in 1689. More than three centuries later, do we still need to be reminded? I would add that in addition to civil rights (protection *by* the law), no one should be denied civil liberties (protection *from* the law) for any reason, religion or otherwise.

If all of this sounds prescriptive, that's because it is. By simply settling for the status quo, we're allowing the framework of us versus them to structure the way we view the world and everything in it. This concern isn't just for "bleeding hearts." Nor is it strictly an attempt to defend Islam or any other religion for that matter. Islam just happens to be the greatest potential victim today. Many other groups have been targeted in the past.

So what am I prescribing? Certainly not more violence. Rather, what I'm suggesting is that, as consumers, we hold ourselves accountable to engage in at least a minimal level of critical thinking. Stereotyping any demographic (whether Muslims or Jews or blacks or women) is not only insensitive and wrong; it's also dangerous—and we can do better.

A personal anecdote may or may not be in order, but I'll share it anyway. My wife is Filipina, and it was probably three years into our marriage before she finally disclosed to me that most Filipinos (herself included) share the opinion that the majority of Americans are arrogant, rude, and conceited.

The only reason this information finally came out is because we were hosting a dedication for our son in the Philippines, and a disproportionately large number of people made the comment that I was "so nice!" I basically accepted the first one or two comments as compliments and didn't think anything more about it. However, after the ninth or tenth, I started wondering why people kept saying that I was "so nice!" Honestly, I'm not that nice. I try to be kind and considerate, but I doubt I'll win any personality contests for it. So what was up?

I asked my wife afterward, and she told me that when all her friends and relatives heard that she had married an American, they more or less expected me to be a jerk. So now whenever we're at a Filipino gathering or the Philippines embassy or any place where most people are Filipinos (such as Manila), I jokingly say to my wife, "So everyone here assumes that I'm an arrogant jerk?" She smiles and nods her head, "Yeah . . . pretty much."

I offer my personal anecdote to demonstrate that any group can be the victim of stereotyping. And while reports of Americans being attacked by Filipinos are rare—at least for now (if Duterte has his way that may change)—there have been many accounts of violence between Muslims, violence between Muslims and non-Muslims, violence between blacks and whites, and violence against women.

I'm not Muslim, black, or female (or Filipino), but my higher authority instructs me to love all people and to treat everyone with honor, respect, and dignity. As a result I'm ethically and morally responsible for the information that I simply accept as true. I'm also an academic, and as such, I'm required to think critically, which means that I should never allow the facts to be packaged for me. It also means that I must never share these prepackaged facts with others unless I'm absolutely certain that they're true.

Unfortunately, many prepackaged facts are floating around that conflate Islamic extremism with mainstream Islam. In the words of Bernard Lewis, it isn't for non-Muslims to define Islam. Only Muslims can do that. Only they can "decide what to retain of the rich and diverse inheritance of fourteen centuries of history and culture, and how to interpret that inheritance and adapt it to new needs and challenges."[52] Our role is to ensure that nearly two billion people aren't punished for the actions of a few.

The Islamic State or the State of Islam?

It doesn't take a scholar to recognize that the vast majority of violence in the news revolves around Islamic extremism. Unfortunately, due to the us-versus-them framework in which it's presented, it does take a bit of scholarship to parse out the differences between mainstream Islam and the extremist ideology that most people think they understand—but very few actually do.

Hence, a major endeavor of this book is to distinguish between mainstream Islam and Islamic extremism. I'll also (1) identify three principal ideologies in Islamic extremism, (2) explain the origins of these extremist ideologies, and (3) disclose why we need to understand them.

It's common today to hear reporters and politicians use the terms "Islamist" and "jihadist" synonymously. Although it may seem pedantic, it's important to differentiate between the two. The aim of the first group is to reform both government and society in accordance with sharia (Islamic law) by operating within the political process.[53] This goal sets its adherents apart from the vast majority of moderate everyday Muslims who don't necessarily have any desire to live under sharia.

The beginning of Islamist ideology can be correctly dated to the 1920s, when the Ottoman Empire was dismembered after World War I (also known as the First World War for Oil). This event was of supreme significance to Sunni Muslims everywhere because the Ottoman Empire was the last caliphate (Islamic empire), and the sultan was the last caliph (deputy of the Prophet). Even though the caliphate had lost much of its actual power and influence over the centuries, it retained symbolic importance for Sunni Muslims because most believed that there could not be a valid ummah without a caliph to lead it. However, when Ataturk founded the secular state of Turkey, he abolished the office of the caliph.

Conservative Sunni leaders met at a number of conferences to try to revive the caliph, but of course, there was widespread disagreement over who would assume the office. This attempt to bring Islam back into the state marks what many scholars refer to as the beginning of political Islam, or Islamism.[54]

Islamists such as Hassan al-Banna (1906–49) and those who followed sought the reestablishment of the caliph and the reinstitution of sharia.[55] Most Islamists are nonviolent and seek political change through democratic elections. Those who are violent are typically referred to as jihadists.

For most Muslims around the world, the term "jihad" signifies the struggle to be a good person. But unless you've been living under a rock somewhere, you've no doubt been exposed to the widespread misuse of the term.

Without being insensitive to the original meaning, the fact is, the negative connotation has largely become the norm for most non-Muslims. Therefore, for clarification in this book I'll refer to jihadists as a violent subset of the Islamist population. Technically, this classification is true as both groups desire the reinstitution of sharia. However, as we'll soon discover, jihadists have been around much, much longer.

Jihadists reject man-made laws and democracy as deceptions. In fact they reject the entire Westphalian nation-state system and all international political institutions (except the caliphate), arguing that they are merely extensions of Western imperialism. Therefore, jihadists legitimize violence as the only means available to reestablish the caliphate and defend the ummah. This conviction is what sets jihadists apart from Islamists, and many are staunchly opposed to their Islamist counterparts.

The fundamental message in all of this is that Islamic extremism represents only a tiny fraction of the overall Muslim population. While it's impossible to know with absolute accuracy, most reliable estimates calculate total worldwide membership of all Islamic extremist groups to be somewhere between one hundred thousand and two hundred thousand.[56] These figures result from simply adding the *estimated* membership of every Islamic extremist group known to be in existence. I emphasize that this is an estimate because, of course, the actual number is dynamic and constantly changing. However, it is accurate enough to serve our purposes here.

Given roughly 1.6 billion Muslims in the world, Islamic extremists constitute between .006 percent and .012 percent of all Muslims worldwide and between .001 percent and .002 percent of the total population of the planet (based upon a population of 7.6 billion people). Simply put, Muslims are *not* all murderers just because some murderers are Muslim.

Examples of religiously motivated violence abound from the Christian Crusades to Muslim/Hindu conflicts and even Buddhist/Hindu conflicts. No one religion can hardly be cited as the exclusive domain of violence, nor is it possible to demonstrate conclusively that any religion *causes* violence.

My Branch Davidian friends are a perfect example. Individually, most of them were kind and considerate human beings. But as a group, they were dangerous extremists led by a narcissistic psychopath. Where did they get their misguided ideas? From the Christian Bible. Vernon Powell (aka David Koresh) was a master at twisting scripture to support his grandiose scheme of mass slaughter. Does that mean Christianity causes violence? Should all 2.2 billion Christians in the world be held accountable? The answer should be obvious. So why is it so difficult to draw the same conclusion when it comes to Islamic extremists?

How serious is the threat of Islamic extremism? To put the threat in context, only one in seventy-four thousand people worldwide is likely to become an Islamic extremist. Granted, that's still one person too many. But we have to keep the threat in perspective. As stated above, not all Muslims are Islamic extremists, and not all Islamic extremists are involved in terrorism. Most Islamists are nonviolent, and the tiny percentage of those who are violent (jihadists) are mostly insurgents involved in a civil war. The simple truth is that the vast majority of jihadists are not terrorists. Yet people automatically assume (with the help of the media) that every violent attack is an act of Islamic terrorism until proven otherwise. And that's not the worst of it.

The real threat is that, due to both a lack of information and the sheer oversimplification of the facts, the average individual has been encouraged to equate terrorism with Islamic extremism and Islamic extremism with mainstream Islam—painting all Muslims with the same terrorist brush (one suicide vest fits all). This demonization of entire groups of people has historically led to systematic violence on a far greater scale than the comparatively random violence caused by terrorism.

There's another reason why this type of policy is dangerous. In the West it seems obvious to people that no group wants to be discriminated against—nor should they be. What's less obvious to most Westerners (who are in the practice of separating church and state) is how people in the Muslim world are likely to react to such discrimination and oppression.

For 1.6 billion people (nearly 23 percent of the earth's population *and growing*), the separation of church and state is still a relatively new concept. The last caliphate ended only a century ago. Given that the secularization of society is much less institutionalized in the Muslim world than it is in the West, it's considerably more likely to be rejected altogether in times of severe difficulty when Islam can be presented as a preferable option.

Islamist parties don't perform as well as they do in democratic elections because the majority of Muslims prefer sharia. Rather they garner support because a growing number of voters are convinced that Islamist governments will offer a desirable alternative to the corrupt secular regimes they have now.[57] This isn't to say that secular government is inherently flawed. But we simply cannot ignore the fact that many of the democratically elected regimes in the Muslim world have been propped up by Western powers to protect their oil interests.

When nearly 25 percent of the world's population exercise their rights in free and fair elections, we tend to see it as a victory for democracy—unless, of course, Islamist parties win the election. When that happens, Western powers scramble to isolate the party, control it—and if possible—manipulate a different outcome.

Again, the issue has nothing to do with Islam or Islamist parties. The issue is entirely about the control of energy resources. Why doesn't the United States topple the Saudi monarchy and demand that democratic elections be observed there? Because Saudi oil is secure (at least for now). The only places in which the West has insisted on regime change are the states whose leaders have failed to play along with America's neoliberal demands. When those leaders are taken out and corrupt puppetocrats are installed, it only serves to strengthen the jihadist message that man-made laws are an affront to Allah and that corrupt, Western-backed puppet regimes must be overthrown through violence rather than peacefully replaced through the democratic process.

America's own hypocrisy—insisting on elections but refusing to accept the results—strengthens the jihadists' claim. And when the United States does this all in the name of oil, the result is invariably more violence.

CHAPTER TWO

THE FIRST ACT OF TERRORISM

Now the serpent was more crafty than any other beast of the field
that the Lord God had made.

—Genesis 3:1

The Poor Young Farmer

An ancient Chinese parable tells of a poor young farmer who lost his
only possession: the horse that he had inherited from his father. The
members of the village visited the poor farmer and expressed their
condolences for his loss.

"How do you know that losing my horse was a misfortune?"

Sure enough, about a week later the horse returned with a healthy
young mare as its wife. The citizens of the village were shocked, and
they all went to visit the farmer to congratulate him on his good fortune.

"How do you know that gaining the mare is good fortune?"

Again, the young farmer's words rang true. About two weeks later,
as he was breaking the mare, she threw him, and he broke his leg. All
the people of the village gathered around his bed to console him for
his tragedy.

"How do you know that breaking my leg was a tragedy?"

Later that month the Japanese invaded. The emperor sent emissaries
to every village to find healthy young men. All the young men of the
village were sent to the front except the young farmer whose leg had not
yet healed. None of the young men returned. All were killed in battle.

The Fine Print

We live in an era of political correctness that, while necessary and beneficial in many respects, can also be an obstacle at times. This is one of those occasions. With respect to those who may be put off—or even offended—by the religious concepts discussed in this book, it's simply impossible to understand religious extremists without possessing, at the very least, a basic knowledge of the scriptures they claim to represent. Isn't this why moderate religious leaders are often called on to spearhead the deradicalization process? From an academic standpoint, this seems so obvious that it hardly merits mention. Still, a brief disclaimer seems to be in order.

This book has been reviewed by no less than a dozen academics and professional editors (not to mention my own readers and my agency's readers). One common reaction I've received is "religious stories just aren't the sort of thing one expects to see in a book about terrorism." Unfortunately, the very fact that this is true is symptomatic of a much greater problem within the discipline of terrorism studies.

The vast majority of non-Muslims in the West have been led to assume that terrorism and Islamic extremism are one and the same thing—and that they're both fueled by the religion of Islam. Yet the secular nature of Western society (and the emphasis on being politically correct) has made it unpopular to discuss "religion" in the public domain.[1] This restriction both blinds the eyes of many and ties the hands of those who would remove the blindfold.

How then does one dispel these myths and address our need for a deeper understanding of the phenomena? Most people don't want anyone upsetting their neat and tidy perception of us versus them. Ironically, this disruption is exactly what most people need. However, this obstacle is much more difficult to overcome than simple ignorance alone.

If this book were about the Ku Klux Klan, wouldn't some discussion of white supremacy be necessary? If the book were about Hitler and the Third Reich, wouldn't some exploration of antisemitism be in order? If the book addressed Darfur or Rwanda, wouldn't the topic of genocide be a necessary component? As off-putting as such concepts might be to the queasy and the fainthearted, they're absolutely essential for those who want to understand the phenomena we study.

In this case it's necessary to understand the religious beliefs that drive Islamic extremism. As politically incorrect as it may seem to some, this requires an examination of the scriptures and stories from which these beliefs are generated. As crazy as some religious extremists may appear to the average citizen of planet earth, the crazy ones are those who think that religious extremism can be comprehended without the slightest clue regarding the religious beliefs that spur extremists on to kill.

Therefore throughout the remainder of this book, I'll explore and discuss a few key stories that are shared by all three of the world's largest monotheistic faiths. I am in no way attempting to justify violence in the name of religion—I'm actually arguing the exact opposite. By including a discussion of the religious texts on which much of today's extremist violence is based, I hope to bring to light a clearer understanding of what religious extremists want to achieve. More importantly I emphasize the fact that the true source of this violence is not religion per se (or any particular religion) but rather the misinterpretation of such texts by a very small minority of misguided souls.

A Central Theme

Collectively Jews, Christians, and Muslims constitute a substantial percentage of the total world population. And while it may be human nature to focus on the differences between these three great religions, they also share a tremendous amount in common with one another. A central theme in all three faiths is the belief in a single, almighty creator. All three religions also have their own version of the story of Adam and Eve.

Most people are familiar with the story. God created Adam and Eve, and even though they lived in a state of perfection, the serpent (Satan or the devil) tempted Eve into eating the forbidden fruit. As a result the couple was cast out of the Garden of Eden. Of course there's much more to the story. However, details vary depending on one's religious background. Therefore, I'll focus on the more common aspects of the story to avoid privileging one tradition over another.

Again, I'll disclaim up front for the more secular-minded readers that the analysis of this story is meant to inform, not to persuade. A proper understanding of any act of violence necessitates an analysis of the strategic objectives involved (if any). As I'll establish, the story of Adam and Eve contains critical information regarding the strategic objective of many Islamic extremists groups operating today.

Some take the account literally, others figuratively, and still others don't believe there's a thread of truth in any of it. Regardless of one's position, most people tend to just accept the story for what it is without questioning the details. By this I don't mean questioning whether the story is true or not. I simply mean that most don't take the time to deconstruct the text and ask the more difficult questions.

For instance *why* did the devil tempt Eve? Most people just assume that he's the devil and that's what devils do, so they simply accept that he tempted Eve and leave it at that. But why did he do it? What was his motive? Thucydides claims that fear, honor, and interest are among the most compelling motives. I wonder what the serpent's motive was.

Furthermore, and more important from a strategic perspective, is his strategic objective. In other words what was he trying to achieve? I'm going to suggest that this was the world's first recorded act of terrorism. Most terrorism scholars list the Jewish Zealots among the first terrorists. I maintain, however, that the written history of terrorism goes back a little further. And believe it or not, this first recorded act of terrorism sheds considerable light on the Zealots' strategy as well.

The Jewish Tanakh tells us that God gave Adam dominion on the earth. In other words God put Adam in charge. In this sense Adam was sovereign. According to the story, God put Adam in the Garden of Eden and commanded him not to eat from the tree of the knowledge of good and evil. Afterward God created Eve, and it's fairly common knowledge what happened subsequently. The serpent tempted Eve, and she ate of the forbidden fruit. Then Eve gave some to Adam, and he ate as well.

The apostle Paul later wrote in the Christian New Testament that Adam was not deceived by the devil, only Eve was. Needless to say, Paul isn't too popular with most feminists, who I'm sure would prefer to look at Eve's defiance as an act of liberation rather than one of weakness. That's one way to look at it.

Another way to look at it is that once Eve transgressed the command, she became the first human hostage. Even though Eve willingly obeyed the serpent (in a sense she entered into a contract of rebellion with the devil), she was not legally culpable because she was under the dominion of Adam. As has been the case throughout much of human history, women needed the approval of a male guardian for an agreement to be legally binding. This is still the case today in some parts of the world. So it was with Eve.

Therefore, as Eve's legal guardian, Adam had a choice to make. He could confirm the contract and, in essence, enter into rebellion against God himself. Or he could take a position that is popular among political leaders today and refuse to negotiate with terrorists. If he chose the first option, Adam would bear the legal responsibility for Eve's transgression himself. He would, in fact, forfeit his dominion to the serpent. This, of course, is the political concession that the devil was seeking. If Adam chose the second option, he could retain his dominion, but he would lose Eve.

As everyone knows from the story, Adam approved the contract by transgressing the commandment himself. He thus forfeited his dominion and granted the serpent the political concession he sought. And there you have it: the first recorded incident of terrorism in human history.

One can look at this story in two ways. Many fault Adam (and especially Eve) for their part in the transgression—and they did clearly transgress the law. But when we consider who instigated the entire conundrum, an interesting parallel comes into focus between predatory oil companies today (backed by powerful state militaries) and the serpent. The people of the sovereign states that rightfully own the oil can be compared to Adam and Eve. Finally, oil itself can be compared to the Garden of Eden.

The great powers have made a concerted and deliberate attempt to take this oil by any means necessary. When the people affected respond by demanding their fair share, they're banished as criminals or labeled as "terrorists." When the states themselves resist, they're attacked and invaded, and their oil is stolen and privatized. Therefore, the serpent may have been the first "terrorist," but he certainly wasn't the last.

As for the Jewish Zealots, their strategy was a bit flawed. The Tanakh records that before God banished Adam and Eve from the Garden of Eden, he promised that he would send a messiah who would defeat the serpent and reclaim the dominion that Adam forfeited. The Zealots, who based much of their justification and confidence on this promise, mistakenly believed that the Messiah would come and deliver the Jews from Roman bondage. All their hopes were based on this one promise. Their strategic objective was freedom from the Romans. However, their strategy wasn't sound because—according to Judaism—the promised Messiah has not yet come. Therefore, the cavalry never arrived, and the Zealots lost badly to the Romans.

Christians and Muslims also believe in the promised One, and these two religions have extremist factions as well. They too are expecting God to send help from above and sanction their violence. In this chapter I'll uncover the truth about a misguided few, who like the Jewish Zealots before them, got the message wrong.

A Brief History of Muslim Extremist Ideology

When the Prophet Muhammad died in 632, the majority of his followers in Medina elected Abu Bakr as his successor because he had been Muhammad's closest companion. Abu Bakr took the title of caliph but did not claim to possess supreme religious authority. In other words he didn't claim to be the final judge of religious truth. Neither Abu Bakr nor his limited perception of the caliph's religious authority was accepted by everyone, however.[2]

A small minority of Muhammad's followers rejected the election of Abu Bakr, favoring Ali as his successor instead, and they made a number of claims to defend their position. First, they insisted that Muhammad had specifically designated Ali as his successor. Second, they argued that as the first male Muslim convert, Ali had first priority to lead—a sort of right of first refusal. Finally, they asserted that as Muhammad's closest kin by both blood and through marriage (he was the prophet's cousin as well as his son-in-law), Ali was the most qualified to succeed Muhammad by pedigree.[3]

Furthermore, the "Partisans of Ali," or Shia Ali as they called themselves, maintained that religious and political authority must remain united in one man.[4] According to the Shia, that one man was Ali. Additionally, Ali's followers insisted that leadership was hereditary. Therefore, the position should be passed on to the descendants of Ali.[5]

Although the Shia acquiesced to the rule of Muhammad's first three successors (Abu Bakr, Umar, and Uthman), they resented it. In 656 a revolt led to the assassination of Uthman and some of the rebels proclaimed Ali as the new leader. The governor of Syria, Mu'awiyah, was a kinsman of Uthman and sought revenge for his death. Mu'awiyah refused to acknowledge Ali as the fourth caliph until Uthman's assassins were brought to justice. However, Ali was largely dependent on the support of those responsible and refused to surrender them.[6]

A struggle for power within Uthman's clan (the Umayyad) ensued, and in 657 Ali invaded Syria. The indecisive Battle of Siffin resulted in Ali agreeing to allow the matter of succession to be decided by arbitration. Ali's acquiescence sparked tremendous protest among his followers who believed that succession should be decided by Allah alone.[7]

A small group of believers known as the Kharajites (outsiders) withdrew in protest and launched sporadic attacks against both the supporters of Ali and the Umayyad leadership. The Kharajites believed that once a leader succumbed to sin or failure, he could be removed by force. In 661 a Kharajite assassinated Ali, and Mu'awiyah succeeded him. For nearly a century, the "Partisans of Ali" refused to accept Umayyad control of the caliphate.[8]

In 750 the Shiite Abbasids overthrew the Umayyad dynasty. While the new caliphs were kinsmen of Muhammad, they were not descendants of Ali, and they eventually adopted the majority Sunni position. The remaining Shia insisted that the rightful imam was still the supreme, infallible religious leader whether vested with political authority or not. According to the Shiite view, the hallmark of a leader is his supreme religious authority and knowledge, not his political power. Therefore, Shia prefer the title imam over that of caliph.[9]

Both Sunni and Shia believe that the Mahdi (guided one) will one day come to rule the world and redeem Islam.[10] He will fight the Masih ad-Dajjal (false messiah) and rid the world of wickedness before the day of judgment.[11] The Sunni believe that the Mahdi is yet to come and will be a descendent of the Prophet Muhammad, while the Shia believe that he has already been born but has disappeared to one day return.[12]

The legend of the twelfth imam began to spread in the ninth century among a group of Shia known as the "Twelvers" after Muhammad al-Mahdi allegedly disappeared. The "Twelvers" believe that al-Mahdi is the promised messiah and that he will one day reappear to bring justice to the world.[13]

While most Sunni and Shia are content to wait for the Mahdi to arrive on his own, a few misguided souls have somehow misinterpreted the message. Like the Jewish Zealots of old, these Islamic extremists believe that they can usher in the end of days by preparing the ummah for the coming of the Promised One. How are they to do this?

The notorious militant group Islamic State believes that the first step is to establish and expand the caliphate. IS also believes that it must purge Islam of apostates and banish all non-Muslims from the territory of the caliphate so that the Mahdi can return.

Like Christian extremists such as the Branch Davidians, Islamic extremists truly believe that they're a select group—specifically chosen for this purpose. No doubt there are some who are just along for the cheap rent so to speak. But many are true believers, and like the Jewish Zealots, they're relying on the Promised One to come and fight beside them, strengthen them, and give them victory over their earthly enemies. They too will lose badly.

Three Types of Islamic Extremism

In chapter 1 I distinguished Islamists from jihadists. Another important distinction can be made between jihadist and takfiri groups. While jihadists maintain that violence against the apostate regime is necessary for instituting sharia, takfiri groups make no distinction between the government and the governed. In their estimation *shirk* (idolatry) is *shirk*, and it doesn't matter who commits it.

These groups justify their actions on the takfiri doctrine, which basically argues that anyone who does not agree with a particular interpretation of the faith should be excommunicated and killed. The doctrine dates back to the Kharajites in the seventh century who opposed the Umayyad dynasty, claiming that they were not true Muslims.

The doctrine has since been invoked by Ibn Taymiyyah, Muhammad al-Wahhab, and Sayyid Qutb; more recently it resurfaced in Egypt in the 1960s with an offshoot of the Muslim Brotherhood, Takfir wal-Hijira (Excommunication and Exodus). In the late 1980s and early 1990s, the group's followers spread the doctrine to Peshawar, where it influenced a number of jihadists including Zarqawi.[14] The most notorious adherent of the takfiri doctrine is Baghdadi's Islamic State, which has inspired literally dozens of other groups to follow its example.

Imagine a large circle consisting of mainstream Muslims. Inside the large circle is a much smaller circle containing Islamists. Inside the small circle is a tiny circle containing jihadists, and inside the tiny circle is a dot that represents takfiri groups.

All three wish to establish sharia. While the majority of Islamists are willing to contest in democratic elections, the relatively small number of jihadists reject democracy as an usurpation of the sovereignty of Allah and are therefore willing to employ violence against existing regimes to impose sharia. At the far extreme, takfiri groups believe that by killing individual apostate Muslims, they're doing the will of Allah and preparing the way for the Mahdi.

While not every group fits into this typology perfectly, it serves as a methodological starting point from which one can discern an actor's strategy. I'll make this very important distinction again and again—from the Islamist approach advocated by the more moderate faction of the Muslim Brotherhood to the jihadist agenda outlined by al-Qaeda and finally the takfiri doctrine embraced by the Islamic State, al-Shabaab, and Boko Haram. These three broadly defined ideologies inform how actors view their strategic environment. This view, in turn, greatly affects the strategy these groups employ to achieve their goals.

Distortion

Despite these important distinctions between the three main categories of Islamist ideology, the media tends to lump them all together and call them "terrorists." What's worse, much like the old maps of the world that were drawn to make Europe the largest and most central region of the earth, media coverage today distorts reality to make the small number of Muslim extremists appear to be the majority in Islam.

So when did all this begin? Hassan al-Banna and Sayyid Qutb are widely recognized among the forefathers of modern Islamic extremism, and the argument that their teaching helped fan the flames of violence is not entirely without merit.

One reason for crediting the two with this distinction is the tumultuous times in which they lived (both were alive when the caliphate ended). The division between the house of peace (Dar al-Islam) and the house of war (Dar al-Harb) was much easier to discern while the caliphate was still in existence. Therefore, the primary purpose of jihad was considerably less contestable.

Today entire populations no longer fall either within the caliphate or without, so the classifications of Dar al-Harb and Dar al-Islam have become much more problematic. Consequently, the concept of jihad has also become much more controversial, making the writings of al-Banna and Qutb more relevant.

A second reason for listing the two among the forefathers of modern Islamic extremism is that the group in which they were both so influential, the Muslim Brotherhood, still exists and continues to influence Islamists and jihadists around the globe.

So, on the one hand, one could argue that *modern* Islamic extremism began in the early twentieth century with the movement to reinstate the caliphate and the rule of sharia.[15] The flip side of this argument is that the concept of jihad has been debated by Islamic scholars and militants for centuries. Therefore, this chapter seeks to trace that debate back in time beyond al-Banna and Qutb to Muhammad al-Wahhab, Ibn Taymiyyah, and even the Prophet Muhammad himself in an effort to gain greater illumination on this controversial concept and on how a number of other controversial issues (*takfir, ijtihad, jahiliya, bid'a,* etc.) first crept in.

My purpose is *not* to defame Islam in general or to in any way associate mainstream Islam with its more radical, fringe elements. In fact my goal is to demonstrate the exact opposite. Every religion has its extremists, and there are also many other types of extremism in the world. To paraphrase G. W. Heck, is it fair to blame 1.6 billion Muslims and more than 200 million Arabs for the misguided ideas of a handful of extremists?[16]

First of all, there is little consensus on the definition of extremism. One common component is the possession of hostile beliefs toward members of another group and the willingness to act on those beliefs.[17] In this sense extremism is an intense form of ethnocentrism, which is nothing more than the tendency to perceive (and judge) the world around us according to the standards, customs, and preconceptions instilled in us from birth. Ethnocentrism is a reality of the human condition. As social creatures steeped in their own culture, human beings can't help but filter everything through socially distorted glasses.

Some view ethnocentrism as the tendency to view all other cultures as inferior to one's own. It isn't. It's the inability to see aspects of other cultures objectively. Hence, most people tend to feel more comfortable with the familiar and less comfortable with the unfamiliar. Isn't this the basic idea behind advertising?

Airports

A case in point is airports. In the immediate aftermath of 9/11, soldiers armed with M16s patrolled America's major airports. My first encounter with this sudden new reality was surreal. It felt as though I'd just walked into North Korea. But over the years, travelers became accustomed to increased security at airports. At first most people were shocked, and many were too frightened to fly. The airline industry faced a $24 billion drop in revenue as a result.[18] But eventually the collective perception of the threat became more realistic. Society simply needed time to assimilate this foreign and largely unfamiliar (if not new) state of affairs.

Still, there are limits. However compliant travelers have become with security at airports, most people wouldn't be comfortable with armed guards at McDonalds or 7-Eleven. That is not unless they live in Manila, where armed guards are nearly everywhere—even at hospitals.

I remember flying into Manila on a two-week furlough for the birth of my son. A passenger on the plane had a heart attack and died as we passed through Typhoon Glenda (one of only two category 5 super typhoons ever recorded in the South China Sea). Once I was in Manila, torrential downpours flooded the streets (the water was up to my waist in some areas). My baby picked the perfect time to enter the world—Manila was underwater, and getting to the hospital was nearly impossible. Still, my wife was as calm as she could be.

"Don't worry, baby. This is the Philippines. It rains like this every summer." Her reassuring tone and peaceful demeanor sustained me as the taxi crawled through the flooded streets, stalling routinely at every intersection.

We finally made it to the hospital, and all was forgotten. Absolutely nothing compares with the wonder of holding your newborn baby for the first time (and the overwhelming fear that you might drop him). Still, my elation was temporarily deflated by the armed guards stationed at the exit. They insisted we show proof of payment before they let us leave. I fumbled through my pockets for the receipt the cashier had given me a few hours earlier, and they waved us through. At the exit adjacent to us, an elderly couple was detained. They didn't have a receipt.

The entire concept of being held hostage at a hospital until you can pay your bill was completely alien to me (I'm from America—land of the brave and home of 0 percent down). I felt upset. It just seemed wrong. My wife, on the other hand, wasn't the least bit fazed by it as this was the medical system she was accustomed to. And this is an example of what we mean by ethnocentrism: two people, experiencing the exact same reality, yet perceiving it completely differently. One's perception of Islamic extremism is like this as well.

Most normal, well-adjusted human beings acknowledge that Islamic extremists constitute only a very small percentage of the world's Muslim population. And this is absolutely true. Extremists (of any variety) represent a statistically insignificant minority. People who live in the Middle East are probably more aware of this reality than others, but it isn't unlike living in America.

My students always ask me if it's really dangerous to live in the United States. They see reports of the school shootings, police shootings, and mass shootings, and it disturbs them. I tell them it's pretty much the same as watching all the bombings and various attacks that happen in their part of the world. The violence, as horrible as it is, only affects a small percentage of the population. It looks like it's everywhere, but it isn't. The civil war in Syria and the ongoing conflict in Iraq are obvious exceptions; the toll on civilians in cities such as Aleppo and Mosul is overwhelming (but again, closer analysis reveals that Syria is a proxy war and oil—not Islam—is the central issue. Why else would the United States be involved?).

These exceptions aside, most people in the West don't have a proper understanding of the threat. To be fair people who honestly don't know any better can't help but be influenced to some degree by our daily diet of bloodshed and carnage. And while the coverage of the events themselves may (or may not) be accurate, the magnitude of the threat is greatly exaggerated. As a result the media gives the impression that Islamic extremism is all around us. The fear this impression generates is causing the broader social mentality to gradually drift away from a position of openness and acceptance toward Islam to one of isolation and prejudice. This assessment is particularly true in the West, where the various right-wing reactions to the migrant crisis continue to grow in both number and intensity.

I've noticed increasing negativity toward Islam in general among Westerners (both here in the Middle East and in the West). At one time the most dangerous phrase you could say in an airport was, "Hi, Jack!" Today, it's, "Allahu Akbar!" Both are totally innocent and benign statements when taken in the proper context. "Allahu Akbar!" is even an expression of reverence. However, in a world that perceives itself as under attack, it has also become a war cry.

When breaking news of the Ataturk Airport attack flashed across our television screens—36 dead (and counting) and 147 more injured—my first thought was, "How statistically insignificant is this?" I was inclined to go back and delete everything I'd written regarding the statistical insignificance of violent extremism.

On the one hand, it seems insensitive to the victims and their families to downplay attacks such as these. But on the other hand, the worst thing to do is empower those who engage in violence (and their copycat admirers) by public discourse.

To paraphrase the great Fareed Zakaria, terrorism only works when people allow themselves to be terrorized. The entire strategy behind terrorism is to cause a reaction. And while not all violent attacks are necessarily acts of terrorism, the most common reaction to violence is an emotional one.

People are more likely to respond to violence with emotion than with logic because fear is a raw and natural reaction, whereas logic requires us to control our emotions. Referring back to my furlough in Manila, my flight back to Riyadh (Saudia Flight SV871) was canceled because, as we were taking off, the plane skidded off the runway due to heavy rain and strong winds. (Most of the passengers on the flight blamed it on the pilots for texting and flying. Of course, this notion was mere speculation fueled more by stereotypes than actual facts, but such is human nature.) The aircraft was stuck in the mud, and we had to exit the plane right there—ankle deep in sludge with our carry-ons in the pouring rain.

The airline crew packed all 298 of us into two small transit vehicles (you know, the kind with one seat on each end and nothing but poles to hold on to in between). And I mean they *packed* us in. We were squeezed in there so tight it was difficult to breathe, and most of us were drenched from the rain.

The airline staff had no idea what to do with us, so they just left us in those two vehicles for more than forty-five minutes while they waited for a response from their superiors. If you've ever been to the Philippines in the summer, then you can imagine our predicament. Outside it was 86 degrees Fahrenheit with 75 percent humidity. Inside the vehicle, it felt *a lot* hotter. We were wet. We were tired. We were hot and hungry and grumpy. And now we faced the uncertainty of what would happen to us and where we would spend the night.

People started to panic and complain that they couldn't breathe. Others started pounding on the windows, screaming for the airline crew to let us out. The doors were controlled by the drivers, and they were doing their best to ignore us. I can only imagine that they were instructed not to let us out under any circumstances. The last thing the airline wanted was a herd of angry passengers stampeding through the airport.

Fear spread like a wildfire. People felt as though they were suffocating, although I'm pretty certain that there was plenty of oxygen to sustain us. But this is what happens in frightening situations: logic gives way to hysteria, and people start to panic. Clear-headed individuals are absorbed into a mob mentality, and reason gives way to the loudest voices. The point is people don't have to overreact to violent attacks. They can choose not to listen to those who simply scream the loudest and let cooler heads prevail.

The Loudest Voices

Have you ever wondered what might happen if violent attacks weren't publicized so sensationally? Most people wouldn't even know about them. And for those who actually commit true acts of terrorism (i.e., those that demand political concessions), their strategy would fail because there would be very little (if any) reaction to it. For those attacks that are not terrorism, there would be no celebrity status waiting for the perpetrators and therefore less incentive to commit violence in the first place.

So why does the mainstream media publicize violent attacks so sensationally (when it's the absolute worst possible reaction) and yet ignore substantially greater problems that actually need and deserve our attention?

For instance, nine million people starve to death each year. That's nearly twenty-five thousand people *every single day* (roughly one person every three seconds), and most of them are children.[19] A surprisingly high number of these unnecessary deaths occur in oil-producing states such as Nigeria that produce billions of dollars in oil every year but refuse to feed their own people. Oil companies extract the wealth, and what little they give in return lines the pockets of a few corrupt politicians.

Moreover, the World Health Organization estimates that 35 percent of all women worldwide experience physical and/or sexual violence.[20] Again, sadly many of these victims are children. Furthermore, 45.8 million people are enslaved worldwide.[21] *Slaves!*

Why doesn't the mainstream media insist on bombarding homes and offices with this news every ten seconds like it does with "terror" attacks and school shootings? More importantly, if Americans as a society are truly concerned about human rights, freedom, and the loss of innocent lives, why don't they demand more balanced coverage of *all* the issues that affect the human condition?

One can't blame the media. It's up to consumers to hold it accountable. Islamic extremism kills tens of thousands of people every year, and therefore, it's definitely an issue that needs to be addressed. However, it's by no means the most important issue. Nor should one conflate Islamic extremism with terrorism. By far the vast majority of the deaths caused by Islamic extremism occur in civil wars, not terror attacks.

So what's my point? By completely ignoring issues that kill and enslave tens of millions of people each year and focusing on Islamic extremism, which only kills tens of thousands, every unthinking consumer of mass media is culpable. Also, by blaming the violence committed by a tiny fraction of extremists on the entire population of Muslims, we're contributing to the denigration of Islam as a religion. This in turn contributes to Islamophobia, which only serves to empower the extremists.

The mass media is all about communication. At the most basic level, communication involves a sender (the mainstream media outlets) and a receiver (the general public). When the vast majority of the news that the public receives concerns Islamic extremism, the average individual is led to believe that this tiny minority somehow represents the views and intentions of Muslims everywhere.

This message, whether intentional or not, poses a much greater threat to the world than Islamic extremism ever could. People around the world are afraid. The world is primed to react. All it will take now is for the fearmongers to become the loudest voices, and who knows what could happen.

In chapter 3 I'll explore the concept of culture further as I contemplate the very contentious term "jihad."

CHAPTER THREE

THE MEANING OF JIHAD

Do not slay the soul justified by God except for just cause.

—Quran 6:151

The term "jihad" is a highly contested concept.[1] As one traces the evolution of jihad back through the ages from the Prophet Muhammad to the present day, one finds that a number of other controversial issues also spun out of this age-old debate over the legitimate use of violence in the name of Islam.

The word is derived from the Arabic *jahada*, a verb that literally means to struggle or to exert.[2] The more moderate interpretation of jihad, of course, refers to either (1) the individual spiritual struggle against sin or (2) the collective battle against an enemy aggressor. However, according to the second interpretation, jihad must be sanctioned by authority and conducted with restraint.[3]

The moderate interpretation is based on a hadith (account) of the Prophet Muhammad where he's quoted as saying, "Self-exertion in peaceful and personal compliance with the dictates of Islam (constitutes) the major or superior jihad," and the "best form of jihad is to speak the truth in the face of an oppressive ruler."[4]

Pre-Islamic Arabs observed a basic code of conduct in war: don't kill women, children, the aged, or the wounded.[5] Muslim Arabs inherited this practice, and it was encoded in sharia. It's believed that in the days of the Prophet Muhammad, jihad was a very comprehensive term, requiring the submission of all one's resources—both physical and spiritual—to Allah. Therefore, jihad encompassed all aspects of life, including the military.[6]

Some scholars insist that jihad passed through three stages during the life of Muhammad. From 610 to 622, jihad was an internal personal struggle. Between 623 and 626, the relocation to Medina required defensive jihad. Finally, the period 626–632 ushered in the need for offensive jihad against apostates.[7]

These multiple applications of jihad were very practical in the time of Muhammad. For instance, the early Muslims were instructed to reject the idolatry and polytheism of the pre-Islamic Arabs and thus struggle for inner spiritual growth and revelation. When Muhammad and his followers fled to Medina to avoid persecution, they were called on to sacrifice their homes and possessions and to start completely over in the name of Islam.

As the Muslim empire began to coalesce and power was consolidated, the concept of jihad became a matter of state policy—justifying both defensive war and conquest. Especially during times of division when power was contended (as during the Umayyad Dynasty), jihad was also employed to claim political legitimacy over one's opponents.

Various Muslim scholars interpreted jihad differently to deal with different practical realities. For instance Abu al-Walid Muhammad ibn Muhammad ibn Rushd—better known as Averroes—stressed the peaceful and spiritual applications of jihad, while Ibn Taymiyyah emphasized its role in war.[8] In contemporary times its true nature has been widely debated as definitions vary from the sensational to the more benign.

On the far extreme, Islamophobes such as Daniel Pipes insist that there is no such thing as a moderate Muslim. I emphatically disagree. Over the last decade or so, I've lived in a number of Muslim countries. Most of my students, friends, and colleagues are just as moderate and progressive as the Westerners I know. Some aren't, of course—but I know a number of Americans and Europeans who hold rigid and inflexible views as well. As is always the case, it just depends on the person. Extremism is a personal characteristic, not a religious one.

How one interprets the concept of jihad is an individual choice as well. Pipes has concluded that jihad is "unabashedly offensive in nature, with the eventual goal of achieving Muslim domination over the entire globe."[9] In other words with Muslim friends, who needs enemies? Pipes would be correct if he were discussing takfiri groups such as the Islamic State or Boko Haram. Unfortunately he isn't. This is just another example of how mainstream Islam is often conflated with extremism.

David Cook defines jihad as "warfare with spiritual significance."[10] Cook tends to focus on the expansive phase of Islam and emphasize the military nature of conquest. According to this somewhat less extreme definition, the defense of Islam was only a secondary priority, playing second fiddle to conquest.

At the other extreme are those who defend jihad as purely defensive, claiming that the term "holy war" is misleading as it associates jihad with the bloody and barbaric Crusades. These insist that jihad refers to the individual and collective struggle against evil—either to cleanse oneself of sin or to defend Islam against those who would attack and destroy it. Many in this camp compare jihad to the Christian concept of just war and even contend that jihad in the Middle Ages was actually far less brutal than most warfare of the period.[11]

I would suggest that the truth lies somewhere between these two extremes in a dichotomy between jihad for political purposes and jihad for social purposes. The one serves Islamic hegemony and hence is at times violent, while the other serves Islamic society and is focused on inner growth and spirituality. According to this understanding, jihad has both military and peaceful applications. Furthermore, military jihad can be either offensive (as when Muhammad attacked Mecca in AD 630) or defensive depending on the need (as the battles of Badr and Uhud in 624–625 demonstrate).

Furthermore, jihad is not limited to waging war with arms. It can also refer to several other activities in support or defense of Islam such as *jihad bi-al-lisan* (jihad of the tongue), *jihad bi-al-qalam* (jihad of the pen), *jihad al-nafs* (jihad of the soul), *jihad bi-al-nafs* (self-sacrificing jihad), and *jihad bi-al-mal* (financial jihad).[12]

Truth is like beauty; it's in the eye of the beholder. Regardless of how jihad was originally intended to be performed or how it was actually applied, it has since assumed a violent connotation. Especially after 9/11 many politicians have claimed that jihad is nothing less than an attack against humanity practiced by violent and irrational extremists who hate the West and are intent on destroying it. For example George W. Bush repeatedly promoted the idea that the United States was in a battle between good and evil.[13] Meanwhile, many Muslims understandably emphasized the spiritual and nonviolent application of jihad.[14]

Predator or Prey?

> Therefore when you meet in battle those who disbelieve, then smite the necks until you have overcome them, then make (them) prisoners.
>
> —Quran 47:4

As with any sacred writings, opposing interpretations of the Quran abound. Take Surah 47:4 quoted above. On the one hand are those who contend that it was written in response to the persecution of Muhammad and his followers by the Quraysh tribe—a persecution so severe that the early Muslims fled for their lives to Medina—therefore, this text and others like it should be understood only within the proper context.[15]

On the other hand, others remind us that between AD 624 and 632, Muhammad led at least twenty-seven military campaigns against the inhabitants of the region surrounding Medina.[16] Muhammad first attempted to convince the surrounding tribes of the truth and legitimacy of his message through peaceful means. But those who refused to accept it became targets of conquest.[17]

Abu Bakr later united the various warring clans of Arabia following the Ridda wars (wars of rebellion), and by AD 750 the Arabs had conquered territory from the borders of China and India in the East to the Atlantic Ocean in the West.[18]

Of course all war is violent (except perhaps in Thailand, where bloodless coups have become an art form). The fact that Muslims engage in violence during times of war is a matter of historical record and isn't all that remarkable.[19] Therefore, one could argue that Surah 47:4 doesn't sanction Muslims to kill *all* disbelievers, only those confronted in battle. Furthermore, Islam dictates that all wars be (1) declared by a legitimate authority and (2) fought in accordance with the many rules regulating Muslim conduct in warfare. These claims are reassuring. However, as I'll discuss in this chapter, legitimate authority and the traditional rules of battle would be challenged again and again over the centuries.

THREE PHASES OF ISLAM

Gamal Badr argues that Islam has passed through three distinct phases in its history over the past 1,400 years and that jihad has taken on a fundamentally different meaning and purpose in each period.[20] Originally, Muslims saw the world as divided into two realms: Dar al-Islam, which was made up of Muslims, and Dar al-Harb, which was made up of non-Muslims. According to Badr Islam experienced a period of expansion and conquest where jihad was primarily waged as a series of offensive military campaigns against non-Muslims both to spread Islam and to feed its imperial ambition.

The second period was a time of interaction in which a third realm was added: Dar al-Sulh. This third realm consisted of non-Muslims. While the inhabitants of Dar al-Sulh did not recognize Muslim authority or govern themselves according to sharia, they did nevertheless, live at peace with Islam—unlike Dar al-Harb. During this phase jihad was primarily waged in defense of Islam against the attacks of hostile members of Dar al-Harb.

The final stage is the current era of coexistence, in which the main purpose for jihad is highly debated. As useful as Badr's threefold typology is for a general understanding of the evolution of jihad, it's also highly oversimplified. Therefore, it isn't very accurate for our purposes. As one digs a little deeper into the chronicles of Islamic history, one discovers that it tells a somewhat different story. In the pages that follow, I'll examine a number of Islamic scholars who have influenced Islamic extremist ideology.

IBN TAYMIYYAH (1263–1328)

Taqi al-Din Ibn Taymiyyah was a medieval Islamic scholar who lived in the Mamluk Sultanate (1250–1517) during a period of constant threat from Mongol invasions. Because the Mongols had embraced Sunni Islam, jihad was not a legally sanctioned option for the Mamluks as Islamic law prohibits Muslims from going to war against fellow Muslims.[21] However, Ibn Taymiyyah found a way to solve the Mongol problem. The Mongols still upheld their traditional Yassa law. Therefore, Ibn Taymiyyah issued a fatwa (an Islamic religious ruling) accusing the Mongols of being un-Islamic for not making sharia the law of the land and declaring defensive jihad against them.[22]

In much the same way that the Catholic Church insisted that interpretation of the Bible was reserved for the clergy, *ijtihad* (the interpretation of Islamic scripture based on reason) had been prohibited for Sunni

Muslims by Islamic scholars in the eleventh century. However, Ibn Taymiyyah became widely known for his defense of ijtihad. This insistence on the right to interpret the Quran distinguishes Ibn Taymiyyah and his followers from those who view the early interpretations of the Quran as sacred.[23]

Ibn Taymiyyah's famous fatwa declared jihad against an apostate Sunni regime to be legal according to sharia, and it set a precedent that would be cited again and again by Islamists throughout the centuries, including Muhammad al-Wahhab, Sayyid Qutb, Osama bin Laden, and others.[24] Yet Ibn Taymiyyah's fatwa actually echoed the takfiri doctrine, which was introduced by the Kharajites in the seventh century.

MUHAMMAD AL-WAHHAB (1703–92)

Muhammad al-Wahhab attempted to reform the Islam of his day by rejecting all forms of interpretation that had been introduced over the past 1,100 years. He called for strict adherence to the Quran and the example of the Prophet Muhammad and the *salaf* (pious forefathers). The term *salaf* generally refers to the first four caliphs who ruled after Muhammad (Abu Bakr, Umar, Uthman, and Ali).

Al-Wahhab condemned many practices that were popular among the Sufi and the Shia such as saint worship, mysticism, idol worship, reverence for shrines and relics, praying to *imams* and saints for intercession with God, and all other pre-Islamic traditions on the basis that they constituted *bid'a* (religious innovation).[25]

Wahhab's followers, known as Wahhabis, declared themselves to be the only true Muslims and labeled all others (including the Ottoman Sultans) apostates. The Wahhabis pronounced takfir on many Muslims on the charge that they were guilty of *kufr* (false worship). Al-Wahhab cited Ibn Taymiyyah's fatwa against the Mongols as justification, claiming that the same precedent applied—they were not true Muslims and therefore it was legally permissible to kill them.[26]

The clan of Ibn Saud joined the Wahhabis and declared an aggressive jihad on the cities of Mecca and Medina in the early nineteenth century.[27] Again in 1918 with the support of the British, the Saud clan declared aggressive jihad against the Ottomans and expelled them from the Arabian Peninsula.[28]

Al-Wahhab's influence on present-day Islamists is virtually impossible to overestimate. The royal al-Saud family of Saudi Arabia continues to derive its legitimacy through Wahhabism, and the House of Saud spends billions to export the Wahhabist version of Salafi Islam throughout the world.[29]

SAYYID ABU AL-AʿLA MAWDUDI (1903–79)

For Mawdudi—an Indian-born journalist who agitated for Pakistan's independence and later became a leading Islamist theorist—jihad meant the liberation of Muslim states. Insisting that the purpose of Islam is to replace the dominion of man with the sovereignty of God, Mawdudi (Like the Kharajites) saw jihad as the sixth pillar of Islam, the ultimate goal.[30] Accordingly, all the other pillars of Islam: *shahada* (the profession of faith), *salat* (prayer), *saum* (fasting), *hajj* (pilgrimage), and *zakat* (alms) are meant to prepare Muslims for jihad.[31]

Mawdudi established Jamaʿat-e-Islami in 1941 and became its first emir. While Mawdudi embraced the idea of an elected president, parliament, and judiciary, he maintained that social injustice was caused by the corruption of state leadership.[32] Demanding unconditional obedience, he imposed his strict interpretation of a purified Islam in an effort to create a Muslim elite that would be worthy to take over India, not through violence but via the peaceful assumption of control of the state.[33]

Once in power Mawdudi and his party would eradicate inequality and suffering in India and promote a global Islamic revolution. Mawdudi's ideas have been extremely influential, among Islamists both of his time and in the present day.[34]

HASSAN AL-BANNA (1906–49)

The 1919–22 revolt and the subsequent institution of parliamentary democracy in 1923 ushered in a period of tremendous upheaval and transformation in Egypt when the liberal nationalist forces gained control. By 1928 many people from all spheres of society in Egypt felt a severe crisis of identity as a result of foreign occupation and its Western influences.[35]

Hassan al-Banna—who formed the Muslim Brotherhood—began to unite these otherwise diverse segments of Egyptian society under a banner that combined Islamic revivalism with progressive socioeconomic ideals and staunch anticolonialism.[36]

Motivated by his conviction that Islam was both a religion and a state, al-Banna sought the revival of Islam and the establishment of a state governed by sharia—insisting that Muslim leaders had to liberate themselves from foreign rule and educate their citizens regarding the "true" way of Islam.[37] Once these two goals were accomplished, al-Banna sought to create an Islamic caliphate from which Islam would be spread throughout the world.[38]

The entire process would entail seven stages: (1) education of the individual, (2) education of the family, (3) education of Muslim society, (4) assumption of political power through elections, (5) creation of a state governed by sharia, (6) liberation of the Muslim world from foreign occupation—both physical and ideological, and (7) re-creation of the Islamic caliphate, which would then spread Islamic values throughout the world.[39]

While the Muslim Brotherhood adopted the pronouncement of takfir against the Egyptian regime, al-Banna largely aspired to reform Egyptian society from the inside out. His focus was primarily on eradicating jahiliya (ignorance) through education.

The heart of al-Banna's message can be traced back to the influence of Ibn Taymiyyah's ijtihad. As we'll see in the next section, Sayyid Qutb would also draw from this influence but for a much darker objective. The Muslim Brotherhood would grow much more radical under his direction.

SAYYID QUTB (1906–66)

Qutb began as a secular scholar. Influenced by Westernized education and English literature, he originally sought to reconcile Western individualism with the precepts of Islam.[40] However, the two years he spent in America (1948–50) dramatically altered his views. Qutb was also heavily influenced by Mawdudi's writings—which became available in Egypt in 1951—and he openly criticize the West as uncivilized and even backward because immorality such as homosexuality was allowed and women were liberated from their natural duties of childbirth and motherhood and free to engage in relationships based on lust and passion.[41] Later, years of torture in prison turned him into a radical who staunchly opposed the corrupting influence of Westernization in Egypt.[42]

Westernization (also known as "Islamic reformism") entailed many innovations that many conservative Muslims at the time considered offensive. Those who resisted change insisted that Western influences required faithful Muslims to compromise basic Quranic principles. Reforms such as equal rights for women, Western education that prioritized secular sciences and technology over the sacred writings of the Quran, and of course democracy were considered nothing short of heresy by a number of Muslim clerics and their followers.

In an effort to secure their interests, the British were more than happy to cooperate with the Muslim Brotherhood in Egypt. King Farouk also saw the group as useful for countering nationalist movements. Prior to the 1956 invasion, Britain sought to stem the tide of anti-imperialism and Arab nationalism via more covert methods, which largely backfired because the more extreme elements in Egypt became suspicious of the Brotherhood.[43]

A fissure developed between two opposing forces, those who embraced Westernization and the more religiously conservative who rejected it. Qutb essentially viewed both the West and the Soviet Union as morally bankrupt. He openly spoke out against democracy and communism as incompatible with Islam—a religion in which Allah is sovereign, not the people or any particular class of persons. In fact Qutb was one of the first to recognize that the United States wanted to use the Muslim world as a pawn in its chess game with the Soviet Union. The American support of the mujahidin in Afghanistan demonstrated that he was right.

While Qutb was opposed to both the capitalist system in the West and communism, he defended the notion of private property, embraced certain libertarian principles adopted from John Stuart Mill, and opposed the exploitation of the poor. Still, while Qutb's writings drew on Western philosophy and even Marxism to a degree (actually, he argued that Marxism drew on the principles that Islam had established hundreds of years earlier), he ultimately dismissed capitalism, socialism, and communism as fundamentally flawed.[44]

In *Social Justice in Islam*, Qutb writes, "The nature of European and American philosophy does not differ essentially from that of Russian; both depend on the supremacy of a materialistic doctrine of life." As an alternative he argued in favor of governance based on sharia—a position that many Islamist groups share today.[45]

As the Muslim Brotherhood grew more radical, its secret apparatus began to engage in ever more defiant acts of violence. In 1948 the group allegedly carried out a series of bombings in Jewish areas of Cairo that killed seventy and wounded two hundred others.[46]

Prime Minister Mahmoud an-Nukrashi Pasha led a crackdown on the organization in December 1948, and a few months later the group assassinated him. Later that year al-Banna was also assassinated by the secret police in what appears to have been retaliation for the prime minister's death. The Brotherhood was banned, and its members were either arrested or driven underground.[47]

Qutb allied himself with the Muslim Brotherhood after returning from the U.S. in 1951.[48] Not long afterward Gamal Abdel Nasser ascended to power in the 1952 revolution. Many of his nationalist forces—the Free Officers—had long-standing ties with the Brotherhood.[49] Incarcerated members were released, and Qutb began to rise through the ranks.[50]

He became the intellectual leader of the group, and for two years the Brotherhood flourished. However, when the group began to oppose Nasser's policies (particularly the 1954 Anglo-Egyptian pact), the relationship took a turn for the worse. When a member of the Brotherhood attempted to assassinate Nasser, he outlawed the group, executed six of its members, and arrested thousands more.[51]

Qutb was arrested and sentenced to fifteen years' hard labor.[52] While incarcerated Qutb was tortured and abused. By the time of his release in 1964, he had completed *In the Shadow of the Quran* and *Milestones along the Path*, the second and third major works in what is now regarded a trilogy.

Qutbist scholars note the radical turn in his writing after he was imprisoned. For example in *Social Justice in Islam* (the first completed work of the trilogy which he wrote in 1949 before Nasser's persecution of the Brotherhood), Qutb explicates the many contradictions of Western society. And while he offers Islam as the ultimate solution, both the policies and the goals he expresses in *Social Justice* are significantly more moderate than those expressed in *Milestones*.[53]

In *Milestones* Qutb encourages the use of force to carry out an Islamic revolution. Like Ibn Taymiyyah Qutb emphasized the importance of ijtihad, and *Milestones* offers one of his finest examples.

At the core of Qutb's approach was his reinterpretation of jahiliya. The term is traditionally used to refer to the ignorance that existed before the emergence of Islam and still lives and breathes in the non-Muslim world. Qutb applied the term to the ignorance that has found its way back into the Muslim world such as democracy (sovereignty of the people), Western values (hedonism and materialism), and Western education that elevates science but does not recognize God. Qutb stated that the forces of jahiliya in the Muslim world are the first enemies to be eliminated and that jihad is the means to achieve this goal.

Qutb justified his position by redefining the traditional understanding of the term "Dar al-Islam." Rather than restricting the term to territory controlled by Muslims, Qutb used it to refer to all aspects of Islam—faith, community, and the Muslim way of life—which he claimed were under attack. Since jihad was legally prescribed for the defense of Islam, Qutb argued that jihad should be used to defend all of Islam—not just its territory.

Qutb had long believed that the United States was a major source of jahiliya, but in *Milestones* he claims that the Egyptian state was un-Islamic as well and therefore also guilty of promoting jahiliya. Thus jihad against the Egyptian state was legally defensible according to Islam.

Qutb also defended the state imposition of sharia on the ummah and argued that jihad against individual Muslims who resisted sharia was sanctioned by Islamic law. In this respect he was essentially upholding the takfiri doctrine.[54] Several among the Muslim Brotherhood denounced Qutb, calling him a heretic and a Kharajite.[55]

Qutbist scholars were not the only ones to notice the radical turn in his writings. Qutb was arrested on charges of treason and executed on August 25, 1966, for advocating the overthrow of the secular Egyptian regime.

While both Qutb and al-Banna favored an Egyptian state in which sharia was the law of the land, Qutb's vision differed greatly from al-Banna's regarding *how* to establish such a state. Al-Banna wanted to educate the Muslim people in the true way of Islam, starting with the individual and progressively working through the family and so on.[56] Once the people had learned the true way of Islam, they would be ready and able to create an Islamic state and share the pure religion of Islam with the rest of the Muslim world.[57]

In contrast Qutb taught that a revolutionary vanguard should carry out an Islamic revolution and use force to create an Islamic state in Egypt. The new Islamic state would *impose* true Muslim values on the Egyptian people and then export Islamic revolution to the rest of the Muslim world by waging jihad against anyone who opposes sharia as the sole rule of law.

Generations of Islamists have been influenced by al-Banna and Qutb. As we will see, the tension between al-Banna's more conciliatory bottom-up approach and Qutb's authoritarian top-down approach would continue to be a factor in shaping the strategies of Islamist groups to follow. Two individuals in particular would be instrumental in passing the torch: Abdullah Azzam and Ayman al-Zawahiri.

ABDULLAH AZZAM (1941–89)

Abdullah Azzam was born in the West Bank in 1941. His experiences during the Israeli occupation in 1967 deeply motivated his desire to liberate his fellow Muslims.[58] It's difficult to imagine the shame that many Muslims have felt and continue to feel as a result of Israeli or American (or British or French or Italian) occupation. Most people in the West have never experienced long-term foreign occupation. There are, of course, exceptions such as the European states occupied by Nazi Germany during World War II and the more recent conflicts in the Balkans. However, relatively few Western lives today are still scarred by these wars as compared to the millions of Muslims who are currently displaced or otherwise suffering due to foreign occupation.

During the Lebanese civil war—not long after Israel invaded Lebanon in the summer of 1982—I became friends with a young Lebanese man named Nassib. Because of his red hair and thick red beard, Nassib had acquired the nickname "Red Leb." The fact that his nickname included his nationality is telling of the enormous number of foreigners in Lebanon at that time (French, Syrians, Palestinians, Israelis, Americans, etc.).

Nassib had lost much in the war, but he never lost his hope or his humanity. While others around him were consumed by hatred and the desire for revenge, Nassib reached out to the others in his crumbling world—the outsiders who had forced their way in: the militants, the journalists . . . me—and he demonstrated that true strength is measured in resilience, not force.

I only knew him for a short time, but Nassib taught me many things. Above all he helped me to see that the human spirit is capable of the torment of hate and the elation of love, the despair of war and the solace of peace, the lust for violence and the pursuit of healing—but never both at the same time. We're either instruments of one, or we're agents of the other.

Nassib chose to be the latter. He could see that the various armed factions and militants operating in Lebanon were *all* contributing to the destruction of his country. All of them were depriving the Lebanese people of their homeland, regardless of the cause they claimed to be defending. What did it matter who won if there was nothing left once the fighting was over? Many Syrians I meet today feel exactly the same way. Unfortunately, Nassib's voice was not the loudest. His message was drowned out by the screaming fanatics of the time.

Azzam, on the other hand, made certain that his voice was heard. He studied Islamic law in Damascus, where he found inspiration in the writings of Ibn Taymiyyah, Muhammad Faraj, and Sayyid Qutb. After moving to Jordan to join the Palestinian Liberation Organization (PLO), Azzam soon realized that he was opposed to its secular and socialist agenda. He left Jordan in 1970 when security forces cracked down on the organization and moved to Cairo, where he completed his PhD in Islamic law in 1973.[59]

After accepting a position as professor of Islamic philosophy at King Abdulaziz University in Jeddah, Azzam mentored the young Osama bin Laden. He eventually became known as Amir al-Jihad (Prince of Jihad) and grew famous for promoting universal militant jihad amongst his students. Rather than simply focusing on liberating Muslims from this state or that, Azzam taught that all Muslims everywhere had an individual duty to wage jihad until the entire international Muslim community was free.[60]

Azzam argued that every able-bodied Muslim was morally obligated to engage in global armed jihad to liberate fellow Muslims.[61] When the Soviets invaded Afghanistan, Azzam was adamant that supporting the mujahidin in Afghanistan was an individual duty for every Muslim—those who could should go and fight.[62] He also insisted that once the war in Afghanistan was won, jihad should be taken everywhere that had once been under Muslim control. Azzam justified his position by taking the debate on warfare beyond *jus in bello* (legitimate means in warfare) to include *jus ad bellum* (legitimate grounds for warfare).[63]

Offensive jihad—attacking Dar al-Harb (the land of war)—was supposed to be sanctioned by authority.[64] However, with no caliph to speak of, who possessed the authority? Azzam urged his students—including the young bin Laden—not to wait for the establishment of the caliphate to wage jihad but to take up the individual duty of jihad as Allah had commanded them.[65]

After moving his family to Islamabad in 1979, Azzam taught at International Islamic University and continued to preach his message of the individual duty to wage international jihad. In 1984 he established the Islamic Coordination Council, a clearinghouse in Peshawar through which he funneled recruits and donations for the jihad in Afghanistan. It was in Peshawar that Azzam most likely met Zawahiri. Finally, Azzam went to Afghanistan and began to build the organization that the world would soon come to know as al-Qaeda.[66]

Azzam embraced the concept of militant jihad as an individual duty not only to defend the international community of Islam against aggression but also to recapture territory that had been lost to the infidels. In this respect he adopted the concepts of both defensive and offensive jihad.[67]

A staunch opponent of the takfiri doctrine, Azzam issued a fatwa prohibiting it, claiming that the killing of fellow Muslims and civilians is against Islam. Although he clearly supported the use of violence to the ultimate end of regaining lost Muslim territory and establishing sharia, Azzam was opposed to overthrowing a Muslim government. Neither did he endorse the killing of apostate Muslims as an end in itself (an important distinction that would later resurface). He was assassinated in 1989, but his influence remains a major inspiration for jihadists around the globe.[68]

AYMAN AL-ZAWAHIRI (1951–PRESENT)

Zawahiri came from a very respectable family. His great uncle on his father's side (Rabi'a al-Zawahiri) was the grand imam of al-Azhar University in Cairo. His grandfather on his mother's side was both the founder of King Saud University and the president of Cairo University.[69]

Although he studied medicine at university, Zawahiri was also interested in politics. Qutb had a major influence on his early ideology, and he joined the Muslim Brotherhood at the age of fourteen. Zawahiri was convinced that the primary step in bringing about the caliphate was to overthrow the corrupt Arab regimes—beginning with Egypt. He was among the members of the Muslim Brotherhood who were arrested with Qutb in 1966, and he was incarcerated until 1971.[70]

Zawahiri and four colleagues from secondary school founded an underground group dedicated to the overthrow of the Egyptian government. The cell merged with the Egyptian Islamic Jihad founder, Muhammad 'Abd al-Salam Faraj, in 1979. Faraj's main goal was to institute sharia in Egypt, necessitating the elimination of the near enemy of the time, Anwar Sadat.[71] Attacking the near enemy would remain Zawahiri's main strategy for many years to come.

Zawahiri was arrested again in 1981; this time he served three years in prison for collaborating in the assassination of Anwar Sadat (even though he claims to have learned of the plot only a few hours beforehand and actually to have advised against going through with it). After his release in 1984, he assumed the leadership of Egyptian Islamic Jihad, and he viciously denounced the Muslim Brotherhood for its apostasy in accepting man-made laws over sharia.[72]

Zawahiri fled to Saudi Arabia in 1985 to escape Hosni Mubarak's crack down on Islamist dissidents. It was in Jeddah that Zawahiri first met bin Laden. Zawahiri later moved to Pakistan, where he openly disagreed with Azzam. Unlike Azzam Zawahiri embraced the takfiri doctrine as it applied to corrupt Muslim rulers.[73] He took a more moderate approach concerning fellow Muslims, however. Falling more in line with al-Banna than Qutb in this respect, Zawahiri believed that the ummah should be taught the true way of Islam from the ulama.[74] This point in particular would prove to be a decisive one between the al-Qaeda leadership and Zarqawi.

Zawahiri merged Islamic Jihad with al-Qaeda in 1998, much to the rest of the group's surprise and chagrin. Islamic Jihad had been committed to the overthrow of the near enemy (the Egyptian regime); however, bin Laden had been successful in winning Zawahiri over to targeting the far enemy first—whether by ideological persuasion or financial incentive is uncertain.

The Evolution of Islamic Extremism

In this chapter I've defined extremism as the possession of hostile beliefs toward members of another group and the willingness to act on those beliefs. If hatred is at the core of extremism, then fighting fire with fire is clearly not the best way to eliminate it. People have to refuse to stoop to the extremist's level and take responsibility for their own actions.

I've also distinguished between three broad categories of extremist ideology (Islamist, jihadist, and takfiri) and traced their origins as far back as possible in an effort to determine when and how a number of the more controversial issues (*takfir, ijtihad, jahiliya, bid'a*, etc.) first crept in.

I began with a discussion of the highly contested concept of jihad and traced this notion through the ages from the Prophet Muhammad to the present day. As I traced the evolution of jihad, I identified a number of other controversial issues that had also spun out of this age-old debate over the legitimate use of violence in the name of Islam.

By the demise of the Ottoman Empire and the rise of the Muslim Brotherhood, the evolution of these ideas came full circle as proponents faced persecution and sought asylum in Saudi Arabia. Largely because of the Soviet invasion of Afghanistan, these same ideologies were dispersed from the Arab peninsula a second time by groups such as al-Qaeda, adopted by yet another generation, and passed on to the next. In chapter 4, I'll uncover the real reason why any of this still matters today.

CHAPTER FOUR

THE CRIME OF THE CENTURY

History teaches us that history teaches us nothing.

—Hegel

This quotation is attributed to the German philosopher Georg Wilhelm Friedrich Hegel (1770–1831). Hegel viewed all of human history as one long saga of alienation—from ourselves. The cause of this alienation? According to Hegel our true nature is Geist (mind/spirit), and we can reconnect with our true selves only through philosophy.[1] In other words our consciousness determines our being.

Karl Marx (1818–83) approached the human condition from a very different perspective. According to Marx we can truly understand ourselves only through a proper understanding of our material and social condition. "It is not the consciousness of men that determines their being, but, on the contrary, their social being that determines their consciousness."[2]

Marx observed that history consists of a series of class struggles. In his theory of historical materialism, Marx noted that human society had passed through three stages.[3] The first stage was a primitive one in which hunters and gatherers struggled for daily survival. Since the concepts of class and private property had not yet been introduced, people were basically equal except for personal attributes such as strength, skill, intelligence, and beauty.

The second stage appeared as people learned to domesticate animals and develop agriculture. The concepts of private property and government were introduced as men acquired vast swaths of territory for themselves and enslaved others to work the land. Captives of war became slaves as did those who couldn't pay their debts. Laws were also enacted to protect the wealthy and reinforce the status quo, which was now largely based on class.

Since private individuals owned property in this stage, they could bequeath it to their descendants. Hereditary classes emerged. One no longer merely became enslaved through debt or war—class was determined at birth. Thus the third stage of society according to Marx was feudalism, a socioeconomic arrangement based on agriculture in which the rich inherited the poor along with their property holdings.

As modernization occurred, the division of labor became more complex. Trade emerged, and along with it came the concept of profit. Market economies developed, and the serfs—once tied to the land under feudalism—eventually became factory workers in the cities. Rather than being inherited by wealthy landowners, the poor were now free to sell their labor on the open market.

As Marx pointed out, this development was wonderful for capitalists (the owners of capital) as they were able to maximize their profits. The workers (what Marx called the proletariat) didn't fare quite so well. Paid a dismal wage for their labor and forced to endure terrible conditions, the poor barely survived.

Worse yet they were stripped of the freedom to provide for their own needs. According to Marx in the earlier stages of history the majority of people were free to work and produce for themselves. The poor could farm, fish, or hunt to meet their basic needs, and they could also produce goods on a small scale to trade in exchange for their other necessities and desires. Engaging in these activities gave human beings a sense of identity and purpose.

Under the capitalist system, however, workers toil away at meaningless and repetitive tasks—often without ever even seeing the finished fruit of their labor—in exchange for wages with which they must purchase all their basic needs from someone else. Marx maintained that this loss of self-sufficiency and purpose caused humans to become alienated from themselves.

According to Marx the wealthier capitalists became, the more concentrated wealth itself became. In other words the rising tide did not lift all boats. The status of the elite was elevated, while the poor sank further into despair. A consolidation of ownership was taking place, leaving a growing number of the world's population with little, if anything, of their own. The gap between rich and poor expanded dramatically.

Marx foretold that a revolution—led by the disenfranchised proletariat—would one day sweep the globe, eventually leading to a classless society in which the workers control the means of production.[4] Indeed, Marx's prediction appeared to be coming true as communist regimes sprang up across the globe in the twentieth century. With their central planning and command economies, communists were anathema to free-market capitalists—but this was not the utopia that Marx envisioned. Many of the communist leaders that emerged were brutal, totalitarian dictators with as much lust for oil as the West. As they pursued their own economic and geopolitical interests, they clashed with the new world order envisioned by the United States and its allies. This inherent conflict of interest led to the Cold War.

The Baghdad Railway

Geologists had already discovered oil in Mesopotamia (modern-day Iraq) in 1871, and by the turn of the twentieth century, contemporary geopolitical realities were already beginning to take shape. In 1904 France (which had colonized much of West Africa) and England (which dominated East Africa) signed the Entente Cordiale. The agreement granted France control of Morocco (along with the Straits of Gibraltar) and Britain control over Egypt (including the Suez Canal).[5]

Britain now controlled an empire that covered much of the globe— from Canada to India and East Africa to Australia. Germany had also recently emerged as an industrial power following its victory over France in 1871. The newly unified state's alliance with Austro-Hungary, Bulgaria, and the Ottoman Empire posed a major threat to Britain because it provided the kaiser with an open door to the Persian Gulf.

Germany had acquired some oil fields in Iraq. However, in order to avoid the powerful British Navy, it required a land route. A railway from Berlin to Basra was just the thing. It would supply the German war machine with a steady flow of oil and at the same time allow German corporations to transport their products to the Persian Gulf. From there they could be exported to the coveted Asian markets.[6]

Germany started construction on the Baghdad Railway in 1903.[7] At that time Britain controlled Egypt, along with the Suez Canal, which was critical to the island empire as it basically cut the distance to India in half.[8] Control of the Persian Gulf would give Germany a military and economic advantage that Britain was not willing to gamble.[9]

The railway also created concern for Russia as it would have provided Germany access to the Caucasus Mountains—bringing it closer to the oil-rich Caspian Sea than Russia felt comfortable allowing.[10] Clearly, neither Britain nor Russia wanted to see Germany reach the Persian Gulf. So the two secured an uneasy agreement via the Anglo-Russian Entente of 1907—settling the long-disputed territorial boundaries of Iran, Afghanistan, and Tibet, which served as a buffer between them. By splitting Iran into three separate spheres, Britain secured control of the Persian Gulf while allowing Russia to retain control of the Caspian Sea.[11]

France also had an interest in stopping Germany. It hoped to regain control of Alsace and Lorraine—along with the region's wealth of coal and iron—which it had lost to Germany in the last conflict. Coal, of course, was the oil of previous centuries, stoking the engines of both military and commerce.

The First Balkan War (1912–13)

Germany's plans were thwarted, however, with the outbreak of the First Balkan War. Greece, Serbia, Montenegro, and Bulgaria annexed nearly all of the Ottoman Empire's European territory—effectively slamming Germany's open door in its face. Both Russia and Britain directly benefited from this development, of course.

The First Balkan War was a proxy war. Russia openly backed the Balkan states against the Ottoman Empire, while Austria-Hungary backed the Ottomans. Even Germany had some skin in the game, backing Bulgaria in a bid to devour a slice of the Ottoman pie. Still, much more was at stake than the Ottoman Empire's eastern European backyard—these Ottoman territories were the smaller prize. The true reward was control of the Persian Gulf and the Caspian Sea—control that Britain, France, and Russia all had a vested interest in protecting.[12]

Therefore, Britain supported Arab nationalism and backed an Arab revolt against the Ottomans in the South (Saudi Arabia, Iraq, and Syria) in an effort to drive the Ottomans away from the Persian Gulf.

Meanwhile, Russia supported Balkan nationalism and encouraged the Balkan League to attack the Ottomans in the West in order to block the construction of Germany's Baghdad Railroad.

In addition to protecting the Caspian, Russia also wanted control of Constantinople, the Bosporus, and the Dardanelles, which would have granted it access to the Mediterranean Sea (and potentially the Suez Canal). Despite this risk Britain signed the Constantinople Agreement and promised to relinquish control of Constantinople and the two straits to Russia.[13]

The Master and the Mistress

The marriage between the British Empire and its corporate mistress forever altered the course of history when Winston Churchill—then First Lord of the Admiralty who also enjoyed close personal and professional relations with senior oil executives at the Burmah Oil Company—made the decision that the Royal Navy would begin using oil as its primary fuel rather than coal.[14]

In 1901 British millionaire William Knox D'Arcy obtained the exclusive right to prospect in Iran. After investing seven years and nearly all his wealth, D'Arcy was ready to give up. He had already sold the majority of his prospecting rights to the Burmah Oil Company (originally the Rangoon Oil Company), which also secured an exclusive contract to supply the British Navy in 1904.[15] Burmah Oil secured its contract with the Royal Navy through Churchill's good friend Sir John Fisher, who was at that time First Sea Lord. Fisher had been pushing for the Navy's full transition to oil since 1902 (for obvious reasons).[16]

In May 1908—in a final act of desperation—D'Arcy sent a telegram to his prospecting team, ordering them to return to Britain at once. D'Arcy's head prospector ignored the order, however, and on May 26 the team finally struck oil in the small Iranian town of Masjed Soleiman.[17] The race for Middle East oil was on.[18]

Burmah Oil established its subsidiary, the Anglo-Persian Oil Company, in 1909, and in 1913 it completed construction of the largest refinery in the world at Abadan.[19] Meanwhile, back in Britain Churchill was securing a few deals of his own.

While oil offered a myriad of improvements for the British Navy, Churchill zeroed in on the need for speed—faster battleships that could out-maneuver the German fleet—which he insisted could only be obtained through oil-powered engines. The truth be told, Britain's *Queen Elizabeth*–class battleships only gained an additional four knots by switching to oil. But Churchill's appeal to national security proved convincing even though the slight increase in speed came with a huge strategic disadvantage: Britain boasted massive coal reserves but no oil.[20]

Britain would need to secure vast supplies of foreign oil, and Churchill knew exactly where they would come from. He assembled a royal commission and concluded that in order to maintain competition in the Persian Gulf, the British government should invest directly in the Anglo-Persian Oil Company (APOC), which, of course, was owned by none other than Churchill's good friends back at Burmah Oil. The British government bought up 51 percent of APOC (which later became British Petroleum, now BP), and Churchill negotiated an exclusive (and extremely lucrative) twenty-year contract. APOC later rewarded him with a cushy position as a paid consultant to lobby the British government for exclusive rights to Persian oil.[21]

Oil quickly became the most sought-after commodity on the planet, and the race for energy was framed as a matter of national security.[22] Ironically, the true threats to national security were the massive oil conglomerates themselves. The world's frenzied addiction to oil meant that the mistress would eventually become the master.

The Great Resource Wars

It should come as little surprise that when World War I broke out in 1914, Germany, Austro-Hungary, and the Ottoman Empire allied against England, France, and Russia (Italy joined later in 1915 after Britain and France promised it a share of the spoils).

Toward the end of the war, the 1916 Sykes-Picot Agreement also promised France an inheritance for its part in the war. Basically dividing the oil between them, Sykes-Picot granted Iraq to Britain and Syria to France. After the war the Treaty of Versailles denied Germany control of the Baghdad Railway, which was first used in 1940.[23]

By 1920 the young Soviet Union was desperate for oil. The Caucasus—an oil-rich region between the Caspian and the Black Seas—offered the perfect solution. The Soviet army invaded Baku, Azerbaijan on April 27 and drove out the western forces stationed there to protect their oil interests. The Soviets took Armenia in December and attacked Tbilisi in February 1921.[24]

Back in Tehran tension began to build over APOC's blatant piracy of Iran's national treasure. D'Arcy's original deal with the shah was quite favorable (for D'Arcy). In exchange for the exclusive right to prospect for sixty years, D'Arcy paid only £20,000 in cash and another £20,000 in stock. Furthermore, the shah would receive 16 percent of any future profits. This may have been acceptable in 1901, but by 1920 it was causing an uproar.[25]

Tehran demanded that the terms be revised to grant Iran a greater share of the profits and total control over transport of the oil. In 1932, after several years of fruitless negotiations, Reza Shah canceled the contract with D'Arcy. Britain responded by taking the matter to The Hague.[26]

Reza Shah retracted, and in 1933 the two parties basically agreed to disagree. APOC had Tehran over a barrel, and Reza Shah knew it, so he signed a new contract granting APOC (now the Anglo-Iranian Oil Company [AIOC]) exclusive extraction rights for yet another sixty years—under terms that were nearly as favorable for AIOC as those in the first contract. AIOC sweetened the pot a bit by agreeing to pay Iranian workers a higher wage and invest in infrastructure, hospitals, and schools. But with the windfall profits it was raking in, it never found the time to honor its end of the bargain.[27]

World War II was also waged over oil. While it is true that Hitler entered North Africa to support his ally Mussolini, he had a more self-serving motive as well.[28] Germany imported some 85 percent of its oil, and the British naval blockade severely restricted its access to foreign imports.[29] Consequently, Hitler fought the battle for North Africa over access to Middle Eastern oil and control of the Suez Canal.[30]

By then European armies had become fully mechanized—converting oil into a critical strategic commodity. Britain and France were not at all excited about the prospects of Hitler looting the oil that they had rightfully stolen. But if they wanted to maintain possession of their ill-gotten gains, they would have to stop Rommel's panzer divisions first.

Hitler also invaded the Soviet Union out of desperation for oil.[31] This time Hitler had his sights set on Baku.[32] Immediately, London allied with Moscow against Berlin. Coveting the Trans-Iranian Railway as a necessary supply route from the Persian Gulf—and suspicious of the shah's friendly relations with Germany—the Allies demanded that Iran deport all German nationals as a pretext. When Tehran refused, Britain and the Soviet Union invaded, arrested the shah, sent him into exile in South Africa, and replaced him with his son, Mohammad Reza Pahlavi.[33]

A King and a Coup

A few years earlier, an American company (Standard Oil of California) struck oil in Saudi Arabia.[34] The discovery generated renewed interest in the Arabian Peninsula. Prior to that discovery, only the coastal areas were controlled by Britain and the Ottomans to secure vital shipping lanes. All that was about to change. In 1945 FDR met with King Abdulaziz, and the rest is modern history.

By 1950 four major energy corporations (Standard Oil, Texaco, Exxon, and Mobil) had purchased shares of ARAMCO, which today is the largest oil and gas conglomerate in the world.[35] King Abdulaziz threatened to nationalize Saudi Arabia's oil, forcing ARAMCO to share its profits with the monarch on a 50/50 basis.[36]

Word spread quickly, and in March 1951 the Majlis (Iranian parliament) decided to nationalize AIOC. Nationalists in the Majlis nominated Mohammad Mossadegh—a vocal advocate for nationalization—as prime minister. Mossadegh was the founder of the National Front (the pro-democracy opposition party), and he was extremely popular.[37] So the following month, the shah bowed to popular opinion and appointed Mossadegh prime minister despite the risk to himself and his foreign patrons.[38]

AIOC had no intention of playing Iran's game. That July it threatened to evacuate its employees and spark an international boycott of Iranian oil if the plan to nationalize went through. Refusing to be intimidated, Mossadegh called AIOC's bluff. Left with only its "honor," AIOC made good on its threat to withdraw its personnel. Shortly afterward it organized a worldwide boycott of Iranian oil. Production at the Abadan refinery came to a screeching halt as the world largely followed Britain's lead.[39]

In a shortsighted panic, the shah made the mistake of attempting to replace Mossadegh, but the people rioted and the Shah himself was perceived as a puppet of the West. A power struggle ensued. At the same time, the boycott created an economic crisis (known as the Abadan Crisis). Iran suffered an enormous loss of revenue as a result.[40]

AIOC also suffered. Honor or no honor, something needed to be done. The British government even considered another invasion to occupy the oil fields. Truman blocked the move, however, suggesting instead that Britain threaten to bring the matter before The Hague again. This time Iran stood its ground, and on July 22, 1952, the International Court of Justice ruled that since AIOC was a private company and not a government, the dispute should be decided by Iranian domestic law. Small victories aside, Tehran would soon learn its place.[41]

In 1953 the CIA and British intelligence agencies cooperated to overthrow Mossadegh and strengthen the shah.[42] After the coup the United States became a strategic ally of Iran, sharing close economic and military ties.[43] Iranian crude again flowed freely, lubricating the engines of the military-industrial complex—this time via a consortium of companies including AIOC (now British Petroleum), Royal Dutch Shell, and the companies that would later be known as Total, Chevron, Exxon, Mobil, and Texaco.[44] These seven oil conglomerates would soon be known as the Seven Sisters. Up until the oil crisis of 1973, these seven monster multinationals controlled 85 percent of all known oil reserves.

The traditional colonial arrangement between government and capital persisted until the devastation and carnage of World War I and World War II rendered the old model inoperable for most European capitalist countries. They were too broke and their armies too decimated to continue to plunder and pillage on behalf of the industrial elite. Nor could most afford to maintain their colonies any longer. As the crumbling empires of the West set their former captives free, the wealthy industrialists desperately sought a way to continue to exploit the resources and the markets of these newly independent states. But they needed another approach—a backdoor so to speak into these regions. They needed a Trojan horse.

The Trojan Horse

The Trojan War of Greek mythology was sparked by Paris, prince of Troy, after he took Helen, the queen of Sparta, to be his own. Legend has it that the goddess Aphrodite made Helen fall in love with Paris. The jaded King Menelaus sent his brother Agamemnon with an army to collect his adulteress wife. After a hopeless decadelong siege of Troy, the Greeks decided on a new strategy. They built an enormous wooden horse and hid soldiers inside it. Then they sailed away, leaving the mammoth trophy behind. The men of Troy brought the great statue into their city and celebrated their supposed victory. Later while the city slept, the Greek soldiers emerged from within the giant horse and unlocked the gates. The Greek fleet returned by night and slaughtered the inhabitants of the city. What they couldn't gain by force, they won through deception.[45] In the wake of World War II, the neocolonialists were about to attempt the very same thing.

Humbled by decades of war and depression, the great colonial empires of Western Europe had no choice but to grant many of their colonies independence, but the corporate powers behind these empires had no intention of relinquishing control over the vast wealth of resources that lay hidden within the former "protectorates." Assembling in Bretton Woods, New Hampshire, the true victors of World War II openly planned to take over the world. Just who were these conquering heroes? The same industrial elites who had been pulling the strings all along. They contrived an elaborate web of international organizations that would turn the Westphalian system of states on its head.[46]

By tying the hands of nation-states with layers of international laws and agreements, the New World Order transferred many of the traditional powers of the states to international organizations such as the United Nations, the World Bank (WB), the World Trade Organization (WTO; formerly the General Agreement on Tariffs and Trade [GATT]), and the International Monetary Fund (IMF). Each of these organizations was strategically designed to strip a specific facet of sovereignty from the state and then wield that power on behalf of corporate elites.

Try to imagine a group of billionaire thugs (the type who make Donald Trump look like an amateur), sitting around a table, smoking stogies and drinking cognac while beautiful hirelings stroke their egos. Life was good, but they had a problem. They wanted to tap the untold treasures of oil, gas, minerals, and other natural resources that lay just beyond their reach. The problem was that their old henchmen had grown weak and unreliable. They needed a new plan.

A slew of newly independent states was emerging on the world's stage. How better to secure their resources than through lies and deception?

Lured by the promise of international acceptance, enhanced trade, and a pile of much-needed cash, these new states were putty in their hands.

The World Bank offered hundreds of millions of dollars in development loans—money that would literally go directly back into the industrial elite's pockets as they secured the construction contracts. The IMF aimed at stabilizing currency-exchange rates, making international commerce less volatile by restricting states from devaluing their own currencies. Rather than simply printing more money, when times got hard states could apply for stabilization loans. Thus the IMF protected elite bank accounts from wild fluctuations in the value of foreign currencies. Meanwhile, the UN outlawed war, and the WTO outlawed trade wars—both making the world a safer place for capitalism.

Like pieces on a chess board, each organization had its own unique role to play in securing a neoliberal new world order. The UN stripped states of the power to declare war, the WTO eroded much of their power to impose trade barriers such as tariffs and quotas, and the two lending organizations (WB and IMF) made loans contingent on strict limitations of the recipient government—eventually insisting that they become neoliberal states and privatize the majority of their public sectors.

Privatization, of course, equated to enormous profits for the corporate elite. But it sentenced much of the rest of the population to dire poverty as public goods and services would no longer be offered for free or at discounted prices. Private schools, hospitals, and banks sprang up overnight. Meanwhile, subsidized food, fuel, and other necessities disappeared from the market.

Nowhere was this scenario imposed with such efficient brutality as in the oil-producing regions of the world, where citizens waited in long lines for gasoline. The IMF and the World Bank reduced the developing states to indentured servitude. The only winners were unmistakably the oil conglomerates. In fact oil economies enslaved the developed West just as readily as everyone else. The world's insatiable addiction to oil forever reversed the traditional relationship between the states and their corporate mistresses.

Marx was right after all. Free-market capitalism has been overthrown—but not by the proletariat. Instead, it's been replaced by monopolistic corporate empires that continue to consolidate the wealth of the world into the hands of fewer and fewer elites. Corporations emerged as the new empires—the neocolonial era had begun.

Was It Really the End of History?

Like all the great conflicts of the twentieth century, the Cold War was also fought over oil.[47] After World War II, the U.S. lacked sufficient oil reserves to endure yet another protracted conflict.[48] Cold War plans placed a high priority on access to Middle East oil fields.[49] Archival evidence reveals that the Soviet Union had similar designs.[50] Competition over the world's oil reserves kick-started four decades of economic and political conflict. The Soviet Union not only blocked Western corporations from accessing the coveted crude in its own backyard; it also financed its weapons program with it—substantially upping the ante in the resulting arms race between the two superpowers.[51]

In an ironic twist of fate, the Bear's rapacious hunger for oil also sealed its doom. In 1983 Reagan convinced Saudi Arabia to flood the market and drive oil prices to historic lows.[52] Like a polar bear on a melting iceberg, the Soviet Union tried desperately to balance skyrocketing military costs with a shrinking economic base. Unable to keep pace with the United States, the USSR collapsed. The Cold War was over.

With the fall of the Soviet Union and the rise of communist China as a global capitalist dynamo, the general consensus was basically that Marx was wrong; capitalism had won. Perhaps Marx was wrong, but not for the reasons that everyone assumed. Marx believed that the free-market capitalist system would ultimately be overthrown, and in this respect he was right on the money. The free-market capitalist system has been overthrown. The revolution occurred. It just didn't happen in the manner that Marx expected it to.

Everyone's heard of globalization—the world is flat and all that—but I'm afraid this tale has a much darker ending. While Marx's stages of history were descriptively correct, there's a more instructive lens through which we can view history: the lens of empire. Not to oversimplify (although it's nearly impossible not to in under ten thousand pages), there have been three basic stages of empire: imperialism, colonialism, and neocolonialism.

In the days before industrialization, armies conquered distant lands—looted and pillaged—and then went home. They took everything of value from goods to livestock—especially slaves—and this is how they ran their economies. Rather than tax their own citizens, they taxed foreigners and required a steady flow of booty to avoid the army making another painful visit. Just think of ancient Israel—repeatedly getting sacked for its refusal to pay tribute to foreign kings—and you get the basic idea.

But the armies themselves and the resources needed to go to war had to come from somewhere. The cost of the king's exploits tended to fall on wealthy landholders (and later merchants). Initially (under feudalism) landowners and knights were rewarded with the spoils of war and royal titles. But it wasn't enough.

Eventually, the upper classes tired of being taxed to fight the king's battles (what else might you call a loan that is never repaid?). So the nobles began to insist on having a say in how their resources were used. If the king was going to continue to "borrow" their valuables, they wanted their interests to be represented (this, of course, is where the idea of parliament came from).

Under imperialism the Crown's armies raped and plundered foreign lands. The basic economic arrangement was that the elite supported these conquests and in return received goods and slaves as spoils of war. It was a primitive form of capitalism as the wealthy invested their capital in ventures that they hoped would pay off.

Colonialism was an entirely different prospect altogether. If imperialism was like coming home and finding you've been robbed (albeit, with a ransom note demanding annual payments so that the perpetrator never returns), colonialism was like coming home and finding the perpetrator on your sofa—watching your TV and telling you to go make him a sandwich.

Colonial powers didn't just sack and steal like their imperial cousins. Rather than dragging huge quantities of booty back home to be consumed by the elites, colonialists established regional bureaucracies abroad. Without getting too thick in the weeds, I can cite one main reason for this difference: industrialization.

While the imperial nobles lounged around all day drinking wine and having orgies, colonial nobles largely ran industries and were driven by profit. Therefore, they not only shipped the stolen resources back home; they made finished goods out of them in their factories.

They then shipped those products back to the colonies and forced the people to buy them at hugely inflated prices (then they drank wine and had orgies).

This entire arrangement was part of the great bargain between capital and government. The wealthy industrialists provided revenue to the government (via taxes on the labor of the working class), and in return the government used its military might to rape and pillage on behalf of the corporate interests of the filthy rich—securing both resources and markets (just as Lenin predicted they would).[53]

It was a win-win scenario: the rich grew richer and capitalist governments grew stronger. Only the poor got screwed, but nobody cared about them anyway. In the American constitution "we the people" originally meant "we the white, landholding males"—women, nonwhites, and all poor people were excluded. Anyone following the 2016 American presidential election could see that very little has changed.

The Saudi Sweep

Riyadh is renowned for some of the deadliest traffic in the world. One infamous maneuver has affectionately been baptized the "Saudi sweep" by Westerners who—despite our own bad driving habits—shudder in fear over the apparent lack of any traffic rules whatsoever in the kingdom.

The Saudi sweep is essentially when a driver overtakes another vehicle at a ridiculously high speed and then pulls a hard left turn from the far right lane just inches in front of that vehicle. This is a very common practice in Riyadh because many of the highways are built in such a way that turning around requires a U-turn rather than exiting off the highway and entering again in the opposite direction.

A similarly abrupt left turn occurred in economic policy during the 1930s. Classical liberal economics suggests that an equilibrium exists in the economy. Basically, given the right price, consumer demand will always exceed production—overproduction and underproduction are not sustainable in the long term. When companies produce too much, excess inventory will cause prices to drop until consumers purchase the excess supply. Alternatively, if companies produce too little, deregulation will allow competitors to bridge the gap.[54]

Thus the classical liberal economic model emphasizes increasing wealth for the upper classes, who because of minimal regulation and low taxes will invest their wealth in the production of goods and services. The consequent increase in private goods and services (as opposed to those provided by the government) creates competition, better quality, and lower prices. Liberal economic theory is associated with economists such as Adam Smith, who called for small government, low taxes, and minimal government interference in the economy—a position generally championed by conservatives on the right.[55]

Keynesian economics suggests the exact opposite, maintaining that the key driver in any economic system is demand because in a contracting economy, unemployment (demand) is the main problem not production (supply).[56] Simply producing more or less can't solve the dilemma. During the global economic meltdown known as the Great Depression, we found ourselves speeding out of control down the supply-side superhighway to economic collapse. There was no off-ramp. The world needed to make a U-turn, so it pulled a Saudi sweep.

When consumer demand began to dry up due to high unemployment, John Maynard Keynes asserted that the government needed to step in and stimulate the economy by creating its own demand for goods and services (e.g., the massive spending of FDR's New Deal). Keynesian economics emphasizes the purchasing power of the lower and middle classes—and it is most commonly associated with big government, high taxes, and redistribution of wealth through social spending.

Rising up from the ashes of the Great Depression, many Western European governments swung to the left as they strove for full employment, competitive wages, universal education, and comprehensive health care for their citizens. Meanwhile in the United States, a cease-fire was reached between capital and labor with the 1946 Employment Act, making employment, production, and purchasing power the responsibility of the federal government.[57]

Even fiscal conservatives jumped on the Keynesian bandwagon. Following more than two decades of relative prosperity in the wake of WWII, Keynesian economic principles appeared to be the silver bullet for the international community's economic woes.

A New Monetary World Order

A new international monetary system was established at the Bretton Woods Conference in 1944 in which the forty-four states in attendance agreed to peg their currency to the dollar. The value of the dollar, in turn, was fixed at thirty-five dollars per ounce of gold. All international balances were settled in dollars, and the U.S. was required to exchange gold for dollars on demand.[58] This arrangement assumed that the United States would never devalue its currency by simply printing more dollars—the dollars in circulation were not supposed to exceed the total value of U.S. gold reserves (oops!).

Initially, as Europe and Japan rebuilt their postwar economies, demand for U.S. goods was high. International demand for dollars was also high. Since the United States held about 75 percent of the world's gold reserves, the combination of high demand for dollars and U.S. wealth prevented a run on U.S. gold reserves.[59]

Cracks in the Bretton Woods system started to appear in the 1960s when foreign exports began to compete with American products. As the U.S. market share decreased, so did the demand for U.S. dollars. Unfortunately, due to Cold War military spending and foreign aid, America's balance of payments also began to suffer.

The Great Inflation (1965–82) was a sign of the times. Four additional recessions—complicated by two energy shortages—could mean only one thing: the Bretton Woods system was failing. Nixon announced price and wage controls to check inflation. These measures acted as a temporary speed bump to slow rising prices. However, they also exacerbated food and energy shortages. Long lines at the pumps became a necessary evil.[60]

Concern over a run on gold grew given that dollars in foreign accounts amounted to eight times the value of America's reserves. Suspicion that the United States might devalue the dollar also encouraged the international community to cash in its dollar holdings for gold. By the summer of 1971, speculators were rampantly transferring dollars to foreign currencies, and central banks were converting dollars into gold at an alarming rate.[61]

Richard "Tricky Dick" Nixon faced both a run on the bank and the dilemma of how to pay for the Vietnam War. He complained that other countries were shirking their share of the military burden, and he also blamed America's balance-of-payments deficit on unfair trading practices.

Nixon pulled a fast one on the American people and the world: he took the United States off the gold standard and discontinued the exchange of gold for U.S. dollars. He also imposed a 10 percent import tax on foreign goods to address the balance-of-payments deficit.[62] Meanwhile, the Nixon administration simply printed more money to pay for the war (a tradition that's been upheld by every administration since).

Closing the gold window triggered an international reaction, and monetary authorities from developed countries around the world gathered at the Smithsonian in December 1971 to decide what could be done. In response to America's irresponsible printing of currency, the dollar was devalued to thirty-eight dollars per ounce. Foreign states also agreed to ease existing restrictions on trade, while key allies promised to assume a greater share of the military burden. But it was essentially too little, too late.[63]

Gold prices soared, and by February 1973 the U.S. had again devalued its currency to forty-two dollars per ounce. Speculation against the dollar grew so fierce that by summer 1973, nearly all major foreign currencies were floating against the dollar. The United States had stepped up to the challenge of maintaining a sound international monetary system—and it had failed.[64]

The recession of 1973–75 represented the worst economic downturn since the Great Depression.[65] A devalued dollar equated to higher prices on imports and a steady decline in purchasing power. Exogenous factors also contributed to rising prices. The Arab oil embargo of 1973 drove the price of crude up roughly 400 percent (a price that would basically hold until 1979, when oil prices tripled due to the Iranian Revolution).[66]

By 1980 inflation had reached 14.5 percent, and unemployment was inching near 8 percent.[67] Stagflation—a combination of high inflation and high unemployment—was the final nail in the Keynesian coffin. The die was cast. The only question left was, "what to do next?"

Keynesians had generally assumed that inflation is indirectly correlated with unemployment (a concept known as the Phillips Curve).[68] In other words you could have either runaway inflation or high unemployment but not both at the same time. Therefore, conventional Keynesian wisdom decreed that any attempt to reduce inflation should also raise unemployment.[69] This notion certainly sounds straightforward enough. The only problem was that it was wrong.

Given rising inflation, the government can take measures to slow the economy. But if prices fall too low, profits lag and businesses suffer (which then raises unemployment). Without government intervention the results can be catastrophic (as we saw during the Great Depression). Alternatively, efforts to ease unemployment were sure to boost inflation. The greatest challenge facing Keynesian policy makers (or so they thought) had been how to maintain a balance between the two. But now they were facing both high unemployment and rampant inflation. To paraphrase Ludwig Bemelmans's Miss Clavel, sumsing was not right!

Two basic tools are available to governments for influencing economic activity: monetary policy and fiscal policy. Monetary policy involves raising or lowering interest rates, while fiscal policy involves raising or lowering tax rates and the overall level of government spending.[70]

An expansionary monetary policy lowers interest rates to discourage saving and encourage spending.[71] The goal is to boost economic activity by increasing consumption. Increased consumption equates to increased demand, which—at least in theory—should raise prices and lower unemployment. A contractionary monetary policy increases interest rates in order to encourage saving and discourage spending. The goal in this approach is to decrease consumption and dampen inflation.[72]

Fiscal policy attempts to achieve the same results via the mechanisms of taxes and government spending. To stimulate the economy, governments can lower taxes and/or increase spending. Both actions are intended to increase consumption and therefore demand, which again, at least in theory, should raise prices and lower unemployment.[73] Alternatively, in times of soaring inflation governments can raise taxes and/or decrease spending in an effort to slow economic activity.

In addition to the two basic tools available for influencing economic activity, there are also two standard macroeconomic theories concerning how best to achieve optimal results. The first is called supply-side economics, which asserts that increased production is the main driver of economic prosperity. As Say's Law states, "Supply creates its own demand."[74] Therefore, supply-side economic policy focuses on production rather than attempting to stimulate demand.[75] According to this theory, an increase in the supply of goods and services will increase competition.[76] Increased competition will improve quality and drive down prices. Low prices will encourage consumption, and consumption will in turn drive production.[77]

The supply-side economic model is based on three principles: low taxes, minimal government regulation, and stable monetary policy. First, tax rates are not the same as tax revenues (an idea expressed by the Laffer Curve).[78] Simply put there's an optimum tax rate for generating revenue.[79] Neither taxes that are too high nor taxes that are too low will maximize revenue. Just as in the story of Goldilocks, the trick is to get them "just right." Still, lower income tax rates are generally believed to increase government revenue by motivating individuals to work, while a lower capital gains tax is expected to raise government revenues by encouraging profitable investment of capital. In short the supply-side model suggests that lower tax rates will be offset by a larger tax base.[80]

Supply-siders also view minimal government regulation as preferable because presumably the market is a better regulator than the government—especially concerning both price and wage equilibrium. Finally, rather than viewing monetary policy as a tool for influencing the economy, supply-siders are traditionally conservative and therefore champion small government and nonintervention.

Supply-side economics is the classical liberal economic model in a nutshell, and it was largely the default economic approach to free-market capitalism until Keynesian economics appeared as a reaction to the Great Depression.

Conversely, demand-side economics insists that consumer demand is the principal factor determining economic activity. Rather than focusing on production as the main determinant of economic activity, demand-side economic theory emphasizes purchasing power (wages) as the key variable. This is the Keynesian model, and it insists that during times of economic recession the government needs to increase demand through spending on public goods and services.[81] The claim is that government intervention will keep businesses afloat, minimize unemployment, and safeguard wages.[82]

These descriptions are oversimplifications, of course, and intentionally so. The main point to be made is that one needs to draw a distinction between economic theory and economic policy. As I'll demonstrate, economic theory is grounded in . . . economics. Economic policy, however, is almost always driven by politics.

Monetarism

By the end of the 1970s, the pendulum had swung back to the right. The economic policies of Margaret Thatcher and Ronald Reagan signaled in no uncertain terms that the reign of Keynesianism was over. Supply-side economics burst back on the scene, and the invisible hand was once again free of the shackles of government intervention. While differing slightly monetarism and Reaganomics both targeted the same culprit. Big government was to blame for all the world's economic ills, and neoliberalism would emerge as the cure.

Milton Friedman—celebrated as the guru of neoliberalism—was largely opposed to the use of fiscal policy to manipulate the economy. Still, while he understood that tax cuts could lead to huge deficits, he agreed to them anyway, believing that the result would be a curb in spending.[83]

Friedman suggested that in a competitive equilibrium where the demand for labor equals supply, a natural rate of unemployment will always persist regardless of which economic principles are employed. Therefore, Friedman believed the assumption that inflation is indirectly correlated with unemployment to be false.[84]

While agreeing that an increase in the money supply might decrease unemployment in the short term, Friedman argued that in the long run, increased monetary growth increases prices but has little effect on employment. The supposition that the rate of unemployment can be permanently reduced requires that real wages (or some other variable) also be permanently altered. Without such a change, wage inflation will eventually catch up with actual inflation resulting in no change in real wages or the rate of unemployment. Essentially blaming the Great Depression on unsound monetary policy, Friedman insisted that the best policy makers can do is attempt to minimize the natural rate of unemployment by keeping inflation in check via monetary policy and achieving wage equilibrium through deregulation.[85]

Friedman's approach was a combination of supply-side economic theory and monetary policy called monetarism. Unlike pure supply-siders (who are typically against government intervention and argue that lowering tax rates alone is sufficient), Friedman insisted that control of the money supply through monetary policy was also necessary. He defended the quantity theory of money, which proposes a positive correlation between the quantity of money in an economic system and the price of goods and services. Friedman's money-supply rule contends that if the Federal Reserve Board simply adjusts the money supply according to the rate of real GNP change, inflation will be eliminated. His influence has been extensive.[86]

Reaganomics

With inflation at 14.5 percent and unemployment hovering above 7.5 percent, the 1980 presidential race centered on the economy. Reagan inspired hope by promising that Americans would produce their way out of the economic slump.[87] Through eloquent speeches about American exceptionalism, he painted the image of full employment and affluence from sea to shining sea. And according to Reagan, the transition would be painless.

Paul Volcker—who was strongly influenced by Friedman—became the chairman of the Fed in 1979. He discontinued the practice of targeting interest rates to aggregate demand in favor of controlling the money supply and allowing the markets to set the rates. By 1981 the prime rate had risen to 12.5 percent and the Fed fund rate to 19.1 percent.[88]

Lest we be too quick to assume that perhaps Reagan was sleeping through all of this, Volcker received the administration's full support. Reaganomics rested on the four pillars of reduced regulation, lower taxes, decreased social spending, and tightening the money supply.[89] The "Reagan Revolution" featured a contractionary monetary policy to lower inflation, the continual removal of many Nixon-era price controls, and deregulation of the banks (which greatly contributed to the savings and loan crisis of 1989).

Reagan kicked off his first year in office by signing both the Budget and Reconciliation Act and the Economic Recovery Act. Together the two laws comprised huge increases in military spending, deep cuts in nondefense expenditures, and the largest tax cut in American history, reducing taxes by $749 billion over five years.[90]

The Economic Recovery Act lowered personal income tax brackets as promised. However, it especially favored wealthy investors. By accelerating capital depreciation, Reagan shifted the tax burden away from unearned income and placed it squarely on the shoulders of the working class.[91]

Reagan also cut spending as promised—to be more accurate, he cut spending on the poor. In his first year he reduced social spending by $39 billion, but he also raised military spending by 35 percent.[92] By the end of his second term, the national debt had nearly tripled.[93]

Read My Lips

George H. W. Bush originally mocked Reaganomics, calling it, "voodoo economics." However, he reversed course not long afterward. During his acceptance speech at the 1988 Republican National Convention, he vowed not to raise taxes in line with his party's neoliberal economic policy of low taxes and low spending. Of course, we all know the rest of the story (a certain governor from Arkansas made sure of that).

The combination of Reagan's outlandish military spending and his refusal to tax the rich left George H. W. Bush with substantial fiscal constraints. However, even the 1990 Deficit Reduction Act upheld basic neoliberal principles by introducing more social spending cuts and burdening the working class with even more tax increases.

To absolutely no one's surprise, Bush protected his own private oil empire in the Middle East (see chapter 4). Therefore, despite massive reductions in social spending, military spending on the Gulf War was not affected in the slightest—resulting in antiwar chants ("No blood for oil!") that swept across the nation as Americans pushed back against the Washington machine.

Bush also supported other neoliberal endeavors such as NAFTA and the Uruguay Round (which led to GATT becoming the WTO, an organization that would also spark resistance such as the 1999 protests in Seattle). Still, like the Ford administration, the George H. W. Bush administration is easy to forget. When it is remembered, people usually call to mind lingering recession, persistent unemployment, and a growing awareness among the American people that the neoliberal agenda prioritized money and oil over pretty much everything else. However, as I'll discuss in chapter 6, the first Bush administration was not as impotent as it appears. A lot was going on behind the scenes.

Neoliberal Puppet Masters

> I guess I should warn you, if I turn out to be particularly clear, you've probably misunderstood what I've said.
>
> —Alan Greenspan

Alan Greenspan chaired the Fed from 1987 to 2006.[94] Known as Washington's "resident wizard," Greenspan was credited not for preventing the stock-market crash in 1987 but for preventing it from getting worse. He also enjoyed worldwide praise for the economic boom in the 1990s.[95]

Remember the good old days when the government was actually running a surplus? In addition to Greenspan's monetary wizardry, most credit this achievement to the tight belt of the Clinton administration. But fiscal austerity is not generally the kind of policy that one associates with the Democratic Party and its traditional platform of big government, high taxes, and social spending. The neoliberal winds of change were definitely blowing.

Clinton campaigned against the neoliberal policies of Reagan and Bush, promising *A Vision of Change for America*—which would later be the title of his 1993 fiscal stimulus plan.[96] Did Clinton follow through on his promise? Kinda sorta . . .

In his first year, Clinton raised the earned income tax credit for low-income earners, a move that initially appeared to be in harmony with standard Democratic values. However, the increased tax credit would turn out to be an absolute necessity for the millions of Americans forced to survive on the meager wages resulting from NAFTA (the free-trade agreement that would soon be enacted between the U.S., Canada, and Mexico).[97]

NAFTA was supposed to create millions of new jobs, and it did—for Mexicans! In America the result was a net loss of roughly seven hundred thousand jobs. It was a *net* loss because America lost a lot more than seven hundred thousand jobs. However, many of the higher-paying manufacturing jobs were replaced by service-sector jobs paying dismally low wages and no benefits.[98] Thus reality was far more frightening than the numbers suggest.

From the outset Clinton's neoliberal emphasis on market incentives was in full swing.[99] Oh, and remember his big plan to reform the health care system in America? Whatever happened to that? The long answer is that in 1994 Republicans gained fifty-four seats in the House and nine seats in the Senate, giving them majority control of Congress. Newt Gingrich's *Contract with America*—which borrowed freely from Reagan's 1985 State of the Union Address—introduced legislation to balance the budget, cut taxes (mainly for businesses), and "reform" Social Security and welfare.[100] The short answer? Health care reform didn't happen.

The 1996 Welfare Reform Bill passed the economic burden down to the states (as Reagan proposed in his 1982 New Federalism speech) and therefore destined it to be poorly funded from that point onward.[101] For the remainder of the decade, America steadied the neoliberal course of small government and free trade.

The New Deal—long dead—was officially buried. The net result of the *Contract with America* was smaller government, lower taxes, decreased social spending, deregulation, rampant pursuit of free trade, and more of the same monetarist policies (sound familiar?).

Lest we blame all this on the Republicans, let's not forget that a Democrat was in the White House the entire time. If Clinton possessed the infinite reach to bomb a pharmaceutical factory in Khartoum just to distract public attention away from his personal scandal, he most certainly had the ability to help those Americans most in need. He just didn't want to. As a Bill Maher once joked, "Bill Clinton is the kind of guy who'll give you one tic-tac."

So in hindsight Alan Greenspan was only one member in an entire cast of neoliberal actors. Despite the lessons that should have been learned from the 1987 crash—particularly that Wall Street can't be trusted—everyone just continued to skip blindly down the yellow brick road of neoliberalism, certain that the wizard in the Emerald City had all of the answers. However, when the curtain was drawn, the wizard turned out to be just a man after all.

Greenspan's policies are now largely blamed for the mortgage crisis. Throughout his tenure at the Fed, Greenspan cut interest rates and flooded huge amounts of cash into the economy. The result was an expanding bubble in the stock market, emanating from overinflated prices fueled by dot-coms. It couldn't last—and it didn't.

When the market crashed in March 2000, Greenspan cut interest rates even more, eventually dropping them to 1 percent. Since interest rates were lower than the rate of inflation, they were basically negative interest rates. It now actually cost people money to save—not that anyone had anything left to save after more than a decade of institutional larceny on the part of the Clinton administration.

In 2001 Greenspan testified before Congress that G. W. Bush's proposed tax reductions (which were intended to further ease the tax burden on the rich) were necessary to save the system from another crisis. Greenspan essentially warned Congress that running a surplus without debt could result in the government paying off its long-term Treasury bonds before they matured—thus incurring additional costs.[102]

However, when Bush's tax cuts created dangerously high deficits, Greenspan suddenly insisted that it was imperative to balance the budget by slashing social spending. So according to Greenspan, it's absolutely necessary to balance the budget regardless of what that means for the poor—unless a deficit happens to benefit the rich—in which case it's preferable to be in debt.[103]

Greenspan's monetary policies equated to declining real wages for workers and a significantly lower average household income after inflation. For the wealthy it equated to greater risk as investors sought higher returns. Speculation in the real estate market boomed. Average people survived by taking out home equity loans made popular through inflated housing prices.

Despite Greenspan's claim that the Fed didn't cause the housing bubble, reckless subprime lending was rewarded and largely concealed by the fact that many high-risk mortgages were packaged and resold as AAA-rated securities.[104] When the housing bubble burst in 2007, it triggered the credit crisis by generating huge losses for banks and financial institutions around the world.[105] Lehman Brothers went belly-up in September 2008, and the resulting credit freeze nearly brought the global financial system to its knees—yet everyone was surprised.[106]

What was the response? More of the very same neoliberal policies that created the financial crisis in the first place. Ben Bernanke, who succeeded Greenspan as chair of the fed, bailed out Wall Street by dumping $600 billion into the largest banks—most of which rewarded their top VPs with multimillion dollar bonuses while absolutely refusing to assist average Americans who had either lost their home, gone upside-down in their mortgage, or lost substantial equity in their property.[107] But that's common knowledge.

What most people don't know is that these very banks (Citigroup, Bank of America, J. P. Morgan, Wells Fargo, Morgan Stanley, Goldman Sachs, and others) have also recklessly loaned more than $140 billion to oil conglomerates that are owned by Washington insiders, employ Washington insiders, and/or donate hundreds of millions of dollars to Washington insiders.[108] What's worse, these loans will likely also go into default, and those same Washington insiders will simply bill the American taxpayers. This is why the government will never give the bail-out money directly to the American people. Muslims around the world aren't the only ones being displaced.

When questioned before a congressional hearing in 2008, the wizard finally admitted to the people of Oz that he had "made a mistake in presuming" that Wall Street could regulate itself.[109] While most certainly not a wizard, Greenspan was more of a robbing hood—presiding over an era in which enormous quantities of wealth were stolen from the working classes and heaped upon the super-rich. His very name is synonymous with neoliberalism (among other things).

A long line of presidents—from Reagan to Obama—employed neo-liberal policies, military action, and even war to protect and enhance their own private wealth. Much of this wealth is tied to oil, either directly as with the Bush family dynasty or indirectly through the corrupt banking industry.

The Reagan Revolution was first and foremost a neoliberal revolution that succeeded in overthrowing the Keynesian system. From that moment on—from Reagan's New Right to Clinton's New Liberalism and beyond—while subtle differences may have arisen concerning Cuban cigars and whatnot, there has been virtually no meaningful distinction between Republicans and Democrats regarding macroeconomic policy. In chapter 5 I'll explore how the U.S. political system has become so dysfunctional.

CHAPTER FIVE

THE ROAD TO PERDITION

Today, our enemies see weapons of mass destruction as weapons of choice.

—George W. Bush, *The National Security Strategy of the United States of America*

In the previous chapter, I discussed the neoliberal revolution and how Washington and Wall Street elites have manipulated U.S. economic policy to line their own pockets. In this chapter I'll consider an even more disturbing phenomenon: the neoconservative revolution. I'll begin by examining the various political ideologies in play in America and locating the major players within their respective creeds.

The Democratic Party

In American politics there are two basic distinctions: Democrats and Republicans. However, what these two labels stand for has changed dramatically over time. The Democratic Party was founded in 1828, by the supporters of Andrew Jackson. It used to be the party of the South, representing state's rights, advocating small government, and defending slavery. Jackson himself resided on a plantation that stretched for hundreds of acres, and he owned hundreds of slaves.[1]

Democrats prior to the New Deal Era adhered to classical liberalism, a political ideology that champions civil liberties and free-market capitalism (private property and economic competition).[2] Therefore, these early Democrats believed that the government should protect citizens from torture, false imprisonment, and confiscation of property. However, they were largely opposed to civil rights and the welfare state (redistribution of wealth) because they believed that free markets were the best way to produce wealth (à la Adam Smith's invisible hand). In short they were basically libertarians.[3]

That orientation began to change in the twentieth century. By the time of FDR and the New Deal, the Democratic Party was championing social justice (equal opportunity), a mixed economy (government regulation of private enterprise), and the welfare state. By the days of LBJ, the Democrats were also fully backing civil rights, a position that cost them much of their white constituency in the South.[4]

Democrats since FDR have typically been left of center politically. In America this equated to higher taxes to fund social welfare programs, a pro-choice stand on the abortion issue, and a more responsible approach to the environment (e.g., Al Gore's *Inconvenient Truth*).

However, especially since the presidency of Bill Clinton, the party has shifted back to the right on economic policy—once again favoring free-market capitalism and deregulation. Moreover, the Clinton Doctrine—which emphasized interventionism under the euphemism "democratic enlargement"—moved the Democratic Party even further to the political right. In essence the party now champions neoliberalism and neoconservatism, which in many respects are antithetical to the values of the Democratic Party that most Americans still believe exists—but no longer does.[5]

Beginning in the 1960s, conservative-leaning Democrats who disagreed with their party's foreign policy became politically active in Republican administrations.[6] Although the neocons officially "arrived" with the George W. Bush administration, neoconservatism has been around since the 1960s and has been influential at least since the Clinton administration.[7]

Stepping back to get a better look at the Democratic Party today, one sees a bizarre and hypocritical mixture of civil rights and social justice rhetoric (without any action to back it up), the promotion of civil liberties at the barrel of a gun, and rabid neoliberal policies that represent the interests of the wealthy while oppressing the poor and the working class.

The Republican Party

While the Republican Party has been a bit more stable than the Democratic Party over the years, it too has gone through changes. Founded in 1854 by northern antislavery activists, the Republican Party has consistently represented the interests of businessmen and capitalists. This makes perfect sense when you consider that the North was industrialized long before the South. Consequently, Republicans favor neoliberal policies: small government (deregulation), low taxes, and minimal social spending.[8]

Where the party has changed over the years is in the area of foreign policy. Republicans such as Eisenhower and Nixon were well known for their "realism"—a political philosophy that places power at the center of political affairs rather than other considerations such as institutions or regime type. Therefore—and especially during the Cold War—a leader's willingness to cooperate with the United States mattered infinitely more than his human rights record or whether he was democratically elected.

Henry Kissinger referred to this policy as realpolitik. It meant doing what needed to be done in the interests of national security.[9] In a 1975 meeting with the Thai foreign minister, Kissinger announced, "They [the Khmer Rouge] are murderous thugs, but we won't let that stand in the way. We are prepared to improve relations with them."[10] On another occasion, he callously admitted, "If they put Jews into gas chambers in the Soviet Union, it is not an American concern."[11]

Ronald Reagan was a controversial figure to say the least. While some maintain that his policies were based in misguided idealism, many consider him the last American realist president. In his 1980 acceptance speech before the Republican National Convention, Reagan accused the Carter administration of living in a world of make-believe.[12]

Reagan listed realism, strength and dialogue as pillars of his foreign policy, and his administration based its foreign and economic policy on a stable economy and strong national defense.[13] While Carter's perceived strength was the pursuit of peace, Reagan's electoral support originated from his concern for national security in light of Soviet expansion and offensive arms buildup.

Reagan's famous phrase "window of vulnerability" referred to the fact that American intercontinental ballistic missiles were vulnerable to Soviet attack.[14] The cold warrior increased defense spending substantially, initially proposing a budget of 1.6 trillion for the first five years.[15] Reagan's strategy was based in the projection of power: "We will maintain sufficient strength to prevail if need be, knowing that if we do so we have the best chance of never having to use that strength."[16]

Explicitly adverse to appeasement, the great storyteller criticized détente as naive. He often justified increased military spending by referring to the Munich Pact and comparing his critics to Neville Chamberlain. The fortieth president generated unprecedented peacetime deficits, increasing the national debt from $1.14 trillion at the end of his first fiscal year in 1982 to $2.85 trillion in 1989.[17]

Reagan was determined that military superiority—rather than weakness—would be the position from which he would negotiate strategic arms reduction. Hence (while not everyone would agree with this position), realism can be considered the dominant foreign policy throughout the Cold War years—including the presidency of Ronald Reagan.

The fork in the road for Republicans first appeared with the strong neoconservative policies of the Bush administration, policies that many realist Republicans openly disagreed with. Unlike realism neoconservatism (sometimes referred to as neoliberalism by other means) emphasizes that regime type matters.[18] Hence the Bush administration's obsession with regime change—largely in pursuit of neoliberal policies.

G. W. Bush's administration certainly wasn't the first to entertain neoconservative ideas. As I'll discuss, the seeds were planted decades earlier. Clinton's policy of democratic enlargement was a sign that they were beginning to take root. Even though Bush initially criticized Clinton's foreign policy, he largely continued the same ideals and greatly amplified them. Obama more or less followed the Bush administration's game plan—and in many respects Obama is more of a neocon than Bush. Since neocons are also staunch neoliberals, there has been no substantial change in American economic policy since Reagan and very little change in U.S. foreign policy since Clinton.

America's neoconservative foreign policy is based on the three pillars of unilateralism, preemption, and military hegemony, commonly referred to as the Bush Doctrine. In the remainder of this chapter, I'll investigate both the history of this foreign policy and the tremendous influence it continues to exert today.

The Bush Doctrine

The Bush Doctrine can be summed up in three concepts: preemption, unilateralism, and military hegemony. Based on the Bush administration's policy as delineated in both the 2002 and the 2006 *National Security Strategy* (*NSS*) and popularly christened a doctrine after G. W. Bush's public address following 9/11, the Bush Doctrine clearly states, "We cannot let our enemies strike first. . . . We will not hesitate to act alone. . . . We must build and maintain our defenses beyond challenge."[19]

The Bush Doctrine has had its staunch supporters—Barack Obama being the first in line (and Hillary Clinton hoping to have been the next). While openly criticizing G. W. Bush on nearly every front, these two have pursued foreign policies that put them front and center in the cheerleading squad.

Critics argue that far from extending America's global reach, Bush's foreign policy has politically isolated the United States. Others insist that rather than enhancing America's status as the sole remaining superpower, the Bush Doctrine has discredited it in the eyes of the global community. Finally, instead of advancing democracy throughout the world, many claim that the Bush Doctrine has become the very apparatus of American imperialism: "Having spooked ourselves into believing that we have no option but to act fast, alone, unilaterally and pre-emptively, we have managed in six years to destroy decades of international good will, alienate allies, embolden enemies and yet solve few of the major international problems we face."[20]

One big problem with the Bush Doctrine is that it's being emulated. If the United States can justify preemption and unilateralism in defense of its national security, why can't everyone else? This course of action would be catastrophic if allowed to go unchecked on a global scale.

So why did the Bush administration favor such a disastrous foreign policy strategy? And why did the Obama administration adhere to it as well? More importantly, now that Trump is apparently following suit, how is his administration likely to affect America's standing in the international community? These are the questions I'll address in this chapter.

While much in the 2002 *NSS* is to be applauded, particularly given the context of the September 11 attacks (and there are definitely those who applaud it as well as those who do not), we now have the advantage of hindsight. This hindsight has revealed several things, from the total absence of weapons of mass destruction (WMD) in Iraq to the folly of U.S. intervention in the region and the fragile nature of America's credibility among the members of the international community.

With the adrenaline of 9/11 and its resulting foreign-policy blunders now history, it would be wise to reexamine the U.S. position in world affairs. Particularly now that the country has a new commander in chief, the time is ripe to reassess America's leadership role and adapt U.S. foreign-policy objectives to better serve American national security in the ever-changing global security environment. Trump has promised to do just this. Of course, Americans have heard such promises before—and the nation has never been more divided.

To best move forward, one should attempt to understand where the United States is now—and more importantly, how it arrived here. Therefore, in the sections that follow, I'll examine the history of American unilateralism and the twin policies of preemption and military hegemony.

American Unilateralism

Our purpose as a nation is firm . . . to answer these attacks and rid the world of evil.

—George W. Bush, *President's Remarks at National Day of Prayer and Remembrance*

G. W. Bush's mission to rid the world of "evil" was not so different from that of the religious extremists we discussed in chapter 2—nor was the resolve to go it alone if need be. Extremists will always be convinced that they are right and everyone else is wrong. The more the world opposes their position, the more convinced they become that they alone are right. Hence, unilateralism is a close cousin of extremism.

Unilateralism consists of policies or decisions on the part of one actor without the consent of other actors—perhaps even in violation of multilateral treaties. Multilateralism, on the other hand, is the coordination of policy among three or more states. While there is certainly no clear consensus on when unilateralism became the official stance of U.S. foreign policy, few disagree that unilateralism is the prevailing principle today.

Some observers claim that American unilateralism goes as far back as the Plan of Treaties and the Declaration of Independence.[21] Others argue that early American foreign policy was instead based on the principles of peace, cooperation, and the fabric of international law.[22] Still others maintain that American unilateralism is a far more modern phenomenon, beginning with the United Nations. These argue that since the U.S. was opposed to being governed under international law, it championed favorable wording in what eventually came to be known as the Domestic Jurisdiction Clause, which distinguished those legal issues that fell under domestic jurisdiction from those that did not. The U.S. also refused to accept the World Court's compulsory jurisdiction—and with the Connally Amendment, America demanded the right to decide for itself which legal issues fell under its own domestic jurisdiction.[23]

Others trace the phenomenon to influences of the Christian right on U.S. foreign policy following World War II. According to this perspective, American unilateralism prevailed as the U.S. (a "self-righteous superpower") dominated its allies and attempted to dictate their domestic policy during the Cold War and afterward.[24] As Samuel Huntington has observed, "The unipolar moment has passed. Even old allies stubbornly resist American demands, while many other nations view U.S. policy and ideals as openly hostile to their own. Washington is blind to the fact that it no longer enjoys the dominance it had at the end of the Cold War. It must relearn the game of international politics as a major power, not a superpower, and make compromises. U.S. policymaking should reflect rational calculations of power rather than a wish list of arrogant, unilateralist demands."[25]

Far less accommodating still, others mark a clear line of demarcation between Bush's unilateralism and past American foreign policy, calling it a revolutionary approach to U.S. foreign policy. Pointing to neocons such as Cheney and Rumsfeld who were enraged by earlier administrations that failed to act unilaterally and decisively proclaim U.S. hegemony, proponents of this position observe that September 11 provided an ideal opportunity to drastically alter U.S. foreign policy. Even Charles Krauthammer has described Bush's unilateralism as something new: "With ABM and Kyoto, the new unilateralism made its mark. It began with a great gnashing of teeth by our allies: Nations that spent the better part of the last 500 years raping and pillaging vast swaths of the globe now pronounce themselves distressed at the arrogance of the United States for refusing, at the height of its power, to play the docile international citizen."[26]

Thus, there are two broad schools of thought regarding the history of American unilateralism: one views it as preceding the Bush administration, and the other insists it was implemented as an explicit component of foreign policy during G. W. Bush's presidency and recklessly pursued by Obama and now obviously also by Trump.

Whichever position one accepts, the Bush administration was well known for flexing its unilateral displeasure (e.g., its withdrawal from the Anti-Ballistic Missile Treaty, its refusal to honor the Nonproliferation Treaty, and its invasion of Iraq without UN authority, which earned Kofi Annan's public denunciation of the war as illegal). Obama promised change but then reneged ("Yes We Can!"—we just don't want to), and already in his first year in office Trump's unilateral posture is well established.[27] From his decision to pull out of the Paris Agreement on climate change to his decertification of the Nuclear Agreement with Iran, his withdrawal from negotiations regarding the global migration crisis, and his pronouncement of Jerusalem as the capital of Israel (bolstered by Ambassador Haley's threats to discontinue economic assistance to any state that opposed the decision), Trump has made it abundantly clear where he stands on the issue of American unilateralism. As a result worldwide public opinion remains largely negative toward the United States for its adherence to this policy.

The Policy of "Preemption"

We must adapt the concept of imminent threat to the capabilities and objectives of today's adversaries. . . . The United States has long maintained the option of preemptive actions to counter a sufficient threat to our national security. The greater the threat, the greater is the risk of inaction—and the more compelling the case for taking anticipatory action to defend ourselves, even if uncertainty remains as to the time and place of the enemy's attack. To forestall or prevent such hostile acts by our adversaries, the United States will, if necessary, act preemptively.

—George W. Bush, *The National Security Strategy of the United States of America*

Bush's 2002 *National Security Strategy* introduced a preemptive war policy that was basically just a spin on preventive war—a military doctrine viewed as nothing less than illegal by international standards. Bush's 2006 *National Security Strategy* called for more of the same: "We do not rule out the use of force before attacks occur, even if uncertainty remains as to the time and place of the enemy's attack."[28] This position, of course, has prompted much debate over the legitimacy of preemptive strikes and harsh criticism against the Bush, Obama, and Trump administrations.

It is evident from the preceding chapter that not everyone agrees on when the policy of unilateralism became the foreign policy of America. It is, however, widely acknowledged that while American unilateralism may not be one of the country's founding principles, the United States' insistence on going it alone in a number of arenas has clearly grown more stubborn and futile—with 9/11 and the resulting war on terror serving as the sole common denominator and justification for many of America's more recent actions. In this section I'll explore the policy of preemption and attempt to weigh the prevailing attitudes and opinions regarding its origin and implementation in American history.

Preemption can be defined as military action taken against an imminent attack. Preemptive attacks are legal under international law.[29] Prevention, on the other hand, is an entirely different concept. Preventive war can be defined as military action taken against a state that *may* constitute a risk, either now or in the future.[30] The Bush administration conflated the two terms to justify a preventive war against Iraq, which was, of course, illegal according to international law.

While it may be true that the United States has traditionally allowed for preemptive strikes in the case of an imminent threat, Bush's call to adapt the concept of preemption to include preventive strikes was noteworthy, to say the least. As Richard Falk notes, "Pre-emption . . . validates striking first, not in a crisis, but on the basis of shadowy intentions, alleged potential links to terrorist groups, supposed plans and projects to acquire weapons of mass destruction, and anticipations of possible future dangers. It is a doctrine without limits, without accountability to the UN or international law, without any dependence on a collective judgment of responsible governments and, what is worse, without any convincing demonstration of practical necessity."[31]

Obviously, preemption à la the Bush Doctrine is not preemption at all. Given that the GWOT is a war with unknown multiple fronts, unknown multiple enemies, and no end in sight, the long-range consequences of "preemptive" strikes in such a war could endure for generations. G. W. Bush and Obama waged a sixteen-year preventive war against (1) regimes that give sanctuary to terrorists, (2) failed states that breed terrorism, and (3) state sponsors of terrorism. Yet for all the innocent people killed with U.S. tax dollars, the two administrations combined have succeeded only in creating a world with more unstable regimes, more failed states, and more violence. Thus far Trump appears to be happy to perpetuate the madness. "Terrorism" is still flouted as the enemy, and therefore, the GWOT continues. Who can possibly say where this might end?

One can distinguish between the Clinton administration, which launched retaliatory strikes against specific al-Qaeda targets following the 1998 attacks on the U.S. embassies in Nairobi and Dar es Salaam, and the Bush administration, which launched a worldwide, preventive campaign against "evil" following the September 11 attacks—a campaign so unprecedented that the United States' membership on the UN Human Rights commission was revoked.[32]

Instead of pursuing a proportional response, the Bush administration launched full-scale military operations in Iraq. The U.S. shift to its preemptive policy has substantially increased the occurrence of unwarranted and unprovoked attacks. Multiply these attacks across the planet for an indefinite period of time, and the result is a global preventive war—Armageddon (bad for humanity but extremely good for business).

Obama adopted the Bush administration's policy of preventive war and continued the legacy by greatly increasing the use of drones; Bush ordered 57 drone strikes, while Obama ordered 563.[33] Unmanned drone strikes against civilians became a hallmark of the Obama administration.[34] Despite the highly questionable data suggesting that only 14 percent of unmanned drone strikes kill civilians, even if the data were accurate, is this an acceptable risk? One in seven drone strikes kills civilians, yet Obama carried them out like clockwork. Thus what should have been punished as war crimes was instead dismissed as an everyday part of life (and death).

During the election campaign, Trump was less hawkish regarding the use of drones than Hillary Clinton.[35] However, after just three days in office, he ordered more than thirty drone strikes against al-Qaeda in the Arabian Peninsula in Yemen. Worse still Trump has given the CIA the authority to launch drone strikes autonomously.[36]

In April 2017 Trump made history as the first president to deploy the GBU-43 Massive Ordnance Air Blast (MOAB), otherwise known as the mother of all bombs. First tested in 2003, the MOAB (which is comparable to a small nuclear weapon) produced a blast so extensive that the Pentagon ordered a legal review to ensure the weapon didn't violate the Law of Armed Conflict. Trump ordered the MOAB to be dropped on an IS affiliate in Afghanistan's eastern Nangarhar Province, which borders Pakistan.

The policy of preventive war is as unwarranted as it is unprecedented. To launch preemptive strikes against potential enemies leaves one to contemplate just how "potential" an imminent threat can be.

Scholarship on preventive war is far more decisive than the body of literature on American unilateralism. The consensus is that preventive war—while not new as a strategy—is contemporary as a *policy* with liberal democracies. Scholars also condemn America's departure from the rule of law as established under the UN charter.

The bombing of Hiroshima and Nagasaki can truly be debated as both preemptive strikes and preventive war. While some correctly argue that Japan posed an imminent threat to the United States, others insist that alternatives were certainly available. Either way few would try to justify the carnage and brutality of those attacks today. Yet this is exactly what we find ourselves contemplating in this debate over the validity of "preemptive" strikes, particularly when they involve the use of unmanned drones (or twenty-two-thousand-pound bombs) against civilian targets.

Military Hegemony

> Our forces will be strong enough to dissuade potential adversaries from pursuing a military buildup in hopes of surpassing, or equaling, the power of the United States.
>
> —George W. Bush, *The National Security Strategy of the United States of America*

In much the same way as I've questioned the origins and extent of American unilateralism and the policy of preemption before Bush, I also question the origins and extent of American military hegemony before the Bush administration. Obviously military hegemony was the basis of American foreign policy during the Cold War. But with the loss of America's archenemy after the fall of the Soviet Union and the demise of the threat of communism, was the Bush administration secretly thanking heaven for September 11?

Many scholars note that the Bush Doctrine is a radical departure from America's traditional foreign policy of noninterference during times of peace.[37] Others maintain that this great American tradition wasn't actually a "tradition" at all, arguing that America only chose an isolationist policy due to its initial inability to project power. These critics insist that once America grew stronger, it became more willing to establish its military hegemony in the Western Hemisphere as a matter of policy in times of both peace and war. Classic examples are the Monroe Doctrine (1823), the Mexican-American War (1846–48), and the wholesale decimation of Native Americans from the Mississippi to the Pacific Ocean.[38] Still others point to the collapse of the Soviet Union and America's "unipolar moment" as the true beginning of U.S. military hegemony.[39]

One way to measure military hegemony is via overall military spending. Total defense spending during World War II was roughly $296 billion (37.5 percent of GDP).[40] In 1999 the defense budget was $250 billion (the Clinton administration spent roughly 3.5 percent of GDP on defense).[41]

When the Bush administration came to power, however, it initiated the largest increase in military spending since the Cold War. To put this in perspective, actual military expenditures rose from $289 billion in 1998 to $626 billion in 2007. That's 52.7 percent of federal spending compared to 5.6 percent on health and 6.3 percent on education (it's a good thing no child got left behind).[42]

Bush spent an average of $601 billion per year on defense. Ironically, Obama (the peace candidate) spent an average of $687 billion per year in total defense spending—more than Bush and Trump, who proposed $639 billion in defense spending for 2018.[43] These figures demonstrate that while American military hegemony may have emerged earlier, it received a huge boost through massive increased military spending via the Bush, Obama, and Trump administrations.

There is strong speculation that Trump will continue to increase military spending, based on three considerations. The first is Trump's proposed plan for tackling terrorism. The second is Trump's promise to help veterans, and the third consideration is the simple fact that the neocons are still a force to be reckoned with.

It's difficult to imagine how Trump can achieve points 1 or 2 without increasing spending. Alternatively, it's equally difficult to envision how Trump could stem the current tide of spending even if he were so inclined. If the neocons have their way, the United States will likely continue to be a debtor nation for generations to come.

Of course, military spending alone is just one measure, and it by no means establishes the origin of American military hegemony. Another measure is the United States' worldwide military presence. Currently, the U.S. has 2.1 million troops stationed at eight hundred bases in seventy-seven countries around the world. Estimates of the total cost of maintaining military bases and troops overseas exceed $100 billion per year.[44] While the U.S. maintained military bases throughout the Cold War, there's a stark difference between the policy of containment—which was the pillar of American foreign policy throughout the Cold War—and the 2002 NSS's call to "vanquish" America's enemies.[45] The main justification behind U.S. foreign policy since 9/11, is of course, the GWOT.[46] And the main purpose behind the GWOT is to protect U.S. oil interests.

Those who blatantly claim that American military hegemony is the evil offspring of the Bush administration argue that under previous administrations, the U.S. was still largely a status quo power. Under Bush, however, it became a revisionist power—eager to topple political rivals and dominate the international order.[47] Many who subscribe to this view point out that a fundamental difference between the Clinton administration and those that followed is that Clinton classified terrorism as primarily a law enforcement issue while Bush, Obama, and Trump have treated it as a war.

Even greater cynics have proposed a much darker scenario. By tracing the premeditated pursuit of American military hegemony back to the Bush administration *before* September 11, 2001 (and thereby countering the argument that increased military spending was a result of the attacks), many have suggested that the 9/11 attacks simply provided a convenient opportunity to dramatically increase both military spending and America's worldwide military presence.

A popular narrative claims that the threat of communism validated the United States' role as leader of the West. Following the Cold War, Washington experienced a threat deficit. When at long last the 9/11 attacks provided the impetus needed, the neoconservatives were ready and waiting. The GWOT was just the thing to solve Washington's problem.[48]

Prior to the invasion of Iraq in 2003, in an effort to connect Iraq to the Global War on Terrorism, Bush tried desperately to convince the world that Iraq was in bed with al-Qaeda. The Bush administration alleged that Ansar al-Islam (Partisans of Islam)—an al-Qaeda-affiliated guerilla group in Kurdish northern Iraq—was the link between Saddam Hussein and al-Qaeda. Former secretary of state Colin Powell specifically cited the group before the United Nations on February 5, 2003, "as a key reason" to invade Iraq. But as the invasion grew closer, the Bush administration shifted the justification for attacking Iraq from its connection to al-Qaeda to the threat posed by Iraq's supposed cache of WMD. After the war it became common knowledge that both allegations were false.[49] What is not entirely clear is whether these allegations were simply miscalculations or intentional fabrications—although most suspect that it's the latter.

A major reason for this suspicion is widespread skepticism regarding the actual level of threat that terrorism posed. Given Bush's continual rhetoric that America was in a battle with "evil," the consensus is that he generated unnecessary fear (and Islamophobia) immediately following the attacks. The Bush administration then took advantage of that fear to justify holding suspected "terrorists" in detention centers indefinitely without formal charges or representation. Several conspiracy theories even suggest that the Bush administration orchestrated the 9/11 attacks itself simply to incite fear and to justify its intended course of action.[50]

The USA Patriot Act was passed by Congress and signed by Bush on October 26, 2001—just fifteen days after the attacks. Yet the reach of this legislation is unprecedented, overriding some forty-eight state laws regarding the privacy of library records, allowing search and seizure without a judicial warrant, and denying Congress any oversight of how the act is implemented—all to protect Americans from a threat that has killed fewer people over the years than bee stings and lightning.[51]

Beyond the question of the origin or emergence of American military hegemony is the debate over whether it's advantageous, ethical, or moral. Scholars, security professionals, and journalists alike have published countless scathing criticisms of the way that the Bush and subsequent administrations have conducted themselves. Washington invaded Iraq and Afghanistan, interfered with conflicts in numerous other states, and deployed troops around the world to allegedly fight

"Islamic terrorists" who threatened democracy and the West (I'll reveal the real reason for these wars in chapter 6).

The Washington war machine has consistently increased defense spending by the billions every year since 2001 and slaughtered innocent civilians by the tens of thousands. Still, neoconservatives argue that American primacy is the most appropriate and preferable alternative available, claiming that America needs to ensure its primacy by defending its homeland and securing the free flow of oil around the world. Discounting claims that the U.S. should retrench, neocons insist that such a policy would create instability and war.[52]

While American hegemony is enforced via its extraordinary military advantage, its justification is grounded in American exceptionalism. But Americans are not different from any other group of people. While a certain amount of national pride is admirable, when coupled with American military superiority, unilateralism, and the policy of "preemption" (preventive war), the concept of American exceptionalism becomes maniacal. Many in the international community have come to view America as far more dangerous than its rivals. In fact data from various polls suggest that as many as two-thirds of the world's population believe that the greatest threat facing their nation today is the United States.[53]

This may be difficult for Americans to comprehend. Many simply cannot imagine how the greatest democracy in the world could be viewed as such a threat to humanity. One reason may be that Americans are simply unaware of the carnage their government is inflicting. While the American public was bombarded with media coverage of the 9/11 attacks—repeatedly referred to as "ground zero"—American media outlets rarely publicize civilian casualties caused by U.S. attacks. Not only does this deliberate censorship fly in the face of liberal democracy, but the American public has also been intentionally deceived.[54]

Other members of the international community, however, have not been deceived. For example in 2002 the United Nations reported that al-Qaeda recruitment increased substantially in nearly forty countries once the U.S. began preparing to invade Iraq. IS has also enjoyed massive increases in recruitment (many from the West itself) as a result of Western interference in Syria, Libya, Yemen, and other states.[55]

The American military continues to reinforce this negative

perception—largely due to its preference for conducting air strikes and unmanned drone attacks. These two tactics cause substantial civilian casualties but risk relatively few American lives, thus making them a safe bet for politicians but not so safe for people residing in the strike zone. The U.S. has increasingly relied on these unnecessary tactics despite the collateral damage incurred.[56]

Americans, like most other people, tend to be blind to their nation's ill. They automatically assume that the American notion of liberal democracy is the best and more or less only way to govern a nation.[57] But taken from the perspective of others, America is riddled with violent crime, addiction of all kinds, domestic violence, vice, greed, immorality, homelessness, and extreme poverty. America's liberal democracy has not spared the country any of these ills—nor has America's great wealth spared an unacceptably large percentage of its own population from hunger, homelessness, inaccessibility to healthcare, and the consuming nihilism of poverty. Yet America spent an average of $10 billion per month on the war in Iraq alone![58]

It isn't surprising that other cultures want no part of American liberal democracy, yet the United States insists on thrusting it on them anyway, often by force. It does so because the neocons want everyone to believe that America is the best and furthermore that America knows what's best for everyone else.

The concept of "military strength beyond challenge" necessarily subjugates all other countries in the world to U.S. domination. American military hegemony challenges the sovereignty of other states and claims that the United States alone is above international law. Unfortunately, while America has the military strength to impose its will on others (and while the neocons remain in power), America's disregard for the rest of the world will continue. The people of the world need to know that not all Americans agree with this approach to foreign policy.

Beyond the question of whether American military hegemony is moral or ethical, one must also consider whether it's politically advantageous. Neoconservatives may think so, but they're clearly in the minority. To most other observers it's fairly obvious that when America props up corrupt regimes in favor of its own interests and increasingly relies on drone strikes to enforce its will, it fuels the very militancy it's supposedly spending trillions to combat. This scenario may work for

Dick Cheney and the stockholders of Halliburton, but it fails to make any sense to most other people.

While one obviously cannot claim that neoconservatism originated with George W. Bush, there's a great deal of substance to the argument that the neocons are more rampant today than ever. America's military superiority may very well keep the country at the top of the food chain for now. However, by 2025 the world's population is projected to grow to eight billion, with most of this growth taking place in the developing world. This shift could present real problems for a technology-rich but dwindling U.S. military.[59]

Prevailing negative opinions of the United States produced global support for change. Obama promised that change—a promise for which he was immensely popular but ultimately failed to deliver on. Instead, Obama greatly escalated the war on terror. Trump has pledged to make America great again, but unfortunately he too appears to be blind to the greater issue of the day, namely, that the enemies America is creating today will surely be too numerous to fight tomorrow.

What Bush, Obama, and Trump all fail to see is that although superior weaponry minimizes American casualties (a distinct political advantage for warmongers), the continual abuse of military strength will backfire in the long run. In the words of Albert Einstein, "I know not with what weapons World War III will be fought, but World War IV will be fought with sticks and stones."[60]

CHAPTER SIX

THE IRAQ WARS

One of the hardest parts of my job is to connect Iraq to the war on terror.

—George W. Bush

The Wise Old Emperor

As much as people love to make fun of G. W. Bush's slips of the tongue, one can learn quite a bit from them as well. One object lesson is the value of honesty. An ancient Chinese parable tells of a wise emperor who, growing old, decided that it was time to appoint his successor. None of his own children or advisors were worthy, however, as all had become deceitful and interested only in their own glory and honor.

So the wise old emperor decided to invite a group of poor children from the surrounding villages to his palace. He would choose his successor from among them. Giving each one a seed, he instructed them to plant their seed, water it, and nurture it. And he told them all to come back in one year's time.

The following year, as all the children gathered before the throne, the emperor surveyed the array of beautiful plants and trees. Then spotting a young boy, hiding in the back with an empty pot, the emperor commanded him to come forward. Trembling and carrying his pot full of dirt, the young boy approached the throne as the other children pointed and laughed at his apparent failure.

"What is your name?" The emperor asked.

"Ling," the boy replied, nearly in tears.

"Bow before your emperor!" The wise old man instructed as he himself knelt before Ling.

Astonished, Ling didn't know what to say. "But my seed didn't grow," he confessed.

"None of your seeds grew," the emperor explained. I gave you all boiled seeds. *You* were the only one honest enough to tell the truth."

Opponents of the 2003 invasion of Iraq retort that America went to war in Iraq not to establish democracy but rather to pursue the U.S. corporate takeover of Iraqi markets. Naomi Klein refers to Paul Bremer as "Iraq's one-man IMF."[1] Bremer—who was America's top civil administrator in Iraq from May 11, 2003, until June 28, 2004—earned this designation due to his blatant disregard of the Iraqi people. Dismantling state-owned enterprises and replacing them with private contractors, Bremer prioritized protection of the oil infrastructure over the provision of public goods and services.

Other critics of the Bush administration contend that it took advantage of 9/11 as an opportunity to invade Iraq. The idea to invade Iraq was raised days after 9/11 when members of the Project for the New American Century issued a letter arguing that Saddam Hussein must be removed from power whether proven to be linked to the attacks or not.[2] Associates of the American Enterprise Institute—a neoconservative think tank known for advocating deregulation and funded by corporations such as ExxonMobil—also strongly advocated regime change in Iraq. In fact AEI had been agitating against Saddam Hussein for over a decade.[3] It gets interesting when one realizes that both organizations boasted high-profile neocons such as Irving Kristol, Elliot Abrams, John Bolton, Dick Cheney, Paul Wolfowitz, Lewis Libby, Richard Perle, and Donald Rumsfeld as associates.

Bush had firmly decided to go to war with Iraq already in July 2002, and the Bush administration continued to discuss the viability of an invasion in secret meetings until it finally took place in March 2003.[4] Whether the threat of WMD was an intentional fabrication or an honest mistake, this administration wanted to invade Iraq. When it couldn't find WMD, it shifted to a crusade for democracy in the Middle East.

Bush insisted that Saddam was a despot, that he defied numerous UN resolutions, and that he harbored terrorist organizations. Furthermore, the Bush administration argued that Saddam could not be contained—he was just too reckless and too unpredictable.

As for the claim that the Bush administration took out Saddam because of his brutality against his own people, critics are quick to point out that the United States was not concerned with Saddam Hussein's brutality against his own people when he was America's ally, which is when he committed his most brutal atrocities (with U.S. hardware).[5] As for the claim that the Bush administration was concerned with democracy and stability in Iraq, more than a decade later it's clear that regime change hasn't worked.

The neocons compared Saddam Hussein to Hitler, but the two actually shared little in common. Throughout the thirty years that Saddam was in power, he invaded Iran in 1980 and Kuwait in 1990. Hitler, on the other hand, invaded Czechoslovakia, Poland, Norway, Belgium, Holland, France, Greece, Yugoslavia, and the Soviet Union, while his panzer divisions steamrolled across North Africa in a frenzied quest for oil.[6] To date as far as foreign policy is concerned, Hitler has more in common with Bush, Obama, and Trump than he does with Saddam Hussein.

It's also instructive to compare Iraq and several other countries in the region. Egypt started four wars and partook in six between 1948 and 1973. Israel provoked three wars and has issued countless air strikes and military interventions against neighboring Arab states in its brief modern history.[7] So why the urgent need to attack Iraq in 2003? The answer to this question actually begins nearly a century earlier.

Operation Desert Storm

George H. Walker—G. W. Bush's great grandfather—was president of W. A. Harriman and Company, which was involved in rebuilding the Baku oil fields in the 1920s. Walker's son-in-law, Prescott Bush, was senior director of Dresser Industries (an energy technology corporation that merged with Halliburton in 1998).[8] George H. W. Bush and his sons would also develop strong professional ties to the Middle East and engage in massive business deals in Saudi Arabia, Bahrain, and Kuwait.

Bush Sr. used his position as director of the CIA and later as vice president to secure lucrative oil investments. In fact in the Middle East he was known as "the Saudi vice president."[9] Likewise, back in the States, Bush treated the Saudi ambassador like a member of the family.

While corruption certainly didn't begin with Bush Sr., the Bush family is the first oil dynasty to occupy the White House. They may also be the First Family of ordered assassinations.

Jimmy Carter's solution to the oil and gas embargo of the 1970s was to tell Americans to ride their bicycles to work and wear sweaters. Ronald Reagan had a more assertive approach. When Reagan entered the Oval Office in 1981, he railed against U.S. dependence on Middle Eastern oil. His first executive order eliminated price controls on oil and natural gas.[10] Consequently, production skyrocketed and prices plummeted. This didn't sit well with many oil producers, particularly the vice president and his business associates in the Middle East.

Coincidently, the son of a multimillionaire Texas oil tycoon attempted to assassinate Reagan not long afterward. John Warnock Hinckley Sr.—president and chairman of Vanderbilt Energy Corporation—had contributed substantial amounts of money to H.W.'s failed 1980 presidential campaign.[11] Had John Hinckley Jr. been successful, Bush would have become president considerably sooner than he actually did. Members of the two families had close personal and business ties with one another—hosting dinners at each other's homes and investing large sums of money in one another's private enterprises. Was this all just a coincidence? Perhaps.

Another interesting coincidence concerns the 1990 Iraq War. In 1979 Salem bin Laden (Osama's older brother) invested in George W. Bush's Arbusto Corporation, an oil partnership that became Bush Exploration after H.W. became vice president.[12] G. W.'s uncle Jon Bush raised nearly $5 million for the company from political supporters of the Reagan-Bush administration. Among them were William DeWitt and Mercer Reynolds, the owners of Spectrum 7 Energy Corporation.[13]

Due to G.W.'s poor management (and of course, Reagan's deregulation), Bush Exploration performed less than spectacularly. In September 1984, as a favor to Bush Sr., Spectrum 7 acquired Bush Exploration. Despite G.W.'s proven record of failure, DeWitt and Reynolds appointed him as company president, a position for which he received a generous salary and 13.6 percent of the company's stock. Spectrum merged with Harken Energy two years later.[14]

During the Iran-Iraq War, Kuwait loaned some $14 billion to Saddam Hussein in an effort to fend off Iranian hegemony in the region. By the end of the war in 1988, the oil glut (a result of Reagan's deregulation and overproduction by states like Kuwait) was costing Iraq billions. By one estimate every time the price of oil dropped by $1 per barrel Iraq lost $1 billion in annual revenue.[15]

Rather than decrease production, Kuwait petitioned OPEC to increase its daily output by 50 percent. To add injury to insult, Kuwait refused to forgive Iraq its huge debt—despite Saddam's claims that Iran had been contained thanks to Iraq's great sacrifice. Finally, Saddam accused Kuwait of slant drilling, which was essentially stealing Iraqi oil.[16] Coincidentally Hussein estimated that Kuwait's actions had cost Iraq roughly $14 billion.[17]

All these events led up to Iraq's invasion of Kuwait in August 1990. The two states engaged in several negotiations in 1989 but to no avail—an acceptable agreement could not be reached.

In February 1990 (after months of unsuccessful negotiations between Iraq and Kuwait), Harken was awarded a thirty-five-year contract to drill for offshore oil in Bahrain. A close associate of Bill Clinton, David Edwards, was involved in brokering the deal. The fact that Harken Energy had zero experience overseas and had never drilled in water before suggests that the contract was offered purely as a political favor (it certainly wasn't awarded because Harken was the strongest candidate). This begs the question, political favor for what? Interestingly G.W. sold his stock in Harken just prior to Saddam Hussein's invasion of Kuwait, avoiding plummeting stock prices only days later.[18]

The main point in relating this second coincidence is to demonstrate the extensive and long-term ties between the Bush family, the bin Laden family, and Middle Eastern oil tycoons. Bush sold Operation Desert Storm as a war to stop expansionist Iraqi aggression, a battle against barbarous cruelty, and a fight to rein in an irrational Iraqi dictator.[19] In truth it's much more likely that the "Saudi vice president" waged the first Gulf War to protect the Bush family's personal oil interests. Saddam's cruelty was never a concern earlier, so why the sudden campaign for humanity?

The Revolving Door

In 1991 then secretary of defense Dick Cheney negotiated an agreement in which Halliburton would be awarded a set number of contracts from the Pentagon, barring any competition (many of these contracts were extended on a no-bid and cost-plus basis).[20] For his services Cheney received untold millions in what would be considered kickbacks under any other circumstances.

In 1992 a document known as the draft Defense Policy Guidance (DPG), written by Paul Wolfowitz and Irve Lewis Libby (who at the time worked at the Pentagon under Dick Cheney), was leaked to the *New York Times*. The draft DPG called for American unilateralism, military hegemony, and a policy of preemption. It has been described as a Pax Americana—a vision of world domination by the U.S. military. Its intended goal? To "ensure that no rival superpower is allowed to emerge in Western Europe, Asia or the territories of the former Soviet Union."[21] Sound familiar?

Cheney left the Department of Defense to become the CEO of Halliburton in 1995.[22] David Gribben, Cheney's chief of staff at the Pentagon, also moved to Halliburton as a liaison.[23] Meanwhile as CEO Cheney doubled Halliburton's political contributions to his buddies back in Congress.[24] For the meager sum of $1.2 million in political contributions, Cheney locked in over $2.3 billion in defense contracts between 1995 and 2000—elevating Halliburton from seventy-third on the Pentagon's list of top contractors to eighteenth.[25] Still, Cheney insists that the political donations had nothing to do with the Pentagon's decision to ramp up its business dealings with Halliburton.[26]

In 1999 Cheney gave a speech at the Institute of Petroleum, pointing out America's growing need for the Middle East's oil and arguing that the petroleum industry needs to be more politically active.

By some estimates there will be an average of two per cent annual growth in global oil demand over the years ahead along with conservatively a three per cent natural decline in production from existing reserves. That means by 2010 we will need on the order of an additional fifty million barrels a day.

So where is the oil going to come from? . . . While many regions of the world offer great oil opportunities, the Middle East[,] with two thirds of the world's oil and the lowest cost, is still where the prize ultimately lies, even though companies are anxious for greater access there, progress continues to be slow.

Oil is the only large industry whose leverage has not been all that effective in the political arena. Textiles, electronics, agriculture all seem often to be more influential. Our constituency is not only oilmen from Louisiana and Texas, but software writers in Massachusetts and specialty steel producers in Pennsylvania. I am struck that this industry is so strong technically and financially yet not as politically successful or influential as are often smaller industries. We need to earn credibility to have our views heard.[27]

When Cheney left Halliburton to join the Bush administration, he took Gribben with him as director of congressional relations. Cheney has been a lifelong advocate for deregulation of the private sector (for obvious reasons). Yet Cheney contends that there's absolutely nothing suspicious about this revolving door between Halliburton and Washington. He further insists that Halliburton's political contributions to the GOP had zero influence on the party's decision to endorse him as Bush's running mate (or more accurately, to endorse Bush as Cheney's running mate).[28]

In 2001 then vice president Cheney commissioned a report on energy security that was published by the Council on Foreign Relations and the James Baker Institute for Public Policy. The report warned that under Saddam Hussein, Iraq had "become a swing producer, turning its taps on and off" whenever it was in its "strategic interest to do so." The report further warned of the possibility that "Saddam Hussein [might] remove Iraqi oil from the market for an extended period of time." The impetus to act was the fear of a global energy crisis and increased vulnerability to "unprecedented energy price volatility."[29]

Exactly how much input Cheney had in the report is unclear, but what seems clear enough is that securing Iraq's oil fields was as much about controlling Saddam Hussein as it was about protecting energy security. The Bush administration's commitment to military strength beyond challenge was all about projecting U.S. power and hegemony, and the neocons simply weren't going to tolerate someone like Saddam Hussein coloring outside the lines—especially when it affected their profit margins. So they made an example of him.

A Box of Razors

In his 2000 presidential campaign, Bush condemned nation building as an ambition that risked dragging America's military into "insoluble conflicts around the world."[30] Condoleezza Rice summarized the administration's position in a concise article that clearly prioritized national interest over humanitarian interests. Rice asserted, "The Clinton administration has often been so anxious to find multilateral solutions to problems that it has signed agreements that are not in America's interest."[31] Rice specifically noted treaties such as the Kyoto Protocol and the Comprehensive Test Ban Treaty. According to Rice the Bush administration would focus on "power politics, great powers and power balances."[32] It would have no need of the recent foreign-policy tradition of multilateralism.

When George W. Bush selected his top appointees, he named a number of personnel who had served together under his father, George H. W. Bush (some served under Reagan and Ford as well). Richard Cheney, who had served Bush Sr. as secretary of defense, was appointed vice president; Colin Powell, who had served Bush Sr. as chairman of the Joint Chiefs of Staff, was appointed secretary of state; and Condoleezza Rice, once senior director of Soviet and East European affairs in the National Security Council under the first Bush administration, was appointed national security advisor. Another longtime Washington professional, Donald Rumsfeld, joined the administration as secretary of defense. Rumsfeld had served as secretary of state under Ford and as Middle East envoy under Reagan.

Even many of the junior players shared a long history within the inner circle. George Tenet, director of central intelligence, had been an NSC staffer on the Senate Intelligence Committee under Clinton. Tenet became deputy director of the CIA in 1995 and then director in 1997. Andrew Card, Bush's chief of staff, had served on the White House staff in 1987 under Reagan. He also served under George H. W. Bush, managing his presidential campaign in New Hampshire. Card went on to serve under Bush Sr. as deputy White House chief of staff and later as secretary of transportation.

Deputy National Security Advisor Stephen Hadley worked for Cheney in the Department of Defense. Deputy Secretary of Defense

Paul Wolfowitz had been serving in Washington since the 1970s and served as undersecretary of defense for policy under Cheney in the George H. W. Bush administration. Lewis "Scooter" Libby, who served in three positions (assistant to Bush, Cheney's chief of staff, and Cheney's assistant for national security affairs), was a protégé of Wolfowitz. He first served under Wolfowitz in the State Department in the 1980s. Libby also served as deputy undersecretary of defense for policy in the George H. W. Bush administration when Wolfowitz was policy undersecretary for Cheney.

Richard Armitage, Powell's deputy and good friend, had also served in Washington since the 1970s. Armitage served in both the Reagan and the Clinton administrations. And last but not least, Karl Rove's political career extended back to the Nixon presidential campaign in 1972. Rove advised George W. Bush when he ran for Congress in 1978 and George H. W. Bush when he ran for president in 1980.[33]

Having completed only one full term as governor, George W. Bush lacked experience. But what he lacked in experience he made up for in intuition. Insiders reveal that Bush often thought with his gut, trusting his instincts rather than relying on the facts (no wonder!).[34]

Given his lack of experience in Washington, Bush relied heavily on a group of foreign-policy advisors known as the Vulcans. The group was named after the Roman god of fire, a reference to a statue of Vulcan that stood in Rice's hometown of Birmingham, Alabama. The Vulcans consisted of Rice, Wolfowitz, Armitage, Richard Perle (chairman of the defense-policy board advisory committee), and Robert Zoellick (deputy secretary of state)—but not Powell.[35]

However, Bush particularly relied on Cheney, who by many accounts ran the show. Cheney dwarfed Andrew Card in his role as chief of staff, put together a highly experienced staff of his own, and took it upon himself to advance and empower the executive office.[36] Powell once noted that nothing got decided until Bush and Cheney met in private.[37]

Bush relied almost as heavily on Condoleezza Rice, who had served as his chief foreign-policy advisor in the 2000 campaign. As national security advisor, she condensed information for Bush, spent entire days serving at his side, and vacationed in her own private cabin at Camp David. As for Rumsfeld he and Cheney went way back. Cheney had been Rumsfeld's deputy in the Ford administration, when

Rumsfeld served as White House chief of staff. Cheney handpicked Rumsfeld for secretary of defense after several other top candidates were eliminated.[38] Both were powerful, and both were heavily connected in Washington.[39]

Even Powell, the thirty-five-year army veteran who in many respects was the outsider among them, commanded respect for his vast wealth of experience.[40] Powell's background and connections in Washington were also both considerable and impressive. He had previously held several foreign-policy positions, including his service as military aide to Caspar Weinberger in the Reagan administration.[41]

But there were divisions, chief among them the one between Cheney and Rumsfeld, on the one hand, and Powell, on the other. Cheney and Rumsfeld pushed for a foreign policy based on aggressive unilateralism, while Powell faithfully defended the traditional multilateral approach of the State Department.[42]

Powell was hesitant to resort to military force in Iraq. He was especially opposed to attacking Iraq as retaliation for 9/11 because he couldn't see any connection between the two. Cheney, Rumsfeld, and Wolfowitz adamantly opposed him on this issue. Powell's position stemmed from his realist convictions, which often put him at odds with the more powerful neocons in the administration.[43]

Unfortunately for Powell, he never developed a personal relationship with the president. In fact Powell spent little more than thirty minutes alone with Bush during the first sixteen months of the term. Therefore, his influence was generally overshadowed by the others, and he was at times marginalized from the group (for instance CIA covert operations were briefed to Bush, Cheney, Rumsfeld, and Rice but never to Powell). Powell also battled with Rove over political appointees. Powell wanted to designate certain individuals, but Rove closely controlled all political appointees personally.[44]

Rice had her own difficulties with Rumsfeld as their respective staff encountered various altercations, but she navigated carefully among the political power plays between the State Department and the Department of Defense as she nurtured and protected her growing influence with the president. As Colin Powell remarked, "She's not supposed to be in my corner. She's not supposed to be in Rumsfeld's corner. She's supposed to be in the president's corner, and she is, she enjoys his confidence."[45] Bush relied heavily on Rice to inform him of various policy options, and then he made the final decisions.

Differences aside the group presented itself to the public as unified. Even Armitage went on the record (along with Rice) to present a united front with Bush over Iraq.[46] However, public appearances can be deceiving as even this facade crumbled and cracked at times, with Powell cast as the administration scapegoat.

Planning the Invasion

According to the official party line, on the morning of September 11, 2001, when President Bush was informed of the attacks, he decided on his own, right then and there, that the nation was going to war: "I made up my mind at that moment that we were going to war."[47]

The truth is that war with Iraq had been in the cards all along. Former CIA director George Tenet accused Bush and Cheney of having been hell-bent on war in Iraq and of never allowing a serious discussion of whether Saddam Hussein posed an actual national security threat.[48]

On September 12, 2001, Rumsfeld suggested to the war cabinet that the attacks presented "an opportunity to launch against Iraq." Cheney favored the idea but suggested the administration wait for fear the United States would lose its "rightful place as good guy."[49]

Obviously, quite a bit had changed between the spring of 1992, when the draft DPG was first leaked, and September 11, 2001. The controversy caused by the leaked draft DPG led then national security adviser Brent Scowcroft and Secretary of State James Baker to insist that the final DPG be toned down extensively. By September 11, 2001, Cheney had risen to vice president, Wolfowitz to deputy defense secretary, and Libby to Cheney's chief of staff. Rather than tone the DPG down, the neocons would pursue it to the fullest. G. John Ikenberry writes, "According to this new paradigm, America is to be less bound to its partners and to global rules and institutions while it steps forward to play a more unilateral and anticipatory role in attacking terrorist threats and confronting rogue states seeking WMD. . . . In that respect, the war on terrorism must be seen as a facade for a much more ambitious strategy of projecting US military power around the world."[50]

The Bush administration may have begun with a foreign policy based on realism and selective engagement, but it ultimately pursued a neoconservative agenda of Wilsonian-style nation-building. In his first year in office, Bush pursued what former UN ambassador Richard Holbrooke called a "radical break with 55 years of bipartisan tradition."[51] The most important break with organizational tradition came with the push toward an imperial presidency (an uncontrollable executive branch that exceeds constitutional limits).

The Bush administration's shift to the imperial presidency was marked by a number of developments ranging from an intensification of secrecy to the rejection of international treaties requiring Senate ratification to the doctrine of preventive war. The administration's strong push to empower the presidency demonstrates a major break with organizational tradition.

But which actor, if any, emerged as the clear leader in this administration? Cheney clearly called the shots regarding military intervention—a major pillar of the Bush administration's foreign policy. Cheney "harbored a deep sense of unfinished business about Iraq." The vice-president was in favor of what George Schultz coined "hot preemption."[52] Finally, it was Cheney who worked so arduously to empower the executive branch.

The administration secretly planned and prepared for war while carefully hiding it from the public. As former Nixon aide John W. Dean has declared, Bush and Cheney were more secretive than Nixon during Watergate.[53]

By at least one account, planning for the invasion began in November 2001 and included upgrading airfields in various Gulf countries, moving supplies to the region, and constructing necessary facilities. By November 21, 2001, Bush was completely focused on Iraq. Cheney thought the weapons inspections in Iraq were useless. He wanted to strike immediately.[54]

Rumsfeld agreed. Imminent threat would no longer be necessary; preventive war was the way to go. Powell disagreed. Cheney saw Powell as a problem. He later stated, "Colin always had major reservations about what we were trying to do."[55] Despite Powell's initial argument for containment, however, he did relatively little to stem the ambition of Cheney, Rice, Rumsfeld, and Wolfowitz.

While Bush didn't agree with Cheney's cynicism toward the United Nations, he certainly did not share Powell's naive trust in it either. Bush wanted Saddam out. He was not happy with America's pre-9/11 containment policy toward Iraq, and he didn't like having his options constrained. Containment was placing heavy requirements on the military with an average of thirty-four thousand sorties per year being flown to enforce it.[56]

The administration's argument was that Saddam must have WMD. Why else would he put up with a decade of sanctions? The threat of WMD justified going to war. Democracy in the Middle East was worth pursuing, even if via the barrel of a gun. The group trumped up their allegations with a largely fabricated ninety-two-page National Intelligence Estimate (NIE), which neither Bush nor Rice had read in its entirety. At the same time, members of the Bush administration made public appearances to support the NIE's allegations.[57]

One such appearance occurred on September 8, 2002, when Cheney basically lied on *Meet the Press*, claiming that no one who had seen all the intelligence he had would doubt the threat presented by Iraq.[58] But Cheney hadn't seen any intelligence at all that supported going to war with Iraq because it didn't exist. But in the end, the truth didn't matter. The administration forged ahead with its own agenda.

John D. Rockefeller, the vice chairman of the Select Committee on Intelligence, expressed serious concern regarding the Bush administration's disturbing pattern of cherry-picking intelligence data to support its decision to go to war. According to Rockefeller the administration continually discounted any intel that suggested the war was unnecessary.[59]

By April 2002 the administration was also hiding its plans and preparations for war from Congress. Bush had instructed General Tommy Franks not to make financial requests through Washington, assuring him, "Anything you need, you'll have."[60] The money would no longer be appropriated through Congress. By the end of July 2002, Bush had approved more than thirty projects totaling over $700 million. Congress had no knowledge or involvement.

By August 2002 the Bush administration's foreign policy had changed dramatically. Republican realists were deeply concerned with the administration's break with the realist tradition. Individuals such as Scowcroft and Baker voiced their disagreement with the administration. They saw Powell as their only remaining ally inside the inner circle. Scowcroft warned that a war with Iraq "could turn the whole region into a cauldron."[61]

Retired General Anthony Zinni was present when Cheney gave a speech in Nashville on August 26, 2002. He said that when he listened to the vice president insist that Saddam had weapons of mass destruction, he "nearly fell off his chair." Zinni "had seen nothing to support Cheney's certitude."[62]

Still, in spite of nearly universal opposition, Bush ordered the invasion of Iraq. He argued that the United States had to intervene in Iraq to prevent terrorists from training there, to prevent terrorists from obtaining and using weapons of mass destruction against America, and to bring democracy and freedom to the Iraqi people.[63]

Wolfowitz, who had considered Iraq a threat as early as 1979, was also a strong advocate for toppling Saddam. Wolfowitz had been the preeminent neoconservative in the group. He had earned his PhD in political science from the University of Chicago, a cradle of neoconservative thinking and opposition to détente during the Cold War.[64]

By December 2002 even Rice (who had initially been optimistic that weapons inspections and WMD elimination could work) was recommending that the U.S. go to war against Iraq. Bush and Rumsfeld agreed to start secretly deploying troops into the theater to avoid attracting the attention of the press or the rest of the world. The first deployment order went out on December 6, 2002, and deployments continued every two weeks or so thereafter. Troops were given less than a week's notice at times.[65]

In January 2003 the Bush administration arranged for much of its humanitarian relief to be disguised as general contributions to conceal its war planning from the NGO recipients. Yet when asked about Iraq, Bush's favorite response was "I have no war plans on my desk."[66] At one point or another after the planning began, nearly every member of the administration publicly denied any plans to go to war with Iraq.

A widely known account regarding the decision to invade Iraq is the alleged conversation between CIA director George Tenet and Pentagon advisor Richard Perle at the White House on September 12, 2001. In a now-famous interview with CBS's *60 Minutes* in 2007, Tenet told his side of the story.

According to Tenet Perle told him, "Iraq has got to pay a price for what happened yesterday, they bear responsibility." But Tenet explicitly denied the existence of any intelligence connecting Saddam Hussein to al-Qaeda: "We could never verify that there was any Iraqi . . . complicity with al-Qaeda for 9/11 or any operational act against America. Period."[67]

Yet the Bush administration publicly linked Saddam Hussein to al-Qaeda in an effort to blame 9/11 on Iraq. Tenet also denied the existence of any explicit evidence that supported Iraq's supposed possession of weapons of mass destruction. Tenet insists that he consistently reported that, in his judgment, the earliest Iraq might have had a nuclear weapon was 2007.[68]

As for chemical and biological weapons, the intelligence community believed Saddam had the capacity to produce them, but it had no knowledge that Saddam possessed them. Still the Bush administration heavily justified the war in Iraq based on the alleged existence of such intelligence.

In fact Colin Powell reported to the United Nations, "Our conservative estimate is that Iraq today has a stockpile of between 100 and 500 tons of chemical weapons agent."[69] What is even more incriminating for Tenet than for Powell is that Tenet was present at the briefing.

Furthermore, although the CIA denied the existence of any intelligence supporting Saddam Hussein's alleged attempts to obtain uranium from Africa—even demanding that the allegation be removed from two previous presidential speeches—Bush made the accusation anyway in his 2003 State of the Union Address. The Bush administration clearly used policy to drive intelligence. It selectively used only intelligence that supported its agenda and completely disregarded the intelligence community's recommendations and judgments.[70]

Mohamed ElBaradei, the director general of the International Atomic Energy Agency, emphatically insisted that "Iraq's weapons capabilities had deteriorated badly since the time of the Desert Fox raid." He further asserted that weapons inspections had produced "no evidence of ongoing prohibited nuclear or nuclear-related activities in Iraq."[71]

Powell indicated after the fact that he had felt pressured and manipulated, and Tenet also indicated afterward that the Bush administration had misrepresented the intelligence data. While the invasion of Iraq sparked the largest demonstrations since the Vietnam War, Bush continued to insist that this was a war against "evil."

The Bush administration (like the Trump administration) has been compared to the regime of Hitler, who used the burning of the Reichstag to justify military intervention. It's claimed that Bush likewise capitalized on the 9/11 attacks. Nelson Mandela referred to the Bush administration when he stated, "Anybody, and particularly the leaders of the super-powers, who takes unilateral action outside the framework of the U.N. must receive the condemnation of all who love peace. . . . That country and its leader are a danger to the world."[72]

Nelson Mandela wasn't simply uttering eloquent phrases in pursuit of a photo op. Many scholars and security experts agree that his words are eminently practical.[73] While most of Europe was operating under the collective leadership of the United Nations, neoconservatives in the Bush administration believed that America's unrivaled power exempted it from the obligation to cooperate with others.

Yet Bush argued that America *was* acting multilaterally.[74] When faced with resistance to the presence of troops in Iraq and Afghanistan, Bush claimed that U.S. forces overseas were a symbol of America's commitment to its allies.[75] Perhaps the most fitting criticism of the Bush administration is actually an indictment against America itself.

On the fifty-seventh anniversary of the Hiroshima bombing, Hiro-shima mayor Tadatoshi Akiba condemned America's response to the September 11 attacks, claiming that the result in Afghanistan, Pakistan, India, and the Middle East was only more victimization of women and children, the elderly, and those who cannot defend themselves. Akiba insisted that the United States has no right to force Pax Americana on the rest of the world or to unilaterally determine its fate.[76]

This very angry and heartfelt denunciation strikes many people as both timeless and timely at once. The unimaginable horror of Hiroshima and Nagasaki becomes all too imaginable as we approach the precipice of that nightmare yet again in hotspots around the globe. Experts assure us that there were alternatives to the use of the atomic bomb (as there are alternatives to drone strikes today), but the Truman administration chose to ignore them, as did Obama and as Trump does as well.[77]

Why Did We Do It?

There's a certain amount of debate over the question of why the United States invaded Iraq. The standard knee-jerk reaction is that the U.S. wanted Iraq's oil—and while it isn't preposterous, it is a bit naive.[78] It's certainly true that British and American corporations controlled three-quarters of Iraq's oil production until it was nationalized in 1972; after that they were left out in the cold.

Still, the United States is the largest consumer of oil in the world (consuming roughly 25 percent of the oil on the market). In 2002 it was also the second largest producer of oil—Iraq was only the twelfth largest producer. Prior to the invasion, the U.S. imported roughly 15 percent of its oil from Canada, 14 percent from Saudi Arabia, 15 percent from Venezuela, and 12 percent from Mexico. Only a small percentage of its oil came from Iraq through the oil-for-food program.[79]

Bottom line, America didn't need Iraq's oil. Nor does it appear that America wanted it all that much. The U.S. didn't import much oil from Iraq before the invasion, and it imports even less today. Given the exorbitant cost of the war in Iraq, it isn't logical to conclude that the United States invaded Iraq for its oil—not directly anyway.

According to *World Energy Outlook* for 2001 (published by the International Energy Agency), Iraq's foreign contracts—and particularly its contracts with Russia—had the potential to reach over a trillion dollars.[80] In 1997 Lukoil, Russia's largest oil company, landed a $20 billion contract to drill the West Qurna oilfield. Meanwhile, the Russian state-owned giant, Zarubezhneft, was awarded a concession worth as much as $90 billion to develop the Bin Umar oilfield.[81] So not only had American and British corporations lost out, but Saddam was offering huge contracts to Russian competitors. The neocons didn't like this.

Another theory is that Bush invaded Iraq to defend Israel. G. W. Bush's constituency consisted of a large block of conservative Christians—and particularly a right-wing brand of Christians who supported the war in Iraq as necessary to defend Israel. Many of them believe that the second coming of Jesus is linked to the reestablishment of Israel as a nation. Given the hostile relations between Israel and Iraq since 1948, some Christians were all too happy to see Saddam overthrown.

However, it hasn't gone unnoticed that Bush's "arc of instability"—in addition to being home to a number of political rivals—also includes most of the planet's largest oil reserves.[82] Therefore, while the neocon's claimed to be spreading democracy and defending Israel, the knee-jerk reaction again is that they simply wanted to privatize the world's oil fields.

Others argue that the war in Iraq was mainly about U.S. hegemony and the Bush administration flexing its power. This claim is absolutely true, but the neocons didn't invade Iraq for the geopolitical reasons they insisted were in play (WMD, links to terrorism, etc.). Iraq has the second largest oil reserves in the world, and France and others continued to purchase oil from Iraq despite U.S. sanctions. Worse yet Saddam bucked the system by his preference for euros over dollars and funneled hundreds of billions into unregulated offshore accounts. He just wasn't playing according to the neocons' rules, and they didn't like that.

A fourth argument is that the war in Iraq was largely a smoke screen to engage in crony capitalism under the pretense of national security and the promotion of democracy. Simply put, the war in Iraq was good for business. Privatization is a mainstay of neoliberal policy. By taking over publically held operations, the U.S. Coalition Provisional Authority could grant multibillion-dollar contracts (funded by Iraqi petro dollars) to friends and political supporters alike—such as the $1.66 billion contract awarded to a subsidiary of Halliburton (Kellogg Brown and Root).[83] This was just one of the many contracts offered to Halliburton, totaling some $39.5 billion (including $30 million to build Guantanamo).[84] But can one demonstrate that these contracts constituted patronage rather than procurement?

The Center for Public Integrity reported that all seventy-one companies that were awarded contracts in Iraq and Afghanistan contributed more than $500,000 each to Bush's 2000 presidential campaign, and 60 percent of these companies enjoyed close ties to the Bush administration.[85] Furthermore, Lockheed's vice president and financial chair was also chief fund-raiser for Bush's first presidential campaign, and Lynn Cheney was a member of Lockheed's board of directors (recall that Lockheed itself was notorious for charging American taxpayers $640 per toilet seat).[86]

Finally when all was said and done, the war in Iraq equated to roughly $40 billion in profits for Halliburton, a corporation in which Cheney and his cronies owned substantial amounts of stock and from which he continued to receive a "deferred" six-figure salary the entire time he was in office.[87] Still, Cheney denies that his ongoing relationship with Halliburton was in any way connected to the Bush administration's decision to go to war in Iraq in the first place.[88] Was this blatant patronage or simply an example of the efficiency of the U.S. government? I'll let you decide.

Either way it seems reasonable to conclude that the Bush administration had many reasons for invading Iraq; the least plausible is that it wanted Iraq's oil. Only slightly less likely is the threat of nuclear weapons. Bush was willing to engage with India—also "a persistent non-proliferation problem."[89] Why not Iraq? More convincing is the idea that the neocons wanted to project power in the region and punish Saddam Hussein for challenging American hegemony. The Vulcans had no intention of allowing the world's second largest oil reserves to remain under the control of someone who wasn't playing for their team. Beyond that it's equally likely that corporate profits drove the war machine with Halliburton, Cheney, and his cronies being among the top beneficiaries.

Despite Cheney's continual insistence that Halliburton is 100 percent squeaky clean, between 2001 and 2004 alone it was accused of some thirty-two legal violations involving nearly $13 billion in fraudulent activity.[90] Many others, including a large number of Republicans, have criticized the Bush family for its reputation of corruption. Of course this type of corruption is not exclusive to the Bush administration (or the Bush family). In 1961 Eisenhower condemned the military-industrial complex.[91] More recently Hillary Clinton has been accused of using her influence as secretary of state to offer "pay for play" opportunities to myriad state and nonstate actors.

Just How Stupid Was It?

> Don't do stupid shit.
>
> —Barack Obama

Beyond the controversy surrounding the Bush administration's motives for the occupation of Iraq (which has been compared to U.S. colonialism in the Philippines), there was also widespread lack of confidence in its ability to succeed. [92] Unfortunately, Bush didn't have a strategy for victory in Iraq; his strategy was to "prevent defeat."[93] Furthermore, opponents of the war argued that simply invading a country, fighting insurgents, and holding elections was not enough; the U.S. needed an exit strategy, which the Bush administration never developed. The entire war was half-baked from the beginning. Far from creating a stable democracy, the U.S. only succeeded in destabilizing the region. In other words from a strategic standpoint it was really, really stupid. Nonetheless, Bush insisted, "The path we have chosen is consistent with the great tradition of American foreign policy. Like the policies of Harry Truman and Ronald Reagan, our approach is idealistic about our national goals, and realistic about the means to achieve them."[94]

Those who opposed the Bush administration argued that neither idealism nor realism had anything to do with the U.S. policy toward Iraq. If one looks seriously at the foreign policy of either Harry Truman or Ronald Reagan, Bush's words should have given the American public great cause for alarm. On August 9, 1945, after ordering the atom bomb attack on Hiroshima, Truman gave a speech in which he said: "The world will note that the first atomic bomb was dropped on Hiroshima, a military base. That was because we wished in this first attack to avoid, insofar as possible, the killing of civilians."[95] (What?!)

As for Ronald Reagan, the U.S.-backed atrocities committed in Latin America during the 1980s speak for themselves. If this is the "great tradition of American foreign policy" that future administrations strive to emulate, then everyone should be very concerned. Fortunately, just because Bush says it doesn't make it true.

Understandably, the voices calling for an immediate withdrawal of American forces from Iraq were getting louder. The war was not only costing American taxpayers $10 billion a month; it was also destabilizing the entire region. Bush claimed that pulling troops out of Iraq would give al-Qaeda the opportunity to establish a new safe haven, but the truth was that al-Qaeda accounted for only about 15 percent of the attacks in Iraq in 2003.[96] The rest were the work of various Islamic militants from the surrounding region who had flocked to Iraq in defense of their fellow Muslims. The only reason Iraq became so strategically important to al-Qaeda is because the presence of such a large contingent of U.S. troops gave it a relatively inexpensive opportunity to attack the far enemy on a daily basis (see chapter 7).[97]

Bush and Cheney may have been lying through their teeth, but they weren't the worst of America's worries. The American military bombed residential areas, tortured civilians, and basically dared militants from the entire region to swarm to Iraq and oppose it.

Was this sheer stupidity or an intentional effort to escalate the conflict? The war in Iraq was a win-win for both sides. Private contractors made billions.[98] Meanwhile, American atrocities gave al-Qaeda huge propaganda victories which it translated into fresh recruits—and the flow of fighters into Iraq guaranteed that corporate profits would be unprecedented.

CHAPTER SEVEN

FROM BIN LADEN TO BAGHDADI

All these crimes and sins committed by the Americans are a clear declaration of war on God, his Messenger, and Muslims. . . . Jihad is an individual duty if the enemy destroys the Muslim countries. . . . On that basis, and in compliance with God's order, we issue the following fatwa to all Muslims: The ruling to kill the Americans and their allies—civilian and military—is an individual duty for every Muslim who can do it in any country in which it is possible to do it

—Osama bin Laden, *Text of Fatwa urging Jihad against Americans*

The Bush family's ties to Middle Eastern royalty and the revolving door between Wall Street and the Pentagon created a new enemy. The very Islamic insurgents the CIA had trained and armed to fight the Soviets in Afghanistan now resisted U.S. hegemony in the region. Leading the pack was Osama bin Laden, the black sheep billionaire whose own family had supported the dynasty that Operation Desert Storm was fought to defend. Outraged by the presence of American troops in Saudi Arabia, he resolved to do something about it.

Al-Qaeda's Strategic Object

In the previous chapters, I've established that terrorism is perhaps much older than one might have guessed and that a number of the foundational principles of modern jihadism are not so modern after all.

I now continue my investigation by comparing and contrasting the ideological underpinnings of al-Qaeda and Islamic State. I'll begin with a brief discussion of al-Qaeda and then progress to a more thorough discussion of IS. Bin Laden and al-Qaeda have received so much media coverage that it need not be repeated here. Therefore, my discussion of al-Qaeda will be limited to a discussion of its core ideological composition.

Bin Laden largely picked up where his mentor, Abdullah Azzam, left off. He adopted both defensive and offensive forms of militant jihad, as well as the concept that universal jihad was a personal duty. One sees this last influence in bin Laden's 1998 fatwa (quoted above).

The fact that bin Laden embraced the legitimacy of waging militant jihad in defense of Muslim soil is evident in his offer to employ al-Qaeda fighters to protect Saudi Arabia from a potential Iraqi invasion. Bin Laden also clearly embraced the legitimacy of waging offensive militant jihad as is evident by al-Qaeda's basic overall strategy: (1) attack the far enemy in order to weaken the corrupt puppet regimes of the Middle East, and (2) liberate the international Muslim community by toppling those very regimes—at the very top of the list was the ruling family in Saudi Arabia.[1]

Bin Laden denounced the Saudi regime for its willingness to cooperate with the West and particularly for accommodating the American military on what he regarded as sacred Muslim soil. In this regard one can clearly trace the influences of Ibn Taymiyyah and Al-Wahhab in bin Laden's pronouncement of takfir on the House of Saud.[2]

Like Qutb, bin Laden and Zawahiri embraced the vision of a vanguard and the necessity of the use of military force to establish a Muslim state. In no election would al-Qaeda be found on the ticket (you may recall that this was Zawahiri's main contention with the more moderate political aspirations of the Muslim Brotherhood).

However, bin Laden and Zawahiri also wanted to build and safeguard popular opinion among the worldwide Muslim community so as not to tarnish the al-Qaeda brand.[3] To an extent they also believed that the Muslims were largely ignorant of Islam (brainwashed by corrupting influences), and therefore they had to be taught. In this respect they were waging a campaign to win hearts and minds more in line with al-Banna and the moderates in the Muslim Brotherhood that Zawahiri despised.[4]

Finally, al-Qaeda clearly broke with the Muslim Brotherhood's strategy of attacking the near enemy in favor of the strategy spelled out above. This decision was no doubt informed by Azzam's tremendous influence on the young bin Laden. But it was also due to al-Qaeda's sheer inability to overthrow the Saudi regime, which bin Laden attributed to American support. If al-Qaeda could have overthrown the Saudi regime, it most definitely would have. It certainly tried.

I was stationed in Riyadh at an American military base that was attacked by an al-Qaeda suicide bomber. The blast ignited the gas tanks on the base and completely destroyed an entire barracks. Thirty-five men were killed, and hundreds more were injured. This was just one of many attacks intended to drive the Americans out. When that failed, al-Qaeda decided instead to draw us in.

Some analysts have suggested that bin Laden and Zawahiri were originally quite disappointed after 9/11 because the U.S. didn't respond in Afghanistan with an overwhelming ground force but instead relied largely on airstrikes and collaborated with the Northern Alliance.

Fortunately, foreign-policy analysts were warning as early as September 2001 that bin Laden and Zawahiri were attempting to provoke the U.S. into committing a large number of ground forces and getting bogged down in Afghanistan.[5] In this way the U.S. would alienate the locals and provide al-Qaeda with a fresh new generation of recruits as a result.

Furthermore, a protracted war in Afghanistan would bleed the U.S. of its resources and political will just as it had the Soviets. Not to mention that the invasion of a sovereign state would put pressure on America's allies and give al-Qaeda yet another reason to criticize the United States. Most importantly bin Laden wanted the opportunity to launch an attack successful enough to send the U.S. home with its tail between its legs—just as had happened in Lebanon and Somalia. When the U.S. didn't quite play into al-Qaeda's hands as it had hoped, bin Laden and Zawahiri saw another great opportunity in Iraq.

AL-QAEDA'S TACTICAL OPERATIONS

Many have speculated about why al-Qaeda targets America. One theory is that al-Qaeda hates America.[6] In many respects this notion is overly simplistic. What's there not to like? The U.S. has propped up corrupt regimes all over the Muslim world, it has been exploiting the region's oil resources for decades, and it stationed its troops on sacred Muslim soil. What's more, it invaded Iraq and has killed and displaced countless Muslims in the war on terror. Despite all this, the theory is still wrong, not because it isn't true but because it's so disconnected from al-Qaeda's strategic goal.

Remember, bin Laden succeeded Azzam whose mission was to spark universal jihad to liberate Muslims everywhere. This remains al-Qaeda's objective. Bin Laden simply arrived at the conclusion that the most efficient way to accomplish this goal was to eliminate the U.S. from the Muslim world first and then go about toppling apostate Muslim regimes. Whether bin Laden hated America or not is completely irrelevant.

A related theory is that al-Qaeda is opposed to the freedoms guaranteed by a democratic form of government.[7] Again, aside from being totally irrelevant to al-Qaeda's strategic goal, this suggestion in no way explains why the group would single out America. As bin Laden famously quipped, why didn't al-Qaeda attack Sweden?

A third argument is that al-Qaeda wants to punish the U.S. for its foreign policy in the Muslim world.[8] This notion is absolutely true. In fact bin Laden said as much in his 2002 "Letter to America."[9] However, what al-Qaeda wants and what it's ultimately attempting to achieve are not necessarily the same thing. Al-Qaeda *has* punished the U.S. for its foreign policy, time and time again. Still, it hasn't successfully eliminated American interference in the region.

It has also been suggested that America became al-Qaeda's target after emerging as the sole superpower following the fall of the Soviet Union.[10] Again, this simply isn't relevant to the group's strategic objectives. Azzam encouraged al-Qaeda militants to go to Afghanistan to fight the Soviets because they had invaded a Muslim state, not because the Soviet Union was a superpower. Once the Soviets were forced out, Azzam instructed the mujahidin to switch to aggressive jihad and start taking back lands that were lost to the infidels.

When bin Laden took over at the helm, he had a choice to make. He could (1) follow Azzam's instructions and invade Israel or attempt to retake Lisbon, Cordova, Avignon, the Island of Rhodes, and so on, (2) go after the apostate Muslim regimes, or (3) target the far enemy. While there were clearly tactical advantages in landing a major blow against the only remaining superpower on the planet—and bin Laden took full advantage of them—they were not the main reasons behind the attacks.

Last, several analysts have alleged that, as part of the new generation of terrorists, al-Qaeda has no rationale behind its actions at all. It's purely irrational, and it just wants to kill a lot of people.[11] If that truly were the case, wouldn't it be a lot easier and cost effective to just stay home and kill everyone there?

Alan Cullison, who had the rare opportunity of purchasing Muhammad Atef's laptop and Zawahiri's desktop computer, concluded that al-Qaeda's main reason for the attacks on September 11, 2001, was to galvanize the group's militants.[12] Al-Qaeda's leaders remembered how fighting the Soviets brought a sense of unity to the fighters in Afghanistan.

Beyond that bin Laden hoped to (1) provoke the U.S into overreacting and committing human rights atrocities, which would cost it legitimacy in the eyes of the global community, and (2) draw the U.S. into a long and costly ground war that would erode America's political will to stay involved in the region. One can correctly apply the same strategic objective to each and every attack against American interests. The goal is to get the U.S. to leave the Muslim world alone.

Fortunately, based on my brief strategic assessment here, it can be determined that al-Qaeda *does* have a strategy. What's more, despite the slew of claims to the contrary, it has been following that strategy for the most part. There are, no doubt, a number of tactical maneuvers that are more difficult to explain than others (blunders and absurdities, to paraphrase Emerson). Still, a working knowledge of the group's strategic goal allows one to understand much more readily why al-Qaeda has made many of the tactical decisions that it has.

For example the 1992 Yemen hotel bombings, the 1993 World Trade Center bombing, and the 1998 bombing of the U.S. embassies in Kenya and Tanzania were all obvious measures of coercive diplomacy intended to pressure American policy makers to evacuate the Middle East. Al-Qaeda didn't launch these attacks because it hates the U.S. or because it hates freedom. Nor did it perpetrate these attacks because it's crazy. And while the attacks did punish the U.S., and the group definitely gained some street credit, this was not al-Qaeda's strategic objective.

The analysis above is fairly straightforward. But it becomes a bit more convoluted when one considers less obvious attacks such as the November 2003 suicide attack outside Riyadh that killed eighteen and wounded over one hundred more, most of whom were Saudis.[13] The reasons behind these attacks are not so easily identified without a proper understanding of al-Qaeda's strategy.

Bin Laden's 1998 fatwa instructs every single Muslim to kill Americans wherever they may be found. Given the emphasis on militant jihad as an individual duty and the understanding that jihad is universal, it shouldn't be surprising that attacks against tourists around the world increased dramatically after bin Laden released his fatwa.

There has been tremendous speculation regarding the November 2003 suicide attack outside Riyadh. Some suggest that al-Qaeda hit the softer Saudi target because the American targets in the city were already sufficiently hardened. Another theory is that al-Qaeda was hoping to demonstrate that the Saudis cannot protect their own people. Still others speculate that al-Qaeda attacked the housing complex to scare the roughly six million foreign workers in the kingdom into fleeing, hoping to cripple the Saudi economy.[14]

All these suggestions could be accurate. Or they may not be. Who knows? Without a working knowledge of al-Qaeda's strategy, all one can do is speculate. However, understanding al-Qaeda's strategy enables one to make better sense of its tactics. Therefore, given al-Qaeda's concern for public opinion, the first option is plausible but highly unlikely.

The group did launch a similar attack on an American compound in May of the same year. However, al-Qaeda enjoyed considerable public support in Saudi Arabia at that time—even among some members of the royal family.[15] And when we consider bin Laden's justification for killing Americans—namely, that America has killed so many Muslims worldwide—it would be counterproductive to intentionally target a site comprised solely of Muslims.

The second option is also plausible but highly unlikely for much the same reason. How much sense does it make to kill the very people you claim to defend just to prove that your enemy can't protect them? That's no way to win hearts and minds. Not to mention that the U.S. and Saudi Arabia are allies. To demonstrate that the Saudis can't protect their own people might put pressure on the U.S. to increase its presence in the region and provide more support to the Saudi regime.

This brings us to the third option. Given al-Qaeda's strategy of attacking the far enemy, it makes perfect sense for the group to attempt to frighten foreign workers as this plays right into its game plan. However, to jeopardize popular support by attacking Saudi Muslims doesn't fit al-Qaeda's strategy.[16] So why did it do it?

A little digging uncovers the fact that the housing complex al-Qaeda attacked was once used to house American employees of the Boeing Company. Therefore, a fourth theory might be that the attack was based on outdated information. Given al-Qaeda's focus on the far enemy—and especially considering that it launched a suicide attack on an American compound in May of the same year—this last explanation makes the most sense.

If you've ever been to the kingdom, particularly Riyadh, it's easy to understand outdated information. The first thing that you miss (besides pork and alcohol if you're so inclined) is civil society. There isn't even an empty space where civil society should be as you find in some former totalitarian states. It's as if Riyadh were intentionally constructed to keep personal interaction outside the home to an absolute minimum.

A fortress mentality pervades the city. Everything is walled in, gated up, or locked. New construction is going up all the time, only to remain vacant. Brand new malls stand empty. Even the nicest buildings are surrounded by huge piles of sand and gravel. In spite of some of the worst (and deadliest) traffic in the world, the entire city feels deserted. So, of the four possible explanations, the last one is the most plausible given our understanding of al-Qaeda's long-term goals.

In this first portion of the chapter, I identified al-Qaeda's strategic objectives and demonstrated how a proper knowledge of these can help one to make better sense of the group's tactical operations. From this discussion it's clear that al-Qaeda is a jihadist organization that has relied solely on violence as the primary means for attaining its strategic objectives.

Some may take issue with my designation of al-Qaeda as a jihadist group rather than a takfiri group. For example Tom Quiggin points out that al-Qaeda regularly makes use of the takfiri doctrine to discredit its opponents.[17] Likewise David Kilcullen, who expressly prefers the term "takfiri" over that of "jihadist," also labels al-Qaeda a takfiri group.[18] However, both take an overly simplistic view in my opinion. There is a distinct difference between takfirism and jihadism, so one cannot simply use one term in place of the other regardless of preference. And while it's true that al-Qaeda discredits political leaders whom it views as apostate by pronouncing takfir on them, al-Qaeda does not endorse the killing of apostate Muslims as an end in itself as do takfiri groups such as the Islamic State, al-Shabaab, and Boko Haram.

Recall that Azzam was a staunch opponent of the takfiri doctrine. He was so opposed to it that he issued a fatwa against the doctrine claiming that the killing of fellow Muslims and civilians is against Islam. Yet Azzam clearly supported the use of violence toward the ultimate end of regaining lost Muslim territory and establishing sharia.[19] And while it's certainly true that al-Qaeda targets American civilians, the goal is to drive the Western militaries—and particularly the U.S.— out of the Muslim world. The main difference between jihadists and takfiri groups is that the first group employs violence against civilians to coerce political concessions from a target government, while the second kills civilians because it believes that they are apostates. For the first group, violence is a means to an end. For the second violence is an end in itself. This is a critical distinction that people will likely never hear discussed in the mainstream media because it doesn't fit within the framework of us versus them or the ten-second sound bites used to advance it.

In the second part of this chapter, I'll examine the strategic goals of the Islamic State as well as compare and contrast the ideological underpinnings of al-Qaeda and IS.

The Islamic State

The group we now know as the Islamic State began in 1999 as Jama'at al-Tawhid wa-al-Jihad, "The Organization of Monotheism and Jihad" (JTJ). It was founded and co-led by Abu Musab al-Zarqawi and Abu Ayyub al-Masri. Based in Iraq JTJ mainly focused on training suicide bombers in Pakistan and Afghanistan.[20]

Zarqawi was born Ahmad Fadil Nazal al-Khalayel in the town of

Zarqa, Jordan, on October 20, 1966.[21] A high school dropout, he went to prison for five years at the age of eighteen for sexual assault and drug possession. While in prison he was exposed to radical Islamist influences.[22]

In 1989 Zarqawi moved to Afghanistan to fight the Soviets. However, the war was basically winding down by then. So he settled in Peshawar; he was most likely exposed to the takfiri doctrine here because it was circulating in the area at that time. It was in Peshawar that Zarqawi earned the nickname al-Gharib (the stranger).[23] Here he is believed to have developed his tremendous animosity toward moderate Muslim governments and his intense hatred toward Shia.[24] It's also possible that Zarqawi first met bin Laden in Peshawar.[25]

We know considerably less about al-Masri. He was born in Egypt, became a member of the Muslim Brotherhood, and later joined Egyptian Islamic Jihad in 1982. He received explosives training at bin Laden's Al Farouq militant camp in Afghanistan, where he presumably met Zarqawi.

When Zarqawi learned that the U.S. planned to commit troops to Iraq, he began to set up a network in Iraq and reached out to al-Qaeda for support. Zarqawi's vision was the exact opposite of bin Laden's, however.[26]

Bin Laden was convinced that the establishment of the caliphate had to wait until America was driven out of the Middle East and the corrupt puppet regimes in the Muslim world were overthrown. Only then would Muslims be strong enough to establish the caliphate. Zarqawi insisted that Muslims were only as strong as their leaders. He wanted to set up an Islamic state immediately. Rather than attempt to win the hearts and minds of the majority of Muslims as bin Laden wanted to do, Zarqawi wanted to wage a brutal campaign that would instill fear, not win popular support. Here again we see the tension between al-Banna's more conciliatory bottom-up approach and Qutb's authoritarian top-down approach.

Perhaps of greatest importance was Zarqawi's position on excommunication. Zarqawi believed that takfir should be pronounced on all Muslims who did not strictly adhere to the Salafi tradition. Zarqawi had no desire or intention of tolerating people he regarded as heretics, whether they be the House of Saud, Shia, or common everyday Sunni. In his view the near enemy was not just the corrupt puppet regimes propped up by the West. Zarqawi believed that the near enemy was composed of every single apostate Muslim in the region and that this enemy posed a far direr threat to Islam than the West.

In Zarqawi's perception all apostate Muslims were the enemy, and therefore they must be eliminated. Zarqawi would make no effort to gain legitimacy in their eyes. He planned to achieve his objectives through violence and violence alone. Zarqawi's radical view of takfir and his brutal campaign of terror would also become the hallmarks of his successors in the Islamic State.[27]

Zarqawi clearly embraced Qutb's broader definition of Dar al-Islam to include both the physical territory controlled by Muslims and faith, community, and the Muslim way of life. And Zarqawi argued that jihad should be used to defend Islam first and foremost from apostate Muslims.

Bin Laden was concerned that Zarqawi's sheer brutality would tarnish al-Qaeda's image and thereby jeopardize the future success of his own political program. Still, bin Laden and Zawahiri recognized a great opportunity in Iraq to expand their influence. So bin Laden originally agreed to cooperate with JTJ but not to take it on as an al-Qaeda affiliate.

The U.S. Invasion of Iraq

In March 2003 the United States invaded Iraq along with a coalition of troops from allied nations, removed Saddam Hussein from power, and destroyed much of Iraq's infrastructure. By May 2003 the American-led multinational coalition had ousted the Baʿath Party and proceeded to occupy the country.

Along with dismantling the Iraqi army and attempting to rebuild it largely by arming militias, the coalition installed an interim government that was ineffective to say the least. Major cities suffered shortages of electricity, clean water, phone service, and garbage collection for at least a year after the invasion. Looting was also a major problem.

The U.S. also appeared to have little or no respect for the Iraqi people or their culture. Former minister of defense Ali Allawi recalls that American soldiers conducted full body searches of women, searched Iraqi homes without a male head of the household present, and publically humiliated the elderly.[28] Pulitzer Prize–winning journalist Fred Kaplan further recounts that the American military's counterterrorism strategy largely entailed, "killing suspected insurgents, surrounding whole neighborhoods, pounding down doors in the middle of the night" and other clever attempts at winning hearts and minds.[29] A colleague of mine who was also there during the occupation witnessed horrendous atrocities at the hands of American military; perhaps the most disturbing account involved the "searching" of incubators in a hospital. My colleague reported that the soldiers "pulled out and tipped over the incubators with the babies still in them."

Hostility against the American occupation was such that in April 2006, a poll revealed that 97.9 percent of Sunni either opposed or strongly opposed the U.S. presence in Iraq.[30]

I befriended the family of a Baʿathist officer who had been killed during this period. The family had managed to move to the United States but continued to relive their own personal nightmare as they watched events unfold on television. They used to spend hours describing to me what it was like to live amid continual shelling, power outages, water shortages, and of course constant fear.

During this time tens of thousands of private security forces were brought in to protect the remaining oil infrastructure. As the military fought increasing numbers of guerrilla units, it rounded up thousands of Iraqi men suspected of being radical militants and imprisoned them. Unfortunately, many of these men were ordinary Iraqi citizens who, while in prison, became radicalized through their interaction with militants such as Abu Bakr al-Baghdadi, the current leader of IS.

In February 2004 Baghdadi was arrested and incarcerated at Camp Bucca, which housed more than one hundred thousand men between 2003 and 2009. The camp was subdivided into compounds of approximately one thousand inmates each. Inside Bucca radical Sunni declared sharia and tortured anyone who refused to obey by cutting out their tongue or gouging out their eyes.[31] Bucca is now regarded as an incubator for IS as many of the worst jihadists detained there eventually joined the group, including Baghdadi, Abu Suja, Abu Muslim al-Turkmani, Abu Jurnas, Abu Louay, Abu Shema, and Abu Kassem.[32]

AQI

In October 2004, Zarqawi applied to al-Qaeda for his group to become an affiliate. This time around bin Laden agreed. By now Zarqawi's brutal tactics were producing results. On the one hand, Zarqawi was too valuable to turn away. He may have been a loose cannon, but he was a cannon nonetheless. On the other hand, bin Laden hoped that he could control Zarqawi and minimize the risk to the al-Qaeda brand.

An important tactical barrier had also been removed. It takes a very different level of capability to attack the United States than it does to attack a local mosque or police headquarters. However, the U.S. invasion of Iraq brought the far enemy near. Bin Laden now had the best of both worlds: the U.S. military was within reach, and Zarqawi's bloodlust would provide bin Laden the opportunity to send U.S. soldiers and personnel home in body bags.

Zarqawi officially changed the name of the group to Tanẓim Qaʿidat al-Jihad fi Bilad al-Rafidayn, "The Organization of Jihad's Base in the Country of the Two Rivers," popularly known as al-Qaeda in Iraq (AQI). The new name was debuted on a video release of the beheading of Ken Bigley, a British engineer.

Scholars differ on the exact relationship between bin Laden and Zarqawi regarding who was courting whom. However, most agree that the two groups used each other. AQI benefited from the fame of the al-Qaeda brand, and al-Qaeda general wanted to spearhead Zarqawi's operation in Iraq. Both groups enjoyed tactical benefits, a wave of fresh recruits, and widespread publicity from the merger. However, it was an alliance of pure convenience and nothing more, and al-Qaeda would soon regret the decision.

Zarqawi quickly demonstrated that he could not be controlled. Rather than moderate his own position, he attempted to radicalize everyone else—especially the Sunni tribal leaders—by provoking widespread Shiite retaliation against the Sunni. He hoped this provocation would radicalize the Sunni, who would then put pressure on the tribal leaders. By attacking both sacred and secular targets and killing mass numbers of civilians of all faiths, Zarqawi hoped to spark an all-out sectarian war.

History has seen this strategy played out again and again, from Charles Manson in the 1960s to the 2010 race riots in Kyrgyzstan, where violence between the Kyrgyz and the Uzbeks continued for three months until Soviet troops intervened. Manson hoped to spark a racial confrontation between blacks and whites in America, while it's rumored that the Kremlin was behind the violence that killed as many as a thousand people in the space of a few months in the former Soviet republic.

An Uzbek friend of mine detailed the horror he experienced during the outbreak of what has been referred to as ethnic cleansing in the Kyrgyz city of Osh: "Someone was banging on our door, trying to get in. . . . Outside everyone was screaming. Eventually, I had to go out. . . . I was terrified. People were fighting all over the city."

As he relived the horror, I was reminded of the Rodney King riots in 1992. I was on a flight from Honolulu to San Francisco as the violence broke out across the state (and the nation). The smoke from the fires that rioters had set ablaze was so thick that we were nearly rerouted to Sacramento. After about a forty-minute delay, the plane did finally land in San Francisco, but on the ground it was sheer pandemonium. As I drove from the airport to Santa Clara, exits were blocked, and fires were burning everywhere. Bush had deployed the military to restore order, and a curfew had been imposed. It was like a scene from *Mad Max*.

Once I reached my destination, I watched as looters broke into stores, and rioters smashed car windshields—all fueled by rage. In the immortal words of David Bowie, I kept thinking to myself, "This is not America." But it was. Ethnicity and race can be powerful rallying forces.

Although Zarqawi's plot didn't immediately produce the extent of sectarian violence that he had hoped for, his cold-blooded brutality and systematic recklessness were successful in both terrorizing and polarizing much of the Iraqi population. An Iraqi friend of mine explained that even something as benign as wearing green clothing in public could spark a violent sectarian reaction.

Zarqawi's notorious beheadings as publicity stunts also won the group enormous worldwide attention.[33] The group released video footage of the beheading of Americans Jack Hensley and Eugene Armstrong. Despite pleas from al-Qaeda general to tone it down, Zarqawi was on fire.[34] A rising star on the Islamist horizon, he was about to go supernova.

The year 2006 turned out to be pivotal. Zarqawi wanted to do something big to escalate the sectarian conflict. He deeply resented what he saw as favoritism for the Shia on the part of the U.S. In January AQI joined a number of other Iraqi insurgent groups to form Majlis Shura al-Mujahedin (the Mujahidin Shura Council, MSM), with Abu Abdullah al-Rashid al-Baghdadi as emir.

In February the group attacked the Imam al-Askari Shrine in Samarra, one of the most important Shiite holy places in the world, sparking reprisals against five Sunni mosques in Baghdad. On May 20, Nouri al-Maliki was appointed prime minister. In Zarqawi's mind the appointment was just further evidence of the U.S.-Shia conspiracy. Even al-Qaeda general appears to have been alarmed.[35]

The move to join MSM backfired on Zarqawi. If there's strength in numbers, there's also a certain amount of increased vulnerability. Due to its brutal treatment of all civilians—whether Shia, Sunni, or non-Muslims—AQI made *a lot* of enemies. Its practices eventually turned even many loyal Sunni against it, culminating in the Sunni Awakening. It's likely due to Sunni displeasure that U.S., Iraqi, and Jordanian intelligence operations were able to obtain vital information on Zarqawi's whereabouts.[36]

The U.S. assassinated Zarqawi on June 7, 2006, and in October of that same year MSM combined forces with several other Sunni forces and formed the Islamic State of Iraq (ISI) again with Abu Abdullah al-Rashid al-Baghdadi as emir and Zarqawi's longtime colleague and successor, Abu Ayyub al-Masri, as leader.

A New Caliphate

ISI claimed to have established the caliphate, and it demanded that all other militant Islamist groups pledge allegiance. But at this point ISI controlled no territory, so the other militants just laughed. How can you claim to lead the caliphate with no territory? Both Baghdadi and al-Masri vowed to uphold Zarqawi's jihad against the near enemy. However, both men were assassinated by the U.S. on April 18, 2010, and Abu Bakr al-Baghdadi emerged as the new leader of ISI a month later.

In 2011 American troops pulled out of Iraq, leaving behind a destabilized country with virtually no infrastructure but awash in American weaponry. This development gave ISI exactly what it needed: weapons, space, and time. Because the group adhered to a strict Wahhabi Islamic doctrine, it also enjoyed financial support from a number of Gulf states. Add to these resources the experience and expertise of a significant number of former Ba'athist commanders from Saddam Hussein's recently toppled regime, and you have a recipe for today's Islamic State.[37]

In 2011 ISI also joined the rebellion against the Assad regime in Syria. In April 2013 Baghdadi declared that ISI was extending its territory to include Syria. The group also advanced into Kurdish areas of Iraq and began to kill and enslave thousands of Yazidis. Countless Yazidi women and girls were taken as sex slaves, while others were given away as political patronage or sold on the open market. Of course Obama responded by authorizing more than ten thousand air strikes, killing tens of thousands and further exacerbating civilian suffering. The official number of civilian casualties in Iraq for the past two years alone exceeds twenty thousand. The actual number is likely much higher (just imagine John Kirby lying through his teeth). No one is even trying to keep an accurate account of civilian casualties in Syria any longer.

The group officially changed its name to the Islamic State of Iraq and al-Sham and alternatively the Islamic State of Iraq and the Levant. Baghdadi also announced that ISIL and Jabhat al-Nusra (JN)—al-Qaeda's affiliate in Syria—were the same organization. JN's leader, Abu Muhammad al-Jawlani, denied the claim and publicly reaffirmed *baya* (allegiance) to Zawahiri.

Al-Qaeda general ordered Baghdadi to return to Iraq and leave Syria to JN. Baghdadi rejected Zawahiri's attempt to control him and publicly denounced al-Qaeda for honoring the infidel Sykes-Picot Treaty. Baghdadi's brutality against apostates also led Zawahiri to publish *General Guidelines for Jihad* in September 2013, attempting to set in stone the rules of engagement for al-Qaeda and its affiliates. Baghdadi ignored these instructions as well.[38]

Al-Qaeda officially cut ties with ISIS in February 2014, and in June of that year, Baghdadi officially changed the name of his organization to the Islamic State after announcing the establishment of a new caliphate. This time no one was laughing. IS now controlled large areas of land and embarked on a blitzkrieg of brutality, capturing entire cities, massacring thousands, and taking as many, if not more, as slaves.

The Islamic State's Strategic Objective

IS maintained the exact same threefold strategy that it had followed from the beginning:

1. Establish the caliphate first. Where al-Qaeda believed that the establishment of the caliphate had to wait, IS insisted that the first step should be to establish the caliphate and then expand it. While no one affiliated with al-Qaeda was qualified to be caliph, Baghdadi claimed to be a descendant of Muhammad's tribe.
2. Reign through terror. As a takfiri group, IS would waste no time attempting to win hearts and minds. Rather, it would reign by sheer terror, mercilessly slaughtering infidels and apostates without hesitation.
3. Promote the fulfillment of prophecy. IS places enormous emphasis on apocalyptic prophecy. The group originally promoted the idea that the Mahdi would appear to usher in the apocalypse within a few months. When this didn't happen, IS changed its message and started promoting itself as the fulfillment of prophecy, stating that after the reign of four or five pure rulers, the Mahdi would come.[39]

Baghdadi maintains strict centralized control over a loosely decentralized regional command structure. For instance he might decide on a target and a date well in advance, but regional commanders decide the rest based on various realities at the time and place. The autonomy enjoyed by regional commanders affords IS the ability to avoid situations where the opponent has the upper hand.

Still, Baghdadi has demonstrated his skill as a military commander by successfully adopting a tactic used by Saladin (1137–93) against the Crusaders. By extending the battle line as widely as possible, IS spreads the enemy thin, which often offsets any imbalances of troop strength. Meanwhile, the group makes full use of the means at its disposal, namely, highly mobile units, suicide bombers, and of course social media campaigns designed to terrorize the opponent with images of the organization's brutality.[40]

In June 2014 IS took control of Mosul, Iraq's second largest city. The following month Baghdadi anointed himself the caliph of the Islamic world. He claimed to be a direct descendant of the Prophet Muhammad, which is quite a claim because neither the Saudi royal family nor bin Laden is descended from the Quraysh tribe.

Baghdadi also holds a PhD in Islamic studies from the Islamic

University of Baghdad. He uses his extensive knowledge of the Quran, ahadith (recorded words and deeds of the Prophet), and sunna (religious practices established by the example of the Prophet) to call attention to the legitimacy of his claim to be the caliph. Virtually everything that IS does is intended to reenact famous battles and demonstrate that the Islamic State is the fulfillment of Islamic apocalyptic prophecy.

Take Baghdadi's appearance for example. IS adheres to traditional Wahhabi beliefs that glorify the first three generations of Islam as the most pure. So he fashions his appearance after the rightly guided rulers of that age: Abu Bakr al-Siddiq, Umar ibn al-Khattab, Uthman ibn Affan, and Ali ibn Abi Talib. He has even taken his name after the first successor of Muhammad. His real name is Ibrahim Awwadty Ibrahim Ali Muhammad al-Badri al-Samarrai.[41]

Another example is the rampage of brutal violence that IS has been engaged in for the past decade. To most outsiders it appears to be random, senseless killing. However, Sunni Muslims realize that the first duty of the caliph is to spread Islam—whether through peace or through war—and beheading was the prescribed manner of execution in the Quran.[42]

Even the name of its propaganda magazine, *Dabiq*, is taken from the name of the Syrian city where the final battle between the infidels and the armies of Allah is prophesied to occur. IS captured this symbolically important city in June 2014 and beheaded an American "Crusader," Peter Kassig.[43]

The campaign against IS has been long and bloody, but the multinational coalition has made significant progress. The group lost Kobane to Kurdish forces and Diyala to the Iraqi military in January 2015. A year later IS lost Ramadi only eight months after gaining control of the city. In March 2016 Syrian forces (backed by Russian air strikes) recaptured Palmyra (although IS took it back again in December).

In October 2016 IS lost control of Dabiq, and in May 2017 the group ceded control of Tabqa. IS lost the battle over Mosul in July 2017, and it was defeated at Raqqa in October. In November the Syrian government announced it had recaptured Deir ez-Zor, IS's last major stronghold in Syria. The same month Iraqi forces took Rawa, the group's last stronghold in Iraq.

Is the Islamic State a Terrorist Organization?

Today the Islamic State is the most widely publicized "terrorist organization" in the world. Of course the term itself is a misnomer as any actor can engage in terrorism. What most people don't realize is that, prior to losing the majority of its territory, the Islamic State was actually a hybrid organization. First and foremost, at its peak the Islamic State was a state that controlled approximately 375 miles of territory. Baghdadi has since seen his empire slowly diminish from approximately 30,000 square miles in January 2016 to roughly 23,000 square miles a year later and next to nothing in January 2018.

While the actual territory under the group's control changed with the fortunes of war, at its height IS directly governed and taxed an estimated two to ten million people. Because collecting accurate data inside IS-controlled territory proved extremely difficult, most analysts shoot for the middle and guestimate the number to be between five and six million.

It's been equally impossible to determine the value of the organization's assets with 100 percent certainty. However, it's believed that IS once possessed a war chest of approximately $2 billion.[44] What's more, the group raked in millions every day through taxes, gas and oil revenues, ransom and extortion, black market enterprises (antiquities, art, and slaves), and the sale of other commodities such as cement, phosphate, and agricultural products.

Second, Islamic State is an insurgent group capable of launching rebellions in dozens of locations. As of December 2015, IS had enlisted forty-three affiliates.[45] Given the group's global brand, IS can technically move operatives as needed or desired. However, there is considerable doubt concerning the extent of actual cooperation between IS and its so-called affiliates. While al-Qaeda has been selective in the groups to which it extends the hand of franchise, IS doesn't seem to have been selective at all. And while there's plenty of evidence that al-Qaeda oversees its affiliate groups rather closely, with the exception of Libya, IS appears to have offered very little if any assistance or oversight to its affiliates.[46] As I'll discuss in chapter 8, this loose association casts doubt on whether IS actually perpetrated many of the attacks Baghdadi has claimed responsibility for.

Finally, the group is most popularly known as a "terrorist organization." I argue here that while IS certainly employed violence to achieve its goals, it employed violence primarily to defend and expand its own state apparatus rather than to coerce another regime to change its policies. In this respect it's no different from any other state that employs violence.

Calculated Madness

I've compared and contrasted the ideological underpinnings of al-Qaeda and IS. In addition to the basic understanding that al-Qaeda is primarily a jihadist organization and the Islamic State is a takfiri group, I noted a number of other important qualities. I traced the influence of Azzam by demonstrating that al-Qaeda adopted both defensive and offensive forms of militant jihad, as well as the concept that universal jihad was a personal duty (evident in bin Laden's 1998 fatwa). I also traced the influence of Ibn Taymiyyah and Al-Wahhab as demonstrated in bin Laden's pronouncement of takfir on the House of Saud.

Like Qutb, bin Laden and Zawahiri embraced the vision of a vanguard and the necessity of the use of military force to establish a Muslim state. However, one can also trace the influence of al-Banna and the moderates in the Muslim Brotherhood, as bin Laden and Zawahiri were concerned with educating the Muslim community and preserving popular opinion. Finally, I have demonstrated that al-Qaeda clearly broke with the Muslim Brotherhood's strategy of attacking the near enemy. I attributed this decision to the influence of Azzam and also the failure to overthrow the near enemy due to support from the West.

The ideology of IS differs from al-Qaeda in several important ways. First, Zarqawi wanted to set up the caliphate immediately. In order to be legitimate, IS needed territory. It also needed someone qualified to be caliph. Al-Qaeda didn't need either.

While both bin Laden and Baghdadi can be considered vanguards in their own right, they're vanguards in a very different sense of the word. Bin Laden led a diffuse global network. Baghdadi claimed to have presided over a state, perhaps even an empire. Second, rather than attempting to win the hearts and minds of the majority of Muslims as bin Laden wanted to do, Baghdadi is waging a brutal campaign to instill fear, not win popular support. Finally, IS claims to be the fulfillment of apocalyptic prophecy—Allah's kingdom on earth. As such it has no room for infidels (Christians, Jews, Shia, or apostates of any kind). The Kharajites' famous cry, "No government but God's!" can still be heard echoing in the aftermath of IS attacks today.

CHAPTER EIGHT

UTTER CONFUSION

They used brick instead of stone, and tar for mortar. Then they said, "Come, let us build ourselves a city, with a tower that reaches to the heavens, so that we may make a name for ourselves"

—Genesis 11:3–4

Open Rebellion

Another story that Christians, Muslims, and Jews all share in common is the story of the ancient Tower of Babel, in which humans attempted to build a tower that reached all the way to heaven. While details vary slightly from one religious tradition to the other, in all three accounts the builders of the tower were in open rebellion against God, and their languages were scrambled as a result.

Why Did They Need a Tower Anyway?

Having forfeited his dominion, Adam became the first human criminal. Earth itself became a penal colony—kind of like Australia only bigger. Generations later humankind was still in rebellion. While the passage from Genesis tells us only that the builders of the tower wanted to reach the heavens and make a name for themselves, one can infer that God was not pleased because he intervened and confused their language so that they couldn't finish the tower.

What I find interesting is what God said in Genesis 11:6: "This is only the beginning of what they will do. And nothing that they propose to do will now be impossible for them." This implies that they were after something more, or at least they would be once they finished the tower. What could that something be?

When read in its fuller context, the story takes place after the flood. Nearly every culture on earth has a story of a cataclysmic flood, and many of the details in these stories are similar. In the Jewish Tanakh, God told Noah and his sons to "be fruitful and multiply and fill the earth." However, as the descendants of Noah spread westward (away from their original state of purity in the East), they settled in the land of Shinar, against God's express command to fill the earth.

The general consensus among most theologians is that they were supposed to spread out, not congregate together in one place. But here they were building a city. Plus they all shared a common language. In other words they were all one people, and they were concentrated in one place. Taken at face value, I can't help but wonder who they were hoping to impress. There weren't any other people on the earth. And why did they need to reach the heavens in order to do it?

Of course, no can answer these questions because motive is not only difficult to determine in this case; it's impossible. And any attempt to speculate is just that, pure speculation. However, to maintain any continuity within the story line, one needs to concede at minimum that (1) the earth was in a state of foreign occupation because Adam had forfeited his dominion to a usurper who now reigned supreme, (2) the people, by continuing to disobey God, were in a state of open rebellion, and (3) they were now also attempting to build a tower that would reach heaven itself.

A person could, of course, bring his or her own religious beliefs to the table, which would undoubtedly result in a stalemate as everyone stubbornly defended his or her own theological position. Or one could simply admit that no one honestly knows what the builders' motives were.

The builders' strategic objective is also a mystery. Did they plan to make war on God? Were they planning to manipulate some sort of concessions from him? Was the destruction of the tower the first act of antiterrorism? Perhaps they were simply concerned that there would be another flood (I can only imagine that flood insurance was crazy expensive in those days). Maybe they were simply building a tower in honor of themselves, a monument to their survival. Since their strategic objective is unknown, no one can begin to understand how building a tower that reached to the heavens might allow them to achieve that goal. Whatever it was, God clearly did not negotiate with them.

Those in terrorism studies essentially face the same problem. Rather than simply acknowledge that it's impossible to make sense of an actor's actions without a basic understanding of its strategic objective(s), many terrorism scholars ignore the actor altogether and instead bring *their own* theoretical assumptions to the analysis. Then they waste a lot of time and space stubbornly defending them. In other words they make their own bricks rather than go out and find the stones that are necessary for building a sturdy foundation.

For example, if I were to analyze the Tower of Babel from one of the many theoretical perspectives common to terrorism studies, I wouldn't be asking what the builders were attempting to accomplish. Rather I would be making a host of other suppositions: Maybe they built the tower because they were hungry or poor or illiterate. Perhaps they built the tower because of inequality (everyone in heaven had mansions while these poor people lived in tents). Maybe they were criminally insane, or perhaps they lacked democratic institutions (no doubt, Nimrod was a tyrant).

Of course, the critical theorists would be making an entirely different set of assumptions. Noting an irresolute position regarding the possibility of a value-neutral conception of reality and espousing a post-positivist epistemology, the perpetrators of this nefarious obelisk afforded no nugatory prominence to the identification and deconstruction of hegemonic discourse. Ergo, they were all ostentatiously atheist and didn't believe that heaven existed in the first place, much less that they could get there by climbing on a pile of bricks . . . (blah, blah, blah).

There's an obvious parallel between this story and the field of terrorism studies. Due to the discipline's overall rebellion against common sense, its practitioners have lost the ability (or the desire) to understand one another. Those in the field no longer speak the same language. Consequently, as a discipline, they don't make any sense. The body of terrorism literature is nothing more than an endless flow of incoherent babbling. This may sound harsh, but it's in line with the rules of engagement because it's both reasonable and necessary under the circumstances.

Paradigms shift. Einstein's theory of relativity replaced Newton's laws of motion, and Einstein's own mass-energy equivalence formula ($E = mc^2$) paved the way for quantum mechanics. However, paradigms don't shift because scholars discover new answers; they shift because scholars start asking different questions. Every serious field of inquiry goes through this process. The transition from one paradigm to the next is usually painful—and there are many who resist—but the alternative is far worse. It's time to start asking the right questions about the war on terror.

The "Looming" Tower of Babel

Terrorism scholars and policy makers alike have been busy building their own Tower of Babel—desperate to arrive at some generic grand theory that can be applied to all violence of which they do not approve. Lawrence Wright's Pulitzer Prize–winning account of the road to 9/11 is a fitting analogy for our own inquiry into how this tower came into being in the first place, as well as the writing on the wall concerning its destruction.

An obvious metaphor is the Twin Towers. If one were to figuratively think of the Twin Towers as the endeavor to arrive at a grand theory of terrorism, then terrorism itself is the planes that took them down. Grand theories simply don't hold up when confronted with the truth of terrorist violence (or any violence for that matter).

One could also compare the vast body of terrorism literature itself to the Twin Towers, but it isn't architecturally beautiful (or sound). Rather, it's more like the huge heap of rubble left behind after the attacks: countless contradictory theories and definitions, all piled on top of one another without any apparent order or design whatsoever.

Finally, one could compare the Twin Towers to the us-versus-them framework and the politicization of violence and hypocrisy that it's built upon. I've discussed in previous chapters how this framework generates fear and how widespread fear opens the door to toleration and even demand for unjust social and political policies.

I've also considered how America's obsession with sensational violence does more to "radicalize" people than al-Qaeda or IS combined.

This is the case because more people are lured by fame than by any religious ideology, Islamic extremism or otherwise. Without widespread publicity, sensational acts of violence would be a fairly inconsequential reality in comparison to "everyday" violence.

For instance, between 1965 and 2015, 75,396 Americans were murdered by other Americans in New York alone.[1] This number constitutes an annual average of 1,478 murders per year for the fifty-one-year period leading up to and including 2015. That's more than 120 murders per month—every single month for fifty-one years in New York alone. When one compares this to the 3,031 people killed in the 9/11 attacks, it doesn't minimize the attacks, but it does demonstrate that crime is a statistically more persistent challenge than terrorism.

I make this point not to downplay the seriousness or severity of violent attacks but only to point a finger at the true culprits. Domestic crime is clearly a greater problem for the United States than terrorism, yet the country spends billions upon billions of dollars fighting so-called terrorism and largely ignores the much larger problem. Worse yet the Islamic State doesn't create the majority of "terrorists." We do. How? By commemorating every sensational act of violence that occurs, the public turns the perpetrators into instant celebrities. True terrorism isn't senseless, but many of the violent attacks plaguing the world today are. And more will come as long as there's an audience.

American prisons are filled with countless nameless, faceless murderers. People remember only the notorious ones, however, because they celebrate only the truly sensational acts of violence. And the public continues to set the bar higher and higher for those who would commit mass murder for recognition and notoriety. It's this promotion of violence through the media (and not necessarily any particular religious ideology) that not only serves to "radicalize" impressionable and unstable people but also turns them into instant celebrities once they kill.

So what's the way out of this conundrum? How does one bring the twin towers of politics and hypocrisy crumbling down? Surgically removing the us-versus-them framework from the human psyche is a dubious undertaking at best. And far from abolishing the ten-second sound bite, the media is already embracing the five-second sound bite as the onslaught of sensory data continues to compete for the public's attention. All this adds up to the rather dismal conclusion that prospects for changing the status quo are poor, at least until Islamic extremism is replaced by a new enemy of the people. But even then, nothing will have truly changed. Society will just have a different scapegoat.

Still, while we may not be able to change the *way* that most people view the world, we can do the next best thing. We can change *what* people view. In other words we can stop publicizing violent attacks. After all the media doesn't broadcast the one hundred thousand plus "normal" shootings that take place in America every year. It doesn't have to promote sensational violence either.

David Fromkin reminds us that "terrorism wins only if you respond to it in the way the terrorists want you to; which means that its fate is in your hands and not in theirs."[2] Sensational violence craves an audience—the very thing it needs to survive. So what will the international community do? The world's fate is in our hands as well.

The Problem Presenting Itself Today

Nearly half a century ago, Raymond Aron made an observation that was as prophetic as it was poetic: "Strategic thought draws its inspiration each century, or rather at each moment of history, from the problems which events themselves pose."[3]

What are the problems presenting themselves to the world today? Most obviously, there has been a spike in violent attacks. What do these attacks have in common? With few exceptions, they were all committed by the Islamic State—or at least that's what the media keeps telling us. No doubt, some of them *were* committed by IS. But to automatically assume that every violent attack is Islamic terrorism, and that the Islamic State is behind them all, is symptomatic of a much larger problem.

This approach is even more dangerous than it is naive because it's creating a society in which anyone can become an instant celebrity by going on a killing rampage. The United States regulates other activities that incite violence. The promotion of violence should be more closely regulated as well, as should the *selection* of violence that the media chooses to promote.

What if nearly every death that occurred was automatically assumed to be caused by the Zika virus, and the media reported it as such day after day without any responsible reaction from the medical community? Not only would a huge number of illnesses be misdiagnosed, but a tremendous amount of resources would also be misallocated. Such a misallocation of resources occurred during a recent Ebola outbreak. As of April 13, 2016, the official death toll from Ebola was 11, 325.[4] However, an additional 15,000 or more people died from other causes due to the misallocation of resources to Ebola and away from other healthcare concerns.[5]

Americans are essentially doing the same thing with their obsession with sensational violence. It isn't just an obsession with violence. It's an obsession with violence committed by Islamic extremists, which isn't even among the world's most serious threats. If death tolls equated to newsworthiness, then the media should be reporting the fact that on average 7.6 million people die of malnutrition every year.[6] But it doesn't.

If starvation isn't violent enough, then the media should be reporting that every single day in America alone 315 people are shot. That's roughly 115,000 people a year just in America—and nearly 20,000 of these victims are children.[7] But again the media only reports sensational murders such as police shootings, school shootings, and so-called terror attacks. The U.S. misallocates billions for the war on terror, while the number of people who die from malnutrition or regular everyday violence continues to grow.

However, one shouldn't cast all the blame on the media. As I've already discussed, the problem presenting itself today isn't just sensational reporting and an utter lack of responsible feedback from politicians and terrorism scholars. The greater problem is the human tendency to interpret reality via an us-versus-them framework. The media is simply reflecting the assumptions that everyone makes—and those assumptions are grounded in the subjectivity of the way people view the world. This same subjectivity is blurring the understanding of Islamic extremism and terrorism (and unfortunately, many people don't want to see the issue more objectively).

For those who do desire a more enlightened understanding of the problem, there are a few basic principles to keep in mind. First of all, people are asking the wrong questions. If no political concessions are demanded, then our first assumption should not be terrorism. Automatically assuming terrorism is comparable to the police filing every single missing-person report as a kidnapping whether there's a ransom note or not.

Second, rather than simply assume that the majority of violent attacks are committed by Islamic extremists, one needs to be realistic about the fact that many of these "terrorist attacks" are nothing more than random acts of violence carried out by copycats and other misguided souls who, for whatever reason, crave their moment in the spotlight.

If there is sufficient reason to conclude that a particular incident was indeed a terror attack, we still need to ascertain who committed it and *then* begin to address the question of why. Unfortunately, people are in the habit of putting the cart before the horse. This practice is by no means new, and it has absolutely nothing to do with any particular religion or demographic group. Instead, it's entirely political. It used to be that al-Qaeda was behind everything, and before that it was Ayatollah Khomeini. Earlier still, the enemy was communism. Before that it was the Jews.

Just because IS claims an attack doesn't mean that the group actually orchestrated it. It's foolish to presume anything based on such claims. These people are killers, and they're perfectly capable of lying as well. For the longest time, all al-Qaeda had to do was hint that it would be active somewhere, and the U.S. scrambled to harden its assets there. Meanwhile, bin Laden laughed his assets off.

As mentioned earlier IS has a number of so-called affiliates.[8] So at least in theory, the group enjoys substantial global reach. However, the actual nature of many of these relationships is nominal at best. I believe that Baghdadi claims responsibility for many of these attacks because it's in his best interest to make his organization appear as global as possible.

More importantly we have to consider the Islamic State's strategy, which is to attack the near enemy (as opposed to al-Qaeda, which has opted for a strategy of attacking the far enemy). So the attacks in Europe and other faraway places simply don't fit the Islamic State's strategy. Is it possible that IS has altered its strategy to adapt to changing circumstances? Absolutely. However, any strategy still needs to serve an overall strategic objective. It's difficult to see how many of the attacks in Europe and elsewhere serve Baghdadi's agenda—regardless of his claims.

Let's examine two incidents as a case in point: (1) the suicide truck bombing in the Karada district of downtown Baghdad on July 3, 2016, which killed more than a hundred and injured nearly twice as many, and (2) the attack against a Shiite mausoleum in Balad, Iraq, five days later, which killed forty and injured seventy-four.

Analysts simply assumed that these attacks were terrorist attacks and then claimed that IS launched the attacks in reaction to losing Fallujah two weeks earlier. To begin with, these attacks were not terrorism any more than the Nazi atrocities were. If they were indeed committed by IS (and I believe that they were), then the first thing that one must understand is that IS targets Shia not as a means to an end but as an end in itself.

In the eyes of IS, Shia are apostate Muslims; hence they're worse than nonbelievers because they misrepresent the true message revealed to Muhammad by the angel Jibril. I seriously doubt that the loss of Fallujah was the main impetus for the bombing in Baghdad. Does anyone honestly believe that Baghdadi thought the Iraqi government was just going to give back Fallujah because he blew up a shopping mall? He deserves a little more credit than that. He's not a stupid man. So if Baghdadi didn't attack the mall in an effort to retrieve Fallujah, what was he after? Remember, terrorism is violence (or the threat of violence) intended to coerce a political concession. What political concession did Baghdadi demand? And more importantly, why should one believe that the Islamic State was behind these two attacks at all?

First of all, both the Karada district and the mausoleum in Balad host a Shiite majority. Second, the attack in Karada was carried out during the last week of the holy month of Ramadan—just days before the Eid holiday—in an effort to both maximize casualties and make the event more religiously significant.

The holiday of Eid al-Fitr (festival of the breaking of the fast) dates back to AD 610 when the Prophet Muhammad was visited by the angel Jibril, who dictated the verses of the Holy Quran. The month of Ramadan was originally established by the Prophet Muhammad to commemorate the generosity and mercy of Allah for sharing his wisdom with humankind via the code of conduct expressed in the Muslim scriptures. Could there be a more symbolic occasion for IS to launch such a devastating attack on Shia than the holy month of Ramadan? Could there be a better way for Baghdadi to demonstrate his power as caliph (and his favor from Allah) than to do it in the Shia's own communities?

I'm in no way celebrating or praising these attacks (or any attacks).

The point I'm making is that the Islamic State has never attempted to coerce political concessions from target states, nor has its violence ever been strictly geopolitical in nature. The group's utilization of violence is also highly ideological: Baghdadi attacks Shia because he believes they're apostates.

Finally, as commonplace as such attacks have become, they still require resources and planning. While IS *could* have planned these attacks within such a short period of time, it's highly unlikely that this was the case—especially given the facts mentioned above. Therefore, I believe that IS was behind these two attacks. However, I do not believe that they were retaliation for losing Fallujah. Finally, they were not terrorist attacks. Why does it matter?

Just like Hitler targeted the Jews, takfiri groups such as IS, al-Shabaab, and Boko Haram target Shia and others whom they view as apostates. Yes, it's horrible and violent, but it isn't terrorism if no political concession is demanded. Poor Neville Chamberlain, boasting, "Peace in our time!" Today the "Munich analogy" is synonymous with shortsightedness and political naïveté. Chamberlain had no idea what Hitler's strategic objectives were, and the results were disastrous. This is exactly what America and its allies in the GWOT are up against today.

Winston Churchill once quipped, "It is sometimes necessary to take the enemy into account." The United States needs to follow his advice, or Baghdadi (and those who follow) will be laughing their assets off as well. This is the problem presenting itself today.

The French Connection

Taking the enemy into consideration means, at minimum, understanding its strategic objective(s). Unfortunately, most analyses of the attacks of late completely ignore strategic objective and focus entirely on motive.

In some ways the situation is reminiscent of the O. J. Simpson trial. *Everybody* had an opinion, and nearly all were based entirely on motive (if even that). In this sense strategic analysis is much like a criminal investigation. The facts (actual evidence) can be equated to an actor's strategic objective, while motive is simply the frosting on the cake.

The O. J. Simpson trial is assumed by many to be a perversion of justice (a murderer walked free simply because he was a celebrity), and the trial is a fitting example for this very reason. First, the trial received so much publicity that public opinion was formed by headlines and not by the facts. Second, once public opinion decided that O.J. was guilty, the facts no longer mattered. When a court of law found him innocent based on a lack of evidence, many assumed it was his celebrity status (or the high-priced defense of Johnnie Cochran and the "Dream Team") rather than his actual innocence that drove the verdict.

The very same is true of violent attacks today: most are so widely publicized that public opinion is formed by headlines, not by facts. Unfortunately, most headlines automatically assume that the Islamic State is the culprit behind every attack. This message has become so popular that the actual facts no longer matter to most people. When the evidence suggests a different interpretation of reality, many simply refuse to even consider an alternative explanation because it doesn't fit into their cherished framework of us versus them.

In the last section, I discussed two attacks in Iraq. My strategic analysis strongly suggests that (1) while these two attacks were orchestrated by IS, (2) they were not terror attacks, and (3) they were almost certainly not planned as retaliation for losing Fallujah. I'm aware that this analysis doesn't agree with the popular consensus, but I'm not aiming for a ten-second sound bite.

Next, I'll consider the attacks in Paris and the one in Nice. Again, my strategic analyses will be based on facts, not headlines. The facts concerning these attacks suggest that the Islamic State was most likely *not* behind them for a number of reasons. One of the main reasons is that neither the attacks in Paris nor the one in Nice (nor the killing of an elderly priest in a small town in France for that matter) align with the organization's strategy of attacking the near enemy.[9] Also these attacks don't serve Baghdadi's strategic objective of defending his caliphate and purging Islam of apostate Muslims. I'll begin with an analysis of the Paris attacks.

PARIS

On a brisk November evening, children bundled up for the weather, as lovers cuddled to keep warm, and window-shoppers walked just a little faster than usual. Not too far away, in a northern suburb of Paris, soccer fans cheered at the Stade de France, while young people partied at the Bataclan Theatre.

It was Friday the thirteenth, but few people pay much attention to such things anymore. Given that it was still early, the weekend was just beginning. Cafés and restaurants hummed with conversation, and public spaces echoed with laughter as families and friends enjoyed one another's company.

In a surreal instant, time stood still as seven separate coordinated attacks shattered glass windows and parted the veil between life and death. Carnage coated the city in blood. Devastation was everywhere, but answers were harder to find.

The immediate reaction was that ISIS must have been responsible. Everyone was asking the same question, "Why did IS attack Paris?" Very few bothered to question *if* IS attacked Paris. Quite frankly, if there's any doubt whatsoever about an organization's involvement in an attack (which in this case there is), speculations about *why* it might have conducted the attack are useless. What matters is whether the attack serves a particular strategic purpose.

From a strategic perspective, it's still not all that convincing that IS did orchestrate the attacks. Still, experts immediately attempted to explain why the Islamic State attacked Paris.[10] Of all the possible reasons offered for *why* IS would attack Paris, only two consider the group's strategic objective (what it might gain). The rest are focused entirely on motive.

One possibility is that IS orchestrated the attacks in Paris to coerce Hollande to pull the French military out of the fight. Another possible strategic objective is that IS wanted to provoke France into deepening its military commitment. Of these two possibilities, the first is more strategically sound as it would benefit IS by reducing the number of forces opposing it.

The reasoning behind the second possibility is that actors will sometimes attempt to provoke a target government into overreacting and thus discrediting itself. Theoretically, this can benefit the actor by affording it more legitimacy as the defender of the people.

While France did increase its military commitment to the fight against IS, there are two main problems with the second possibility. The first is that fifty-nine states were already party to the U.S.-led military coalition against IS. Baghdadi didn't need to provoke even more military intervention to win the support of the people. Second, as I've already discussed, IS isn't trying to gain legitimacy in the eyes of nonbelievers. Those who accept the Islamic State as the caliphate already support it. And in Baghdadi's eyes, those who don't aren't true believers, so they don't matter anyway. Suffice it to say that it's unlikely Baghdadi attacked Paris to provoke a military reaction.

The first explanation makes more strategic sense. But it has one glaring inconsistency. Of all the militaries fighting IS, why specifically focus on coercing France to withdraw its forces? France doesn't have the largest number of troops invested, Paris isn't geographically the closest capital, and it isn't the capital with the weakest security. Other than the claim that the perpetrators had "links" with IS (and honestly, who doesn't these days?), the argument that IS orchestrated the Paris attacks is weak. There's just no conclusive evidence to support it.

A year before the Paris attacks, in September 2014, Paris hosted the International Conference on Peace and Security in Iraq. Some have argued that IS wanted to get revenge for the conference. But Paris certainly wasn't the only city to host such a conference. Also, revenge is normally a motive, not a strategic objective. And it's well known that the Islamic State's strategic objective is to defend its caliphate and unite what it considers "true" Islam in preparation for the Mahdi. Revenge won't advance that goal.

There doesn't seem to be any unique benefit that Baghdadi could have obtained by specifically targeting France over any of the other fifty-eight states in the coalition. If the goal was indeed to coerce Western troops to either pull out of the fight or go all in, it made much more strategic sense to strike Brussels, the home of NATO headquarters.

NICE

Now fast forward to Nice, and once again everyone was asking the same question, "Why did IS attack Nice?" However, the why question deals with motive—and more often than not, it only produces more questions. Why did the perpetrator drive a truck into a crowd on Bastille Day and kill eighty-four people? Maybe he was mentally ill. Maybe he was depressed. Maybe he just craved his moment in the spotlight. Or maybe he was working for someone in the French government. We may never know for certain *why* he did it.

However, if one were to ask *what* his strategic objective was—or perhaps what the Islamic State's objective was (or even what the French government's objective was)—one is likely to conclude rather quickly that the perpetrator had nothing to do with IS. While he may have been influenced by the group or the lure of fame (or the French government itself), it seems fairly certain that IS didn't orchestrate the attack.

How can we be so certain? Based on the Islamic State's strategic objective, it's clear that killing eighty-four people in Nice will not bring the group any closer to its goal. If the Paris attacks didn't produce results (assuming IS was behind them), why would Baghdadi waste his resources on a second attack, especially in light of his ongoing defeat in Iraq and Syria?

Yes, IS claimed responsibility for the Paris attacks. But IS also claimed that it was behind the death of a Catholic priest in Saint-Étienne-du-Rouvray, a small town of twenty-seven thousand people. If this were a game of billiards, we would call it slop (calling the shot *after* the ball goes in). Of course it's *possible* that IS orchestrated these attacks, but it's highly unlikely.

People have to ask themselves, what possible strategic gain could Baghdadi achieve by investing resources in killing an unknown priest in an obscure little town thousands of miles away? Then ask, what would Baghdadi stand to gain by *not* claiming the attacks? Claiming responsibility for the attacks gives IS added publicity and the tactical advantage of fear. If this all sounds a little too cynical, then I have more bad news for you: reality television isn't "real."

Now what did the French government stand to gain by the Nice attack (or perhaps even the Paris attacks)? The honest answer is that we don't know just yet, not specifically anyway. However, more circumstantial evidence points to the French government (or certain members of it) than to IS.

First of all, the perpetrator wasn't a jihadist. The available information suggests that this was not a man who martyred himself for Allah. Second, it was *extremely* suspicious that the vehicle he used in the attack was allowed to enter and *remain* on location. Third, the demand that the evidence be deleted and the ridiculous excuse offered as a reason for the demand (IS might get ahold of it?) suggests the attempt to cover up more than mere police incompetence. Finally, the state of emergency had been a political catastrophe for Hollande. Is it merely a coincidence that the attack occurred just hours before it was about to expire?

Franklin Delano Roosevelt's popularity soared after the Japanese attacked Pearl Harbor. He is the only president in U.S. history to win four consecutive presidential elections. Likewise, G. W. Bush was the most popular U.S. president in history for a brief period following 9/11. Who knows? Perhaps Hollande was a quick study.

A number of attacks have been carried out since Nice—the December 2016 Christmas market attack in Berlin; the January 2017 truck attack in Jerusalem; the March 2017 Westminster attack; the June 2017 London Bridge attack—all involving a vehicle and all assumed to be associated with the Islamic State. I'm not advancing conspiracy theories, but some political parties in Germany and the UK stood to gain more from these attacks than the Islamic State and Baghdadi.

All three attacks occurred at critical political junctures for the countries involved. The attack in Berlin seriously weakened Merkel's position on migration and played directly into the hands of her opponents—such as the Alternative for Germany party—which were quick to use the attack as a political victory for their cause. The opposite is true for Theresa May and proponents of Brexit, who have largely exploited the rage and fear caused by the two attacks in London—not to mention other right-wingers, such as Trump, who milk every opportunity to spread Islamophobia.

Finally, there's the January 2017 truck attack in Jerusalem. Many simply assumed that the Islamic State was responsible for no other reason than that it also involved a truck (should one also assume that every plane crash since 9/11 was orchestrated by al-Qaeda?). Almost immediately after the attack—before any serious investigation could even be initiated, much less concluded—Benjamin Netanyahu officially declared that the attack was likely linked to the Islamic State. There is absolutely no defense for such blatant negligence in any criminal investigation. Given Israel's extensive experience and expertise in counterterrorism, Netanyahu's statement was an embarrassment to say the least.

People need to apply responsible strategic analysis to each and every violent attack. Rather than simply assume a particular culprit based on headlines and popular opinion (or the fact that the perpetrator used a truck), one must begin with the facts (preferably relevant facts). And the most relevant fact is not motive but strategic objective. If one doesn't have all the answers, so be it. At least one has the integrity to admit it and the tools to start looking. Simply giving undue credit to Baghdadi for every single attack won't get us anywhere—except perhaps a place in history right next to Neville Chamberlain. But then again we should know better.

Letting the Data Speak

In the dead of winter, the call to prayer rang out through the frozen silence near the Sayyidah Zaynab Mosque, Syria's holiest Shiite shrine. It was the last day of January 2016. On this particular Sunday, as devout worshippers gathered for prayer, two suicide bombers detonated themselves and a car bomb in the mainly Shiite suburb of Damascus, killing themselves and taking sixty other people with them (the death toll later rose to seventy-one). More than one hundred others were injured in the three separate explosions. The Islamic State claimed responsibility, and like so many other attacks by IS, this one targeted Shia.

Sayyidah Zaynab has experienced several such blasts in recent years; it has been under attack from a number of Sunni militants, and it has been the target of frequent shelling. The media reported the attack as terrorism, and everyone more or less just accepted it as true. But was this a terrorist attack?

Just to demonstrate how difficult it can be to distinguish terrorism from other acts of violence without a basic understanding of what terrorism essentially is, let's analyze this particular attack according to a common generic definition of terrorism. While there are literally hundreds of definitions, most include four basic components: (1) intentional violence (2) committed against civilians (3) by nonstate actors (4) for political purposes.

On the face of it, the attack *looked* like terrorism. It was most certainly intentional. And while twenty-five Shiite militants were among the dead, the rest were noncombatants. Furthermore, the Islamic State is not an internationally recognized nation-state (although at the height of its power it considered itself a state, and it is a belligerent in the Syrian civil war).

So, if one agrees that (1) the Islamic State is not an actual state, and (2) that the twenty-five Shiite militants don't count, and (3) the fact that the Islamic State is at war with the Shiite militants doesn't matter, then the terrorism designation holds up—so far. However, if the twenty-five militants killed in the blast aren't counted, how can one say that the attack was political? What political concessions were demanded? When one considers the number of civilians that the Assad regime has killed, it's difficult to imagine what political concessions IS hoped to achieve by killing a few dozen more. It just doesn't add up.

Alternatively, if one concludes that IS specifically targeted the Shiite fighters, then this attack was an act of war and therefore politically motivated. However, if this is the case, then IS did not target noncombatants, and the civilian deaths were nothing more than collateral damage (a defense that several states have used in acts of war).

Either the attack was politically motivated, or it was perpetrated against noncombatant targets. It can't be both, not in this case anyway because the perpetrator(s) didn't make any political demands.

1. Was the act intentional? It would seem so.
2. Was the act politically motivated? It depends on how one interprets the facts.
3. Was the act perpetrated against civilian targets? Again, it all depends on how one interprets the facts.
4. Was the act perpetrated by a nonstate actor? Technically, yes.

Was this attack an act of terrorism? In the words of Meatloaf, "two outa three ain't bad." (In this case, two outa four).

But the reality is that the Islamic State systematically targets Shia, not as a means to attaining political concessions but as an end in itself. IS believes that apostate Muslims should be eliminated, and Shia are at the top of its list. Technically, that would loosely constitute a type of genocide—not terrorism.

Did IS attack Sayyidah Zaynab to coerce political concessions? Not that we know of. If it had, it could be called terrorism. It's much more likely that IS attacked the mosque as an act of war. However, given the Islamic State's strategic objective, it's equally likely that IS attacked the mosque with the deliberate intent to kill Shia for no other reason than that the group despises Shia and wants them dead.

Terrorism has been around since antiquity (perhaps earlier). The Jewish Zealots employed terrorism against the Romans, the Thuggees engaged in acts of terrorism against the British in India, and it's a tactic that is still in use today.[11] However, terrorism is not always a weapon of the weak, nor is it always employed by illegitimate actors. What's the difference between a suicide bomber detonating a load of explosives in a crowded market and an unmanned drone doing the same thing? Terrorism can be carried out in a wide variety of ways and by a wide variety of actors—including states. In fact when compared with the violence perpetrated by some states (Stalin killed 42 million, Mao killed 37 million, and Hitler killed 20 million), nonstate actors pale in comparison.

Throughout this book I've emphasized the fact that terrorism can be distinguished only by the strategic objective of the actor, not by the violence itself, the actor, or the actor's ideology. In other words you can't just know terrorism when you see it. All violence is not terrorism. Neither is all Islamic extremism terrorism. One needs to understand the actor's strategic objective in order to distinguish terrorism from other acts of violence.

Hate crimes, school shootings, and a host of other random attacks may be perpetrated for any number of motives. However, unless the strategic objective behind the incident was to obtain political concessions, school shootings are not terrorism. Insurgencies that attempt to overthrow a government are not terrorism either. And finally just because violence is perpetrated by Islamic extremists does not automatically qualify it as terrorism. Much of the violence committed by Islamic extremists occurs in the context of civil war, such as the proxy war in Syria.

The Bush administration successfully deceived the American people into believing that terrorism was the greatest threat facing the United States and the world. It did this through blatant lies and clever misrepresentation of the facts. Bush and Obama both violated Americans' trust and used their tax dollars to wage a war against humanity that has raged on for nearly twenty years. So far Trump shows no signs of remorse either.

Had the American people been better informed, they might not have been so easily led astray. Americans cannot continue to allow this or future administrations to wage public wars to protect their own private investments (or the investments of their political supporters).

CHAPTER NINE

NAVIGATING THE DELUGE

Make yourself an ark of gopher wood.

—Genesis 6:14

Although details vary considerably, nearly every civilization shares the story of an ancient worldwide flood, a deluge of epic proportion. Today the world faces a new deluge. A flood of sensational violence is raging out of control, and the tide of propaganda (us versus them) is rising above our heads.

How will the people of planet earth find dry ground? More importantly, where will policy makers discover an olive branch amid the turmoil of violent attacks taking place in unprecedented number around the globe? One thing is certain. The answers will *not* come by maintaining the status quo. The world is changing at an accelerated pace before our very eyes. Look around. It's time to build an ark.

Building an Ark

The three great monotheistic religions of the world all share the story of Noah and the ark that he was commanded to build. There's an interesting correlation between the story of Noah and our current dilemma today. Noah was instructed to build the ark of gopher wood, but no one actually knows what gopher wood is (or was). It appears once in the Tanakh and is otherwise unknown in Hebrew literature. This can be compared to the current understanding of terrorism.

The fact that gopher wood is referred to only once suggests that it was either so familiar at the time that it required no further explanation, or it was unknown to the writer as well so no further explanation was available. Sound familiar? (I am, of course, ignoring other possibilities such as translation issues because this is only an analogy.)

Still, the current understanding of "Islamic terrorism" is similar. It's so familiar that most people believe that they know it when they see it. Yet violence that is routinely labeled as terrorism is almost always something else entirely. So how do people build an ark of gopher wood if they don't know (or refuse to agree on) what it consists of? Likewise, how can people understand—much less put an end to—sensational violence if they can't first identify it for what it actually is?

The reality is that every act of violence is unique, occurring within a distinct historical, socioeconomic, and geopolitical context. However, the current approach to explaining violence is to strip away the majority of the details necessary to understand the context in which it occurs. This tendency to generically categorize all types of violence under the label of terrorism makes it easy to misuse and abuse the term to apply to any violence with which one doesn't agree. The resulting war on terror is only the most recent battle in the war of us versus them. While this is a war that we can never win, we can at least begin to build a stable peace.

Know Thy Enemy

As Sun Tzu asserts, "Victory is the main object of war."[1] Daft as this statement appears, understanding the nature of the war one is fighting has been (and continues to be) critical to victory. For instance in the sixteenth century, the Chinese navy opted to employ the traditional tactics of ramming and boarding rather than equipping itself with the most advanced artillery of the day. Why? Because its main strategic objective at the time wasn't to defend itself against modern enemies from the West but to drive out small bands of Japanese pirates.

Meanwhile, in Europe the skills of professional soldiers were being outpaced by modern weaponry. Technological advances between the eighteenth and the nineteenth centuries shifted the tactical nature of warfare from primarily offensive to defensive. General Field Marshal Helmuth von Moltke (1800–91) is credited as being among the first to master defensive strategy with modern firearms. By World

War II, however, the pendulum had shifted back again with the German blitzkrieg.

Furthermore, Kenneth Waltz's structural realism introduced the idea that international polarity offered stronger explanatory power than factors such as political ideology or regime type because rational actors respond to the international structure according to their own best interest.[2] However, nonstate actors don't necessarily take the international structure into consideration when acting in their own best interests. Thus structural realism—the dominant political theory for the past five decades—no longer necessarily informs the participants about the war that they are fighting.

Prior to the bipolar international structure of the Cold War (and the introduction of nuclear weapons), the ultimate goal of the League of Nations was to "attain a better peace."[3] However, with the emergence of the Cold War and the doctrine of deterrence, the new ambition was to maintain whatever peace was possible. The demise of the Soviet Union and the end of the Cold War marked yet another threshold into an age of nonconventional warfare.

Between 1988 and 1996, the United Nations conducted seventeen new peacekeeping operations—more than it had conducted in the previous forty years combined.[4] Ever since the Vietnam War, the U.S. military has been keenly aware of its need for a low-intensity strategy of warfare. This awareness has only intensified with the wars in Afghanistan, Iraq, and, of course, the Global War on Terrorism.[5]

The GWOT greatly damaged America's international reputation. Even though the Middle East has been the recipient of roughly one half of all U.S. foreign aid, a Zogby poll reveals that popular opinion toward America in the Middle East is considerably more negative than in other developing areas receiving far less U.S. assistance.[6] So what might this tell us about the war that the United States is fighting?

Many argue that defeating terrorism depends on stemming the recruitment of future jihadists.[7] At first glance this seems to be a reasonable strategy. Especially given unpleasant realities such as suicide training centers for children in South Waziristan and improvised explosive device factories in Southern Punjab, fewer recruits definitely seems like the way to go. And as long as people are willing to use the terms "jihadist" and "terrorist" synonymously, there's no problem.

However, these two terms are not synonymous. To simply state that America needs to stem the recruitment of jihadists leaves the country with an extremely vague strategic objective and an even less clearly defined strategy. The entire proposition is reminiscent of the Vietnam War.

Vietnam

Imagine if you will, Bến Tre, a Vietnamese capital city of roughly 150,000 people in the Mekong Delta. The Viet Cong were so well entrenched that the American military commanders insisted it was necessary to destroy Bến Tre in order to save it. So they shelled the entire city into oblivion.

Residents in smaller towns such as My Lai were slaughtered like animals. Men, women, children, babies . . . all of them. The fortunate ones were shot. Others were tortured and scalped. Hands were cut off, and tongues were cut out. This is what happens when people don't know who their enemy is.

To insist that the only way to stop terrorism is to directly challenge radical religious ideology is to take the first step down the slippery slope. Which radicals? Which religious ideology? The evil contagion of the Cold War was communism. The dire threat facing humanity in the GWOT is Islamic extremism—or so we're told. Just as in Bến Tre, My Lai, and hundreds of other cities, Americans still don't know who their enemy is.

As George W. Bush stated, "There are no rules." We'll drain the swamps and "smoke them out."[8] There were apparently no rules in Vietnam either. The American public was told that lawlessness was so extreme that it became necessary to kill everyone. And many Americans believed it.

An MP who had served two tours in country once told me that the Viet Cong often booby-trapped women, children, and even babies. He shared several stories involving exploding toddlers and women with razor blades hidden in their vagina. The terror that such tactics inspired forced the American GIs to respond with savage barbarity—they couldn't trust anyone.

I remember asking myself, "How can a woman strap explosives to her own baby?" What could possibly drive a mother to do such a thing? I simply can't understand it, and I hope that I never do. One thing to keep in mind, however, is that the Vietnamese were fighting an insurgency against the colonial occupation of first the French and later the Americans.

Once again we're faced with the "chicken or the egg" dilemma. Who started the slaughter? The Vietnamese? The French? The Americans? Regardless of who started the cycle of violence in Vietnam, both sides had come to see the enemy in very black-and-white terms. Each side had demonized the other. The Vietnamese endured two decades of slaughter. Entire cities and villages were butchered, tortured, blown up, and firebombed with chemical agents. Meanwhile, French and American troops—many barely eighteen years old—were confronted with the sheer horror of guerrilla tactics that tested the limits of humanity. Who was right? The Vietnamese were trying to rid themselves of unwelcome guests, while (most) of the foreign soldiers were simply following orders.

Desperate people do desperate things. It just might have been more merciful for Vietnamese women to blow up their own children rather than allow the enemy to torture them while they were forced to watch.

Beyond the obvious question of whether the U.S. *should* have been in Vietnam is the more important question regarding *what* America's strategic objective was for being there in the first place. The general public was never given the true answer to that question. Vietnam was a Cold War conflict, and the Cold War was fought over control of strategic resources, mainly oil. Why was the United States in Vietnam? The answer to that question requires a great deal more space than I have here.

The critical question today is whether Americans know what their country's strategic objective is in the GWOT. Or will Americans one day look back to yet another war they shouldn't have fought against an enemy they never identified for an objective they didn't have?

Order out of Chaos

It was one of the most polarizing presidential races in U.S. history, laden with Cold War rhetoric, conspiracies involving the Kremlin, hacked emails, allegations of blood ritual sacrifices, and support from the Ku Klux Klan. Fifteen grueling months of mudslinging, demonization, and presidential debates so devoid of any dignity deserving of the office that by the end of the campaign trail, both candidates had been reduced to the status of your typical guests on the Jerry Springer Show.

Hillary Clinton claimed that Donald Trump "has a long record of engaging in racist behavior" and accused him of calling women "pigs, slobs and dogs," an allegation to which Trump repeatedly insisted that "crooked Hillary" should be in jail.[9] Just when it appeared that no one took either candidate seriously at all, the bomb dropped.

Ladies and Gentlemen, the forty-fifth president of the United States of America, Donald Trump! And then all hell broke loose. Despite the backing of the Obama administration, endorsements from stars such as Beyoncé and Lady Gaga, and massive support from the mainstream media (their polls consistently put Clinton ahead by a decisive margin), Hillary Clinton was simply unable to mobilize sufficient support from her own Democratic base, at least not in time to win the election. Immediately after the election—now that was a different story.

Mass protests broke out across the country. Looting, fighting, and destruction of property erupted almost instantaneously. Social media was saturated with scenes of horror, violence, and bloodshed—blacks beating whites for allegedly voting for Trump and everywhere Americans protesting by the thousands that Trump was not their president. Universities across the nation canceled classes, and therapy hotlines were established from coast to coast

If that weren't enough, Green Party candidate Jill Stein actively agitated for recounts in Wisconsin, Michigan, and Pennsylvania. Even Republican lawmakers jumped on board: a bill targeting the Russian propaganda machine that allegedly rigged the election in Trump's favor passed the house with 390 votes.

Most mainstream media outlets clearly backed Clinton on the campaign trail, but some were unabashedly in favor of Trump. On both sides the majority in the press referred to his campaign as a train wreck—at least until he won. Meanwhile, faithful followers celebrated it as nothing short of brilliant. For many of us watching from the sidelines, Trump's rage against the machine was as refreshing as it was entertaining.

So exactly how did Trump win? This is an important question because—regardless of claims that Hillary won the popular vote and that the Electoral College needs to be eliminated—the 2016 presidential election is one of the first that I can remember where it actually appeared to matter who you voted for. Right up until the end, there were many undecided states. It was an extremely close race—as exciting as any Super Bowl or World Series for the average American—and perhaps even rivaling the World Cup for many non-Americans. But how does one explain the results in light of Trump's infamous unpopularity?

The Road to the 2016 Presidential Election

As I seek to identify Trump's position on the political spectrum, I'll argue that his victory in the 2016 presidential election was not so surprising after all given the circumstances. Nor should one be surprised when other conservative and far-right candidates gain ground in European elections and elsewhere around the globe. In many respects the last four or five decades of American politics are directly responsible for the current right-wing political climate that continues to gain popular support.

Campaigning on a platform of making America great again, Trump stated foreign policy initiatives that included severely limiting immigration of both Mexicans and Muslims, dismantling terror networks, defending Israel, improving relations with Russia, and holding Saudi Arabia accountable for financing Islamic extremism. More broadly Trump promised that the U.S. will no longer involve itself in conflicts that do not directly affect its own national security—claiming that as far back as 1987 the U.S. should have stopped "paying for countries that can afford to defend themselves."[10]

As soon as Trump won, the media was again up in arms over his outlandish Twitter statements and his even more alarming appointments of Michael Flynn as national security adviser and Stephen Bannon as chief strategist/senior adviser.

Like Trump, Bannon is highly controversial for his right-wing views. As the executive chairman of Breitbart—a news website now infamous as the platform for the alt-right movement—many feared that Bannon's influence could potentially prove disastrous for women and minorities alike, particularly given the fact that he was initially given a seat on the National Security Council (his seat was later taken away in April 2017).

Likewise retired Lieutenant General Michael "Lock Her Up!" Flynn is known for his use of inflammatory hyperbole, affectionately dubbed "Flynn Facts" by those who worked with him. Flynn called Obama a "liar" and referred to Hillary Clinton as the "enemy." He also stated in no uncertain terms that she should be imprisoned, leading a crowd at the 2016 Republican Convention in chanting, "Lock her up!" The position of national security advisor is one of the most powerful in Washington, and one that doesn't require congressional approval. So again, the fear was that Trump's right-wing rampage would go unchecked. Flynn was removed from his position as national security advisor in February 2017 over undisclosed contact with Russian operatives. He was replaced by General H. R. McMaster.

The liberal mainstream media interpreted Trump's frequent tweets as reactionary and bizarre—and the appointment of Bannon and Flynn as signs of the end. There has also been substantial alarm over Trump's cabinet of billionaires, including former ExxonMobil CEO Rex Tillerson as secretary of state and Steven Mnuchin, a seventeen-year veteran of Goldman Sachs as secretary of the treasury. Talk about letting the foxes into the hen house!

On the foreign-policy front, Trump is as hawkish as it gets. His pick for secretary of defense, James "Mad Dog" Mattis, has openly stated that he enjoyed killing Taliban members in Afghanistan. Mattis is also extremely anti-Iran and pro-GWOT. For Homeland Security Trump chose retired Marine general John F. Kelly, who has been a vocal opponent to closing Guantanamo. After just six months as secretary of homeland security, Kelly replaced Reinhold Priebus as White House chief of staff.

Reinhold "Reince" Priebus (White House chief of staff, January 20–July 31, 2017) is a less controversial figure who, in fact, openly opposed Trump on several issues including Trump's abusive statements concerning women, his unfortunate (if not somewhat orchestrated) feud with the parents of Captain Humayan Khan, and his allegations that the GOP nomination process is rigged (Priebus chaired the Republican National Committee from 2011 to 2017). Not surprisingly Priebus's tenure in the Trump administration was short-lived.

The appointments of Mattis and Kelly combined with Flynn (and then McMaster) make for what many are calling a military junta. Trump's growing number of hardline military figures in his cabinet not only risks militarizing the executive; it also risks politicizing the military—never a good combination.

Trump's controversial discussions with foreign leaders have also turned a few heads. Take Trump's conversation with Taiwanese president Tsai Ing-wen, for example. Much concern was raised that Trump might have overturned decades of American foreign policy in a single phone call. China's foreign ministry even lodged a complaint over the alleged breach of protocol.

But the truth is that U.S. foreign policy has been far from consistent on the issue of Taiwan. Taiwan remained under U.S. protection from the outbreak of the Korean War right up to 1979, when Carter broke relations with Taiwan in recognition of the People's Republic of China. Trump's conversation with Tsai Ing-wen is comparable to Nixon's infamous 1972 visit to China (I don't recall Nixon asking permission to visit China in defiance of more than two decades of Cold War foreign policy).

Trump's subsequent visit to China in November 2017 generated suspicions that Taiwan would be used as a bargaining chip in ongoing Sino-U.S. relations. Trump is first and foremost a businessman. The art of deal takes precedence. The pendulum of U.S. foreign policy regarding Taiwan continues to swing. Whatever the outcome, it certainly won't be the first time a U.S. president toppled the apple cart. But this isn't our biggest concern.

Beyond the fear that Trump might have single-handedly undone generations of American diplomacy before he even took office, the media also criticized the fact that his hotels seemed to be getting the "green light" as a response to his foreign-policy initiatives. For example three short days after Trump spoke with Argentina's president Mauricio Macri, the long-delayed construction on his Trump Tower in Buenos Aires was fast-tracked. But this too is small potatoes. The media has the public so focused on the fear that Trump is using his position to advance his personal business interests that it has completely distracted Americans from seeing the bigger picture.

The Great Distraction

During the campaign Trump repeatedly attacked Clinton on her foreign-policy platform, claiming that America has made "so many bad deals." While conceding that Clinton has experience, Trump insists that it's "bad experience."[11] Meanwhile, Trump's opponents complain about apparent contradictions in his own foreign policy.

For example, when discussing the ongoing civil war in Syria, Trump suggested letting Assad and the Islamic State fight it out among themselves. Yet he also recommended putting boots on the ground, condemning Obama for high collateral damage (Obama authorized more than five thousand airstrikes in Syria alone). So which is it? Stay out of Syria, boots on the ground, or airstrikes? Far from altering Obama's policy in Syria, Trump has more or less endorsed it—more because April 2017 saw more civilian casualties from U.S.-led airstrikes than any other month since the bombing campaign in Syria began (nearly five hundred dead and countless injured); less because Trump has relinquished control to the military, giving it discretion over the frequency and intensity of airstrikes.

Concerning domestic policy Trump vowed to increase jobs, lower taxes, and staunchly support oil fracking and American coal (which goes a long way to explain his decision to pick Scott Pruitt—an open denier of climate change—to lead the EPA).

Furthermore, Trump flatly stated, "We need to protect all Americans, of all backgrounds and all beliefs, from Radical Islamic Terrorism—which has no place in an open and tolerant society."[12] And yet Americans continue to turn out in record numbers to protest his presidency specifically because of his perceived racism, misogyny, and intolerance toward Muslims.

In his first week at the helm, Trump signed executive orders that approved the Keystone XL and Dakota Access pipelines, pulled the U.S. out of the Trans-Pacific Partnership (TPP), and issued sweeping immigration policies that include targeting sanctuary cities, construction of the wall on the U.S-Mexican border, and a travel ban on all refugees and citizens of Iran, Iraq, Libya, Somalia, Sudan, Syria, and Yemen.

Consequently, Trump's first week was also accompanied by mass protests and demonstrations. Mexican president Enrique Peña Nieto condemned the proposed construction of a wall on the border and canceled his visit to Washington. Theresa May and Angela Merkel also publicly denounced Trump's actions.

The courts have also spoken against the travel ban. One federal judge in New York issued an emergency stay, ordering that people affected by the ban can't be forcibly removed from the United States. A federal court in Washington also issued a stay preventing travelers from being detained and sent back to their country of origin. Federal judges in

Boston ruled that people not be detained due to Trump's executive order. Furthermore, the Department of Homeland Security announced that it would not deport detained travelers in compliance with judicial orders. Just days after Trump issued the travel ban, acting head of the Justice Department Sally Yates also indicated that the department would not defend it in court.

Political opponents were also quick to condemn Trump's opposition to the Trans-Pacific Partnership, which they argue would have empowered energy companies and increased American exports. Trump officially opposes offshoring American jobs, yet his critics claim that he's moved much of his own production overseas. Trump has also been accused of wanting to start a trade war with China, something that the neoliberals in both parties oppose.

Regarding domestic policy Trump could very well be in favor of both oil fracking and American coal while still opposing the TPP for the simple reason that he wants to renegotiate the terms of NAFTA. As for a trade war with China, he is emphatic that America "cannot continue to allow China to rape our country."[13] He has correctly observed (albeit in a politically incorrect way) that the United States is running an ever-increasing trade deficit with China. No matter how you slice it, there's simply no way to significantly increase American exports without affecting U.S. trade relations with China. Jumping to the conclusion of a "trade war" is a bit reactionary, but it makes great headlines.

Everyone agrees that trade is generally a good thing, but there are losers in every trade deal too. The losers in NAFTA have been the millions of Americans (of all racial and religious backgrounds) who relied on manufacturing jobs to support their families—many of whom voted for Trump for this very reason. As a self-professed intelligent businessman surrounded by a cadre of advisors, Trump no doubt understands exactly why businesses are offshoring so many jobs (his own included). Theoretically this insight uniquely qualifies him to introduce legislation making offshore production less attractive to U.S. corporations. Reality paints a slightly different picture, however.

Trump promised to lower taxes on businesses, and the tax bill he signed in December 2017 does indeed lower the business tax rate from 35 percent to 21 percent. Trump also negotiated with Carrier to keep eight hundred factory jobs in Indiana in exchange for some $7 million in incentives. But critics argue that he's simply set a dangerous precedent, encouraging other businesses to threaten to outsource whenever they want to negotiate a better deal with the government.

But all these concerns are simply a diversion. Of far greater concern are the huge megacorporations that are already outsourcing most of their employees overseas. Trump threatened to impose a 35 percent tax on any American business that outsources jobs outside the country. Instead the new tax bill does just the opposite, exempting U.S. corporations from any U.S. tax liability on most future foreign profits. Given the current corporate control of the Washington machine, this should come as absolutely no surprise.

Sleight of Hand

Trump's approach isn't all that original. Every politician promises more jobs, and there are a certain number of magic tricks that any administration can get away with for at least a few years. The most common illusion involves lowering interest rates and increasing spending. Lower interest rates (and increasingly negative interest rates) lead to more borrowing and less saving. Both lead to more spending, but the money has to come from somewhere—especially if Congress also lowers taxes (which it just did). Sooner or later the bottom drops out, and the result is always the same: massive debt.

All that borrowing and spending is great for banks and multinational corporations (MNCs), but it's fatal for the economy in the long run. In the short run it makes everyone feel great—like blowing your entire paycheck on Friday night—but Saturday morning is coming, and you've still got the rest of the month ahead of you.

All politicians play this game because every administration inherits the debt generated by the one before it. Promises to increase jobs mean that the government has to spend more to create those jobs, and it invariably gives that money to big businesses, claiming that it will "trickle down." Instead of spending the money on public goods and services that would directly benefit the people (what John McCain inimically referred to as sharing the wealth), neoliberal governments give it to MNCs in the form of incentives, subsidies, and bailouts. The true beneficiaries are the filthy rich, who then sell those goods and services at market prices.

The problem is that the jobs such policies create are usually temporary, low paying, and without any benefits. Therefore, no one can afford to purchase domestically produced goods anyway. This situation leads to an increase in demand for cheap imports. American companies ultimately offshore even more jobs to remain competitive—and the cycle continues. That's neoliberalism in a nutshell.

Neoliberalism simply means "new liberalism," and it maintains that governments should provide only three services: a military to protect state borders, a police force to reduce crime, and basic infrastructure (roads, water, electricity, etc.). Neoliberalism favors the wealthy by lowering taxes and deregulating private enterprise. This policy equates to small government and virtually no social spending on welfare programs, with the net result that someone like John McCain can keep his $28 million all to himself.

Even more importantly neoliberalism is staunchly opposed to government programs such as free education and free medical care so that private companies can sell these services at exorbitant prices. This elimination of public goods to provide private opportunities to the super-wealthy is what the Washington consensus is all about. In this respect the Democratic Party's economic policy is virtually no different from that of the Republican Party under Reagan (there are a few minor differences between Reaganomics and say Obamanomics—but both were driven by the same neoliberal principles).

More frightening still is the neoconservative foreign policy that has been in play since the Clinton administration. Neoconservatism combines free-market capitalism with foreign interventionism—basically, democracy and free trade by the barrel of a gun.

And that's why Trump, despite all his promises, is unlikely to affect any real lasting changes, 35 percent tax or not. In fact by imposing a tax on the smaller American businesses that still maintain operations inside the country, Trump would only have made them prey to being cannibalized by the mega MNCs, which are beyond his reach.

Nothing New under the Sun

Essentially what we've been witnessing is a steady decline in the standard of living for working-class people around the globe. This decline has been caused by the onslaught of neoliberalism, and the reaction is a growing sense of nationalism. It isn't a coincidence that right-wing nationalist parties are growing in popularity around the globe. The world has witnessed the rise of nationalism as a result of poor economic conditions before—it's certainly nothing new—and the seeds of economic decline have been sprouting for some time now. Therefore, the current political climate cannot be attributed to any one administration alone.

So before we start blaming everything on Trump, we need to step back and acknowledge a few important facts. First, Trump didn't create racism, misogyny, porn, or Islamophobia; they existed long before he did. George Washington owned slaves, FDR imprisoned 120,000 Japanese Americans, Truman was a member of the Ku Klux Klan, LBJ loved to use the "N word," and Clinton? Where does one even begin (or end) with the sexual exploits of Bill Clinton? Talk about the need to be more presidential!

Sadly, racism is still alive and kicking in the United States, where black males are incarcerated at more than five times the rate of white males.[14] After eight years with a black president, something's wrong. We can't blame that on Donald Trump, although many will no doubt try.

Concerning Islamophobia let's not forget that G. W. Bush was also accused of waging a war on Islam. Moreover, the U.S. Department of Homeland Security has already been making it difficult for Muslims to enter the United States for nearly two decades. And last but certainly not least, who can forget the ridiculous uproar over "Obama bin Laden?" Kind of ironic when you consider that Barack Obama— originally accused of supporting terrorists—has dropped more bombs on Muslims than any other president in American history . . . so far (is it ironic or just sad?).

Trump didn't destroy the economy either. If we're looking for a scapegoat, Obama and Bush are excellent candidates, although, as we've demonstrated, the neoliberal agenda goes back much further. We can blame Bush—and he certainly deserves much of the blame—but not all of it. While it's true that unemployment was already high when Obama assumed office, eight years later millions of Americans are still either unemployed or underemployed. Despite Obama's claim to have created millions of new jobs, like the jobs created under Clinton most are part-time, low-paying jobs without benefits or any type of job security.

If Obama truly wanted to help the average "folks" in America, why did he cut tens of billions of dollars in social welfare programs? Well you know, times are tight and the money has to come from somewhere, right? Sure it does, but that doesn't give Obama the right to take food off of American children's plates—especially when the money is coming from American citizens' pockets in the first place. But that's the neoliberal way: take money from hardworking people and give it to corporations so that it can trickle back down to the hardworking people. So where did those tens of billions of stolen dollars go anyway?

We could consider Obama's unmanned drone program a likely suspect. By 2015 Obama had already authorized more than ten times the total number of unmanned drone strikes that Bush authorized, despite the known risk of civilian casualties. These figures don't include the lion's share of attacks in Yemen and Syria, where tens of thousands more were killed in 2016 alone—deaths for which Obama is personally responsible.

But to be fair, Obama didn't spend all of our money on killing children and the elderly. Between 2009 and 2013, he spent roughly $4.5 billion in taxpayer's money on *image advertising*! A 2014 Congressional Research Service study concluded that between fiscal 2009 and 2013, Obama spent a minimum of $4.4 billion on advertising contracts to enhance his public image.[15] This figure is just for 2009–2013 and does not include other in-house advertising and promotional activities such as the $100 million Obama spent in 2016 on Obamacare advertising.[16]

No one should be surprised either, especially when we consider that Obama's 2008 presidential campaign won best marketing campaign of the year—and deservedly so. He certainly *acted* the role of a peace candidate convincingly. He should have won an Academy Award as well. Apparently, with all the other problems facing the country, Obama felt that enhancing his public image was more important than things like food and shelter for the growing number of Americans living on the margins.

So what's my point? Simply that no president is perfect, and no president exists in a vacuum. Trump has inherited some very complex problems for which there are no simple solutions. Add to these the extremely diverse American population, and it becomes evident that it's impossible to please everyone (fortunately for Trump, he doesn't much seem to care).

Trump is certainly not the first president to take a controversial position, and he won't be the last. And now in light of the 2018 tax legislation, he appears to be following the Reagan model of cutting taxes and increasing spending. It seems clear that Trump has also chosen the well-beaten path of amassing hopeless amounts of debt and passing it on to the next administration.

Casino Politics

All the major media outlets are speculating on what Trump will do next and how he'll perform. This might be a crazy idea, but I'm just going to throw it out there anyway. Rather than waste time staring into our crystal balls attempting to speculate on Trump's future achievements (or failures), perhaps it would be more useful (and accurate) to look at the known realities and make some assessments based on the facts available to us today.

It may be too soon to call the next hand, but the game is rigged in the house's favor either way. So does it really matter who sits in the White House? The wealthiest 1 percent certainly seem to think so. Presidential candidates today raise upward of $1 billion just to campaign. The vast majority of this money comes from literally a handful of elites. For instance the billionaire duo Charles and David Koch contributed $400 million to the 2012 presidential and congressional elections in an effort to influence the outcome. Their goal? Reduced regulation, low taxes, and free trade. For years Koch Industries has lobbied against obstacles such as the Environmental Protection Agency's regulation of power plants and the Export-Import Bank, which offers federal financing for high-risk transactions. The Koch brothers had planned to contribute nearly $900 million to the 2016 race, but changed their minds after the Republican Party nominated Trump as its candidate. Charles Koch even briefly considered backing Hillary Clinton.[17]

And why not? With the exception of a few domestic issues, which honestly have very little impact on America's economic or foreign policy, the Democratic and the Republican Parties are nearly identical. Both are highly neoconservative and neoliberal. The main issues that distinguish the two parties are gay marriage, abortion, and gun control—with those in favor of such initiatives voting Democrat and most evangelical Christians and members of the Moral Majority voting Republican (however, there's some level of crossover on these issues as well).

Some would argue that immigration is also a divisive issue. To some extent this is true. But the GWOT has turned it into a matter of national security rather than one of party politics. Both Republicans and Democrats have supported tougher immigration policies under the Department of Homeland Security. Trump's suggestions may be extreme, but they're certainly nothing new.

So why invest so much money toward election campaigns when the two parties are so similar to each other? The sole reason for the huge political contributions that we see today is control. The highest office goes to the highest bidder, and the neoliberal elites are simply hedging their bets. With their man (or woman) in the Oval Office, the corporate sponsors run the show.

As Calvin Coolidge once observed, "The business of America is business." There's no place on earth where this statement is truer than in Washington DC. The facade of a two-party system creates the illusion of choice, but the powers that be determine the course of American politics. So one can vote for a Donald puppet or a Hillary puppet—the puppet masters don't really care as long as they're ultimately the ones who pull the strings.

Unfortunately, many of the people protesting against Trump have absolutely no idea what Barack Obama and Hillary Clinton actually stand for. No doubt there are those who are truly passionate about Democratic Party issues such as gay rights, reproductive rights, gun control, environmental regulation, consumer protections, the DREAM Act, and climate change. My point here is certainly not meant to belittle such domestic issues. On the contrary the fact that Americans are exercising their constitutional right to publicly condemn Trump's policies is commendable. But there are also many others who simply react to the headlines—which as I've argued, are controlled by elite interests. I would encourage consumers of the media to dig a little deeper into all the issues that concern them—both foreign and domestic.

Americans don't have to agree with everything Trump stands for (and I certainly don't), but at least he's rattled enough cages to convince even major players like the Koch brothers to pull out of the game. Right or wrong—agree or disagree—on some level one has to respect that kind of audacity. Only time will tell the result of such a course.

Has Trump made mistakes? Absolutely. Will he make more? Most certainly. Like everyone else, I have my own opinion (that and five bucks will get you a cup of coffee). On some issues I think he's spot on. On others I think he's backing the wrong horse. On still other issues, it's simply too early to tell.

Having made that statement, it's important that I disclaim up front: this isn't a paid advertisement for Donald Trump. I didn't support Trump as a candidate, nor did I support Clinton. I was one of those 46 percent of Americans who didn't vote. Why didn't I vote?

The short answer is political. As an American who loves his country but distrusts his government, I came to the conclusion several decades ago that the two-party system in America is broken. But I didn't arrive at this news flash by watching the news—this isn't a breaking story one is likely to see on CNN. Simply put the mainstream media is not the honest broker that it claims to be. Rather, as a student of American politics who also happens to live abroad, I've watched from the sidelines as the American political machine slowly imploded. In this respect my perspective is somewhat unique from that of other Americans.

Despite allegations that the Russians hacked the election, people shouldn't be at all surprised by Trump's election victory. One reason is that, with few exceptions, the political pendulum in America always swings Republican after eight years of Democratic leadership. After two terms of "Obamanation," the American people were ready for a change—and it was obvious.

The second reason for Trump's success is that he was the only viable alternative to Hillary, and quite honestly, this election hinged on which candidate Americans despised less. After the Democrats sidelined Bernie Sanders—who quite frankly might have split the anti-establishment vote (or at least tipped the scales in Clinton's favor had he run as an independent)—who was left?

So those who breathed a sigh of relief when Clinton lost can be thankful that Sanders didn't run as an independent (no offense to Jill Stein). And the fact that the Republican Party stepped away from its endorsement of Trump only made his anti-establishment persona that much more credible. Still, he was the Republican nominee and therefore the only other viable option to "crooked Hillary." So just when it looked like the cards were stacked against him, the stars were actually aligning in Trump's favor.

The third reason Trump won is the simple fact that over the past twenty-six years, American politics has been converging: aside from a few issues that have absolutely no bearing on economic or foreign policy, Democrats and Republicans exist in name only. Only the machine exists, and no one is fooled by candidates who claim to be "Washington outsiders" anymore. Trump actually had the opposite problem; he really was a Washington outsider, and it was obvious to everyone. Clinton's experience might have served her better if everyone wasn't so sick of the predatory politics she represents.

One of the most common observations about Donald Trump—from both critics and supporters alike—is that he isn't very presidential. Quite frankly, as far as I'm concerned that's his most endearing quality. Anyone capable of openly challenging the deep state and taking on the media (and surviving) is bound to stand out among the lying, two-faced politicians people have grown to know and loathe—and if there's anything on which everyone agrees, Trump has certainly made an impression. But that's not why he won.

In many ways Trump is the Frank Sinatra of American politics. Or maybe Bruce Willis is a better comparison—"Yippee-ki-yay, mother-f*cker!" If he were a rapper, D. J. Trump would be an overnight sensation. As a baller he'd be center-court. But that's not why he won either.

Most people love it when their celebrities are outspoken and color outside the lines. But when a presidential candidate turned president acts this way, most people don't like it at all, particularly the elites because he's not following their rules. This is populism, people—a political ideology with a long and inglorious history (remember that picture of Ronald Reagan dressed as a cowboy?).

A Return to Realpolitik or a Neoliberal Coup?

Rejected by the Republican Party and repulsive to the Democrats, exactly how does one classify Donald Trump? In many ways Trump is reminiscent of Ronald Reagan. Both were celebrities before starting their career in politics, both represent the wealthy, and both were criticized for their willingness to cooperate with the "evil empire."

Much like Trump today, Reagan bemoaned the incompetence of the former administration. He viewed Carter's human rights campaign as irrelevant to national security, and he adamantly resisted outside pressure to press for human rights himself. Trump has indicated a similar disposition toward human rights, making the Bush administration look like a bunch of wussies by insisting that waterboarding isn't *effective enough* and claiming that the United States needs to take interrogation *more* seriously.

Reagan blamed the hostage crisis in Iran and the weakness of NATO on the fact that the Carter administration had allowed the United States to appear complacent in the eyes of the international community. Likewise Trump blames the irrelevance of NATO on the poor leadership of former administrations, referring to NATO as obsolete and threatening to reorganize or even possibly withdraw from the alliance if other members continue to free ride on the United States.

Finally, Reagan enacted huge permanent tax cuts in 1982. Given Trump's own personal wealth and his professed commitment to creating American jobs, it's certainly no surprise that he's also endorsing tax incentives for business interests. While it appears that Trump's plan is to spend America's way back to greatness, at least his insistence that other states start paying their own way is a promising start.

To be sure Reagan had his flaws, one of which was perhaps not being enough of a realist. He tended to view every conflict as a battle between communism and the free world (G. W. Bush had this same problem, viewing everything as a fight between good and evil). But problems in the world involve more complex issues than the typical Cold War or GWOT framework can accommodate.

Perhaps NATO *is* becoming obsolete. Given changing geopolitical and economic realities, shifting alliances is precisely the type of realpolitik response that would make Kissinger proud. If Ronald Reagan was indeed America's last realist president, could it be that Donald Trump will be the next?

Or perhaps Trump represents something entirely new in American politics. After decades of the same ole same ole, the American people were ready for change—not just Obama's slogan "Change!"—but real change. And they turned out in decisive numbers to vote for a populist

Washington outsider because he was the one most likely to shake things up. And he already has—but will it last?

The exact same thing has happened countless times before all over the world. Take Venezuela for example. In many ways the history of Venezuela's two-party system is similar to our own. Venezuela's two major political parties—Acción Democrática and the Comité de Organización Politica Electoral Independiente—were both dominated by elites who literally alternated power between themselves. There was virtually no difference between the two. Both parties represented the same elite interests, while the vast majority of the Venezuelan people suffered in dire poverty. Sound familiar?

These two parties held a monopoly on partisan politics for nearly fifty years in Venezuela. Given the party system's iron grip on the electoral process, politicians had to enter through one of the two parties. To not toe the party line was certain political suicide—at least until Chavez came along.

For those who loved him, Hugo Chavez was the Latin American savior, driving neoliberalism to its knees and forcing out elitist, corrupt partidocrats who had hoarded the power and resources to themselves for decades. His policy on social spending improved living conditions in the slums, revamped education and healthcare, and redistributed more than $20 billion in oil revenue back to the people.

To those who hated him (the John McCains of the world), Chavez was a dictator, a power monger, a friend of terrorists, and a threat to the Western Hemisphere. His 1999 constitution flew in the face of democratic ideals by tilting the balance of power clearly in favor of the executive. But Chavez was immensely popular among Venezuela's poor. He was the poster child of Latin American populism, which was itself a sign of the times.

But times have changed. Just look at Venezuela today. Nationalism only works when a country is economically strong enough to keep the neoliberal wolves at bay. In the case of Venezuela—which nationalized its oil under Chavez—oil revenues were its lifeblood, accounting for roughly 95 percent of export earnings. When oil prices plummeted, so did Venezuela's economy—and immediately the vultures began to circle. The question for us today is whether America is economically capable of sustaining Trump's escapades.

Aleppo Is Burning

The long answer regarding why I didn't vote in the 2016 election is much more sinister, and it has as much to do with neoliberal economics as it does with American politics. The most important reason for Trump's election victory is neoliberalism—plain and simple—but no one seems to be addressing this point. Even more relevant is the state of the world today. We didn't get here by accident. History has been following a long and deliberate trajectory toward this very destination.

Iraq fought its eight-year war with Iran largely as a pawn in a U.S.-led initiative to maintain Saudi regional hegemony and to stem Iranian influence.[18] When Saddam Hussein later refused to regulate oil production and prices to meet Western demands, the neocons decide it was "time for toppling."[19] The resulting instability in Iraq created a power vacuum that has since created a number of other proxy wars.

Political instability in the entire region erupted in 2011 with the Arab Spring, but nowhere was it more bloody and protracted than in the oil-rich states of Iraq, Libya, and Syria (we can also include Yemen in this list where substantial oil finds were discovered in the 1980s). The wars in these regions have been as intense as they've been unnecessary. Countless civilians have been displaced and killed, all in the name of oil. Many more continue to suffer as hegemonic rivals engage in proxy wars so that multinational corporations can privatize the oil fields and maximize their profits.

What does Aleppo (or Mosul or Benghazi or Sanaa) have to do with the election of Donald Trump? Aleppo is a fitting metaphor for the world today. Once Syria's largest city, Aleppo endured four years of senseless violence between the status quo powers in the West and those who opposed them in the East. The neoliberal powers were willing to accept the total destruction of Aleppo—and the wholesale slaughter of countless civilians—rather than cede an iota of power or control. In this respect Aleppo is a microcosm of the all-consuming neoliberal lust for power.

Like Chavez Trump represents the demise of the political machine. His populist appeal is an indication that Americans no longer believe the lies that their government is telling them. But the emergence of a Washington outsider as the president of the United States is an omen of something much more sinister—"domination by a cabal of controlling shareholders."[20] The free-market capitalist system is dead. Trump's election victory was simply the funeral. This should be Americans' greatest concern.

Up until now, I've largely focused on the problems associated with conflict and violence in the world today. In the remaining chapters, I'll consider a potential solution.

CHAPTER TEN

A CULTURAL COMPASS

"Would you tell me, please, which way I ought to go from here?"

"That depends a good deal on where you want to get to," said the Cat.

—Alice in Wonderland

When I first met my friend Ali, my initial impression was that he looked like Baghdadi, the leader of the Islamic State. Ali has a long bushy beard and thick eyebrows, and at the time, he was wearing a *topi* (prayer cap). Even with all my travels and the many years I've spent living in various parts of the world, my American upbringing still informs my primary perception in any given situation. So, of course, my first impression of Ali was based entirely on his appearance and the stereotypes it conjured in my mind.

However, the moment he started to speak, I realized that Ali was an intelligent and peaceful man. I learned that he was a husband, a father, and an engineer. The longer we spoke with each other, the more I sensed that we were a lot more alike than we were different. We faced similar challenges and problems, we had many of the same dreams for our children, and we shared each other's views on a variety of issues. Months later, as we were talking one evening, Ali recited the legend of the young Mongol prince.

In the thirteenth century, a young Mongol prince happened upon a poor old man. Seeing his long beard, the prince held him in contempt. "Answer me correctly," the prince sneered, "and I'll let you live. Which is better? Your long beard or a dead dog's tail?"

Looking into the young prince's eyes, the old man saw that his heart was pure. He felt compassion for the young prince because he could see that he'd been deceived. The old man calmly replied, "If I were to die without *iman* (belief in God), then the tail of a dead dog is better."

Realizing that he had misjudged the old man and moved by his wisdom and courage, the young prince experienced a change of heart. Feeling ashamed for his former ways, he confessed, "I want to be like you."

Some years later the old man died, and the young prince became king. He was a good king—just and compassionate—and he was known for his long beard.

When Ali told me the story of the young Mongol prince, he wasn't just entertaining me; he was sharing part of his culture with me. Ali was granting me an inside view into what he holds as valuable and important: faith, humility, and compassion—the very attributes that he's instilling in his own children.

To the average Westerner, the significance of a long beard is not so obvious. Most automatically associate it with the likes of Ayatollah Khomeini, bin Laden, or Baghdadi. If you've spent any time in Saudi Arabia, you may associate it with the Mutawa (religious police). But to many Muslims, a long beard is a sign of religious devotion and the very qualities the story of the young Mongol prince celebrates. So on the surface, the story teaches the value of faith, humility, and compassion. But when people become a little more culturally aware, they realize that their stereotypical view of others leaves them at a distinct disadvantage if they would like to understand the world for what it actually is rather than what they've been taught to believe.

I've had editors and other academics ridicule me for including stories such as this one in my writing. "What does a Mongol king with a long beard have to do with terrorism?" they scoffed.

Obviously, the two have absolutely nothing to do with each other as far as they're concerned, and that's the entire point. Because of the gatekeeping function of those in control of the various media outlets (books, journals, cable, etc.), few realize the connection because most people rely on the media as their primary source of information regarding social problems such as terrorism and extremist violence. Unfortunately, the media—and even quite a bit of terrorism literature—is laden with stereotypes and misinformation. Therefore, people tend to make assumptions that couldn't be more mistaken—such as I initially did with my friend Ali.

Perception of the Other

As a terrorism scholar, I employ strategic theory to better understand the goal(s) of those I study. While most terrorism literature is concerned with the so-called causes of terrorism and *why* actors engage in terrorist violence (i.e., motive), strategic theory examines *what* actors want and *how effective* their strategy is toward achieving their goals.

Ultimately, the strategic approach sheds considerable light on the *why* question as well because strategic theory requires an in-depth understanding of the individuals or groups under examination. One side of this coin consists of objective fact such as the historical and political context in which the violence occurs as well as the perpetrator's socioeconomic position within that context. Often one can glean enough information from the historical and political context to determine what an actor's strategic goal is, but one is still left in the dark in respect to other important considerations.

For instance anyone even remotely familiar with the Holocaust has been confronted with the disturbing compliance demonstrated by both those who collaborated with the Nazis as well as their victims. Fear of punishment (along with at least some sense of racial superiority) explains much of the former behavior, but how do we explain the passive acceptance displayed by millions of Jews as they faced their own extermination? Objective fact alone only paints half of the picture.

The opposite side of the coin is subjective in nature, requiring insight concerning how actors view themselves and those around them. To fully understand why so many Jews did not resist the Nazis, we need to look beyond the political and historical context and attempt to grasp how the Jews of that time viewed their plight. Only by attempting to view these actors and the world through their eyes rather than through one's own can analysts begin to see a more complete picture.

Therefore, an important component of any strategic analysis is an actor's perception of the other. Strategy is the use of one's resources toward the attainment of a particular goal. How an actor perceives his or her own resources vis-à-vis the resources of another plays as large a role as the strategic objective itself by influencing the decision to engage in violence in the first place (as well as the way in which targets and victims respond). Understanding an actor's perception of the other also affords tremendous insight regarding what that actor considers to be acceptable behavior toward various outgroups.

For example, al-Qaeda and the Islamic State share the same strategic goal of establishing an Islamic caliphate, yet they employ very different tactics in pursuit of this goal. They also target different victims. Why?

Answering this question requires both objective fact and a more subjective type of information to shed light in the shadows. Historical and political realities indicate that the last caliphate ended with the defeat of the Ottoman Empire in World War I. The introduction of Western-style democracy led many Muslims to embrace political Islam as an alternative, thus creating the desire to reestablish the caliphate via the political process. Such objective information only tells us half of the story, however. Perception of the other contributes greatly to one's understanding of how al-Qaeda and IS view others — particularly how they view Muslims who don't conform to their strict interpretation of Islam.

Even though al-Qaeda and the Islamic State both practice a strict version of Salafi Islam, and both share the strategic objective of establishing an Islamic caliphate, the two organizations view the greater Muslim community very differently. In al-Qaeda's eyes the majority of the Muslim community simply lacks proper spiritual guidance. They're lost sheep — led astray by the corrupting influences of the West — and as such, they need to be taught the "true" way of Islam. Meanwhile, IS views anyone who does not accept its rigid version of Islam as apostates — enemies of Allah — who must be eliminated at all cost in order to make way for the Mahdi (enlightened one).

As indispensable as strategic analysis is for understanding the use of violence, it offers only limited utility as a tool in resolving conflict. Learning what the parties in dispute want is only half the battle. One also needs a sound strategy for arriving at an equitable solution. One viable option is to understand the role of culture.

Horizons

The famed cultural anthropologist Terrence Turner once warned that people should never attempt to equate culture with specific geographic boundaries as though it were the exclusive property of a particular group.[1] Yet it's popular to conceive of cultures as separate and distinct from one another—and to some extent this is true. Most people have a dominant cultural lens or worldview through which they process information. However, this is not the same thing as having a fixed and definable culture. And this worldview is certainly no longer bound in space and time, if indeed it ever was. The big question is, where does one draw the line? Which differences really matter and which differences don't?

I'm always puzzled by the arbitrary and seemingly random criteria by which people determine race. Skin color is critical, but hair color and eye color don't matter at all. The size of one's lips and the shape of one's nose is paramount, while the size of one's nose and the shape of one's lips matters considerably less. In a sense people do the same thing with culture. They assume cultural identities based on superficial and often completely unrelated factors.

So what is culture exactly, and how can one truly distinguish one culture from another? Popular definitions commonly include a shared set of beliefs and accepted practices, but explanations such as these aren't all that helpful. On the one hand, they're far too broad and completely ignore subcultures, countercultures, and cultural diversity. On the other hand, they assume far too much. Is it really possible to identify purely American beliefs and practices as opposed to those of Arabs or Filipinos? To what extent has multiculturalism affected the various components of culture such as language, religion, norms and values, food, clothing, and the way people view time? How has globalization altered cultural universals such as rites of passage, ritualism, and taboos?

Jack Gibbs makes a clever analogy about stones and humans; the two are clearly in separate classes and should be distinguishable from each other, but as far as gravity is concerned there's no difference.[2] Why build artificial walls when there are already so many other obstacles to overcome?

Seyla Benhabib eloquently compares culture to the horizon—always in view but never in reach.[3] In an increasingly globalized world, the intracultural condition makes it extremely difficult to understand the phenomenon commonly referred to as culture or worldview.

When my wife and I married, we faced several cultural challenges.

One big one for me was the difference in the way our respective cultures viewed time. I was raised with the value that it's better to be thirty minutes early rather than one minute late. My wife, on the other hand, usually waited until we were supposed to be somewhere to start getting ready. Yet somehow we were never late. It didn't take long for me to realize that I wasn't in Kansas anymore. In the Philippines the concept of time is considerably more flexible than it is in the U.S.

When we moved to Central Asia, we were both shocked. Although the former Soviet republics still maintain the facade of the factory-room floor, the great time clock has been hopelessly broken for a number of decades now. And of course in the Middle East the sands of time pass not in discernable quantum chunks but in an ebb and flow conditioned by status, circumstance, and a myriad of other social conventions as mysterious as the moon's pull on the tide. Time is adrift here in a fluid equation of relativity and spatial complexity. Like jazz or poetry, it has its own rhythm—and white people can't hear Jimi, or can they?

When I was on vacation in the Maldives in 2016, I struck up a conversation with our waiter one evening (his nickname was Charlly). I asked him if he thought the attacks in Europe had caused any noticeable drop in tourism to his country (a Muslim state).

Contemplating the question for a moment, Charlly replied, "No, we're pretty isolated from the rest of the world here. But we do have to be careful what we say around non-Muslims." With a twinkle in his eye he quipped, "We can say, 'God is great' in any language except Arabic."

Charlly's lighthearted response demonstrates that there are more accommodating ways to approach the current political climate. Rather than react with fear and hostility (which only fuels the extremists' cause), an alternative approach is to embrace the good in others. Sure, we may all be different in superficial ways (food, dress, language, and religion). But once we make the effort, we're likely to realize that 99.999 percent of the human population all want the same things. The vast majority of people want to have a better life than their parents had, and they want to give their children a better life than they had.

A colleague of mine was born in abject poverty in Brazil. Knowing that she could never give her daughter the life that she deserved, this woman's illiterate mother made the ultimate sacrifice: she gave her up for adoption. Today, my colleague has a PhD and a good life in

America. Every time she visits her birth mother in Brazil, that wonderful woman is blessed with the knowledge that her baby is safe and happy and prosperous. Isn't that what most people want for their children?

All around the world, there are millions of migrant workers, men and women who are forced to leave their families behind and take jobs in foreign countries. Most of them miss their spouses and children desperately. But what can they do? Like my colleague's Brazilian mother, they're doing what they can to provide for their families—just as most Westerners would do if they were put in that situation (and a growing number are). People are not so different from one another after all.

Culturally speaking the two largest common denominators shared by people are language and religion. While language has been a source of conflict in isolated incidents (such as the war between East and West Pakistan, where Urdu was proclaimed the national language despite the prevalence of Bengali in the East), religion has played a more vital (if not central) role in armed conflict throughout history.

Culturalists suggest that religion can sometimes be absolute and unyielding, and it's often in these occasions that religious convictions (particularly those associated with monotheistic religions) can actually spark violence when their adherents are confronted with contrary belief systems or practices.

In the case of jihadist groups, for example, one obvious explanation for the increase in violence is the strong belief that democratic forms of government are *haram* (prohibited) under sharia. Thus when this foreign and (in their eyes) unlawful institution is imposed on them, they rebel. However, most other scenarios are not so easily understood.

Take, for example, the average Christian. Are you getting a mental image? Neither am I. This is because there's no such thing as an average Christian. Nor is there any such thing as the average American (despite what politicians claim every election cycle). The same is true of nearly all groups. The more familiar people become with others, the more difficult it is to stereotype them.

The Jaggedness Principle states that no one is physically average.[4] While it's true that one can calculate physical averages such as height, weight, and shoe size—along with dozens of other measurements for any particular group—no single individual meets every criteria. Hence, no one person is "average."

If people are all this different physically, just imagine how different they are emotionally, psychologically, spiritually, intellectually, morally, and ethically. For example, each person has his or her own unique set of ethical and moral "if-then" conditions that determines appropriate behavior in various situations. These conditions are informed by culture and religion, of course, but they're also informed by one's environment, upbringing, and personal choices (not to mention myriad other factors). So to claim that religion or culture alone causes certain outcomes is to miss the bigger picture.

Years ago I was stranded in Manila for nearly five months because the Saudi embassy lost my passport. It was a particularly difficult situation because my father became ill and passed away during these months, and I couldn't travel to see him or attend his funeral.

My pleas for help from the Saudi embassy were largely ignored, and I was more or less instructed to obtain another passport. In other words it wasn't their problem. I had two choices: I could go with the knee-jerk reaction and blame it on the "Saudis" (as if all twenty-eight million Saudis were responsible for losing my passport), or I could search for a more intelligent approach. Trust me, I was extremely tempted to give in to the first option (on several occasions), but how would that have helped me?

Thankfully, cooler heads prevailed, and I did eventually recover my passport. Even though it cost me a lot in lost income, fees, fines for overstaying my legal welcome in the Philippines—and worst of all—the chance to say good-bye to my father, the reality of life is that people are human. Everyone makes mistakes. Furthermore, every bureaucracy has its shortcomings, which have nothing to do with culture or religion.

Still, the cultural approach to understanding terrorism is to search for social conventions that either cause violence or allow violence to occur as a culturally viable option. With the prevalence of "Islamic violence" over the past several decades, there has been a surge of interest in Islam itself as part of the search for cultural explanations of the phenomena.

Like all religions Islam can be a strong unifying force. But of course not all variants of Islam are the same. So Islam can also be a powerful dividing force. However, this doesn't make it evil. If you've been paying attention, you'll immediately recognize the inherent problems associated with the assertion that terrorist violence is "caused" by Islam. Still, prevailing attitudes are difficult to change.

In chapter 11, I'll explore the concept of culture further as I examine ways in which people are different, draw meaning from those differences, and attempt to understand how they can lead to conflict. More importantly I'll consider ways in which this knowledge empowers people to practice a more effective means of conflict resolution.

CHAPTER ELEVEN

THE COLORS OF CONFLICT

In the beginning was the Word.

—John 1:1

One of the most common components of culture is religion, which Marx popularly denounced as "the opium of the masses." Actually, the original German translates as "people," but the real misinterpretation occurs regarding Marx's point. Atheists love to quote Marx; however, Marx had no real qualms about religion per se. It was the system of inequality supported by religion that Marx so vehemently opposed. In this respect Marx was spot on: cultures all enforce their own mechanisms of social control, be it via religion, social structure, customs, norms, or mores. Mechanisms of social control exist in every major civilization on earth.

While conflict often appears to be caused by a difference in values, at the root of most conflict is not a difference of values so much as a different set of rules. Researchers in the fields of anthropology, sociology, and psychology commonly distinguish between two principal mechanisms of social control: guilt and shame.[1]

Despite a number of caveats—including the inherent difficulty in defining terms such as "honor," "shame," and "guilt"—the concept continues to resonate intuitively with many researchers, and it has spawned myriad related theories.

One variation on this theme suggests that worldview is expressed through three basic dichotomies: law/guilt, fear/power, honor/shame.

At the most generic level, Western societies are thought to be more guilt oriented; South American and African societies more fear oriented; and Middle Eastern, Asian, and Native American societies more shame oriented.[2]

According to this model, all people experience tension to some degree between the two extremes on each of these three planes. Individual reactions to that tension combine to produce a distinct cultural fingerprint for each person. Just as the three primary colors are able to produce myriad secondary colors, these three primary worldviews blend in unique proportions in every human being on the planet. In an increasingly globalized world, everyone has degrees of cultural similarities and differences. In some ways all people are alike, and in other ways all people are different.

While this model is based on research that has been around for some time, its application to terrorism and extremist violence has largely been ignored. This is unfortunate as I believe it possesses vast potential. Therefore, I've decided to adapt it to terrorism and violent extremism. As the title of the chapter indicates, I call it the colors of conflict model.

As a theoretical lens, perception of the other affords us a sense of *how* actors perceive those around them. The colors approach attempts to delve deeper and determine *why* this is so.

One might ask (and with good reason) how these three mechanisms developed in the first place and why they differ from one society to another. I have my own theory—half-baked as it is. There is some scholarly agreement that foraging communities (hunters and gatherers) tended to have less hierarchical societal structures than their agrarian counterparts.[3] This may be a simple matter of the one having a less complex division of labor, but I believe it has more to do with the effect of surplus.

Imagine you have a family of eight and one large pizza to share among them. Each person gets a slice. There's no surplus, so everyone receives an equal share, and the family moves on to the next activity. Now consider that same pizza with a family of seven. Who gets the extra slice? No doubt it's the one with the biggest belly, but my point is that inequality is almost always introduced when there's a surplus of goods. A small amount of surplus (such as an extra slice of pizza) may not have much visible effect on a community, but over time the acquisition of wealth and the drive for profit effect dramatic alterations to the social fabric of society. Communal values change, and it isn't long before the haves and the have-nots begin to emerge. This is especially true with a more complex division of labor, the introduction of social status, and the ability to store goods due to a stationary lifestyle.

Obviously, the need to enforce social control becomes greater as communities become more complex because there's simply more order to enforce. Alternatively, if there were no privileged members of society (those who benefit from the surplus of commodities), there would be no entitlements to enforce and protect—and no John McCains in the world to object to the redistribution of wealth.

Time and time again, revolutions attempting to replace the inequality of the ancien régime with liberté, égalité, and fraternité have failed. Why? Because of the greed that accompanies surplus. Liberty without economic equality simply means that the rich are free to get richer at the expense of the poor. Furthermore, the inequity of the international economic system has made some "brothers" more equal than others. Worse still the acquisition of wealth has turned into a deadly game of "winner take all" in which not only surplus is gobbled up but the poor are even deprived of their daily necessities.

Social mechanisms enforce the status quo through fear of those in power, public shame, or legal sanctions for violating established norms. Why one mechanism prevails over the others is a bit of a mystery. However, at face value it would appear that the further a society moves from the perception of basic equality, the more prone it is to either fear or shame.

In the heyday of economic prosperity, Westerners enjoyed the benefits of labor unions (competitive wages, decent benefits, improved working conditions, etc.). Even now in the postindustrial era, people at least have the pretense of equality, and because of what social spending remains, few Westerners are starving compared to people in less developed parts of the world where fear continues to be the dominant mechanism of social control.

In many of these places, nature continues to be the greatest threat to survival as natural disasters, diseases, drought, and famine abound. This inability to control natural circumstances is compounded by war and intractable violence. In fact many of the economies in developing areas of the world have grown dependent on conflict. In such an environment, it makes perfect sense to fear those in power and to attempt to gain their favor through whatever means one can.

Alternatively in resource rich areas such as the Middle East, where inequality is blatant and honor is largely associated with wealth, public shame continues to be the dominant mechanism of social control. In honor/shame societies, the best way to avoid public shame is to always "save face" and protect the honor of oneself and one's family.

The experiences I relate in the following sections are just a few examples that illustrate these points.

Power/Fear

In certain parts of the world such as Latin America, Africa, and Central Asia (as well as in some communities in the West), the power/fear dichotomy is the dominant color. In these regions religion is used primarily as a tool of appeasement, a vehicle for obtaining counsel, or a way of making intercession (rather than offering an explication of right and wrong). Examples abound with Native American spirit guides, voodoo (vodou) Lwa, Catholic saints, and Hindu deities. The primary social mechanism operating in this color is fear, and to secure the favor of someone in power is absolutely critical.

A modern example from my own life is the situation in Kyrgyzstan, where the authorities (and especially the police and border guards) are feared more than the criminals. This fear is largely due to endemic corruption, which is itself a product of the power/fear dichotomy. The police in Kyrgyzstan are paid very little (if at all), so they regularly park on the side of the road and randomly pull vehicles over for no reason whatsoever. They then demand payment. If a person can't pay (or if he doesn't have a powerful friend), the police will arrest him (and trust me, you don't want that).

When my wife and I first moved to Kyrgyzstan, we went shopping at an outdoor bazaar. A police officer overheard us speaking to each other in English, and before we knew it six officers were pushing us along and forcing us to accompany them to the other side of the bazaar, where they had a little tent set up. When we arrived at the front of the tent, the officers tried to force us through the tiny opening.

None of the officers spoke English, so I objected as best I could (in very poor Russian). Fortunately, I had a photo of my wife and me with an American captain at the U.S. embassy in Bishkek on my phone. I didn't have any minutes on my SIM card, but I pretended to call the embassy anyway, and the police quickly dispersed. As we made our way back through the bazaar, many of the locals who had witnessed the scene asked us, "*Shkolka?*" They wanted to know how much we had paid the officers to let us go. We later learned that the tent was used to rape and rob foreigners. Once the police got a person inside, they stole his or her passport and valuables. Without identification the person could end up in a Kyrgyz jail or just go missing (and trust me, you don't want that either).

Renewing one's visa in Kyrgyzstan is another eye-opening experience. The person has to leave the country, renew her visa, and then come back in. The closest border to us was the border with Kazakhstan, so we decided to go to the Kyrgyz embassy in Kazakhstan, get our visas renewed, and then reenter Kyrgyzstan. Sounds easy enough until we realized that there are three to four check points on each side of the border, and each check point has at least two guards who expect to be bribed to let anyone pass. If you have an American passport, expect the bribe to be both substantial and nonnegotiable. If a person doesn't pay, they can send him back—or worse, they can detain him for as long as it takes to change his mind—and they also have a little room.

Once we made it across the border, the fun was just beginning. The border guards called their friends on the highway patrol, who then pulled us over every ten kilometers or so. One said we were driving too fast, another too slow. One actually said that our vehicle was too dirty. All of them exacted a hefty bribe. Fortunately our driver, Dima, had warned us ahead of time to bring plenty of cash. In the States we'd call this a protection racket. In Central Asia it's simply the cost of doing business.

One of my friends, Zarif, owned a "gamburger" stand in a highly coveted location. When he told us how little he paid his employees, we were outraged until he told us how much he had to pay the police every day. Of course he also had to bribe the local officials to maintain his business license. A famous proverb states that a good attorney knows the law; a great attorney knows the judge. This is life in a power/fear society. If you can somehow secure the favor of those in power, you have nothing to fear. If not, be afraid, be very afraid—and bring lots of cash.

Honor/Shame

The honor/shame binary is perhaps the most elusive of the three to the Western mind because the definition of honor itself differs in the two worldviews. Take the ancient proverb, "A good name is better than riches." To a Westerner weaned on the law, the proverb is steeped in innuendos of innocence and guilt. A good name is associated with hard work, honesty, integrity, telling the truth, and keeping your word.

To one raised in a culture of honor and shame, however, the proverb means something entirely different. In the Middle East, for example, a good name is associated with *wasta* (influence) and prestige. Arab society has traditionally elevated ascribed status over personal merit; one's tribe and clan were of considerably more importance than one's personal achievements.[4] This is still largely true today.

As a professor I sometimes have students who fail my classes—it happens unfortunately—and when it does, I try to be as sensitive and helpful as possible. Still, there's only so much I can do. As a dedicated professional, I deliver quality education in the classroom and make myself as available to my students as possible outside the classroom. Beyond that each student is ultimately responsible for his or her own performance (you can lead a horse to water—at least that's my personal philosophy).

Some time ago I had an eye-opening experience that taught me firsthand that this sentiment is not shared by everyone. At the end of one particular semester, I received a phone call from a senior officer at the university inquiring about a particular student's grade. Initially, I didn't think that much about it because in my experience grade appeals are quite common in the Middle East, where the "art of the deal" is always very much in play.

This was no ordinary attempt to negotiate a better grade, however. Upon learning that the student had failed, the senior officer instructed me to "double-check" the entry. As it turned out, the student was the senior officer's son—failure was not an option (literally).

Let me disclaim up front that I'm certainly not suggesting that this is a frequent practice in the Middle East. In all my years' here, this is the only time I've experienced such an encounter. Still, the experience challenged me on a number of levels. First of all, higher education is supposed to be the foundation of attained status—the ultimate level playing field. But here this student was clearly getting by on his ascribed status and his family's wasta (and very little else).

Second, as a product of Western academia, I would be ashamed if I failed a class, period. Regardless of whether anyone found out about it, I would be ashamed. However, neither the student nor the parent demonstrated any observable shame whatsoever (at least not any that I could detect). To the contrary they appeared to be quite proud of the fact that they were "above the law."

I'm not claiming that cheating is part of the culture. However, a distinct mind-set seems to pervade just about every aspect of the honor/shame society. From the way people drive to the way they park their cars, it's clear who's above the law and who isn't. I recall taking my family to the mall, and as usual, the parking lot was full—not because there were too many vehicles, but because most of the more expensive ones were parked diagonally and took up between two and three parking spaces. Consequently, I was forced to drive around for twenty to thirty minutes in search of a spot. I eventually found one, way at the end of the lot. It wasn't marked as such, but apparently it was a no-parking zone because when I returned to my vehicle, I had a parking ticket. Slightly outraged I began to check some of the vehicles that were parked diagonally; not one had a parking ticket. Apparently, if you have an expensive enough vehicle, you can park anywhere and anyway you like.

I often wondered about how other traffic violations are dealt with. It's very common to see drivers speeding, running red lights, texting while driving, and making illegal lane changes, but surely the cameras can't distinguish between expensive cars and inexpensive cars, can they?

A colleague of mine came to work one day absolutely furious. She had just returned from vacation and learned that while she was away (in Ireland) she had received a number of traffic citations. She went to the police station with her passport to prove that it couldn't have been her since she was out of the country when the violations occurred. The officer smiled at her and said, "Yes, yes. You pay. No problem." My colleague said that she pressed the officer and eventually discovered that the tickets had been transferred from someone else's registration to hers—and absolutely no one was going to do anything about it.

Not long afterward I was involved in a hit and run. I managed to get the license plate number of the other driver, and I reported it to the police. The officer took the plate number from me and typed it into his computer. He took one look at the driver's information and said, "*Khalas!*" (finished). The police report (written in Arabic) stated that I was at fault. That's the power of wasta.

One last experience that is perhaps the most revealing of how deeply ingrained our cultural colors tend to be occurred on New Year's Eve 2017. My wife and I and our two small children were waiting for an elevator along with another woman with three small children. As the elevator doors opened, an Emirati woman with four maids quickly approached from behind and forcefully pushed my wife out of the way so that she and her companions could enter the elevator first. My wife was shocked and on the verge of tears. "Why are you pushing me?" she insisted. The woman just glared at her in a very condescending manner and said, "You're just a Filipino." With that she pushed the button and closed the elevator doors in our faces.

Several people witnessed the incident including a security guard, but no one said anything except the other woman with the three small children. "Don't put that in your heart," she whispered in broken English, trying to console my wife.

Innocence/Guilt

Islamic scholars often point out that all the prophets (including Jesus) taught pure monotheism based on the unity of God. They claim that Christianity was pure until the apostle Paul corrupted it by adopting a number of pagan Roman practices in order to obtain the favor of those in power.[5] Likewise some accuse Constantine of having forced the Nicene Creed on the church and slaughtering those who refused to accept it.[6] I can't say whether any of this is true or not because I wasn't there. Still, many scholars of all backgrounds argue that Western Christianity has been clearly influenced by the Roman concepts of law, guilt, and innocence wherein even the highest official is subject to the law. Little wonder that some Christian theologians insist that even God is subject to his own laws.

This positioning of the law above everything else is evident in the writings of early Western theologians such as Tertullian, Augustine, and Calvin.[7] Their influence, in turn, shaped much of Western civilization to come.[8] The primary mechanism of social control in Western Europe and the United States is presumably the law—before which all stand as equals (unless, of course, you consider the disproportionate percentage of minorities in Western prisons).

In the Western mind-set, the innocence/guilt dichotomy resonates as just. Meanwhile, as my experiences with the Kyrgyz authorities and the senior officer at the university in the Middle East demonstrate, the other two colors naturally strike most Westerners as unjust. For those christened in the objectivity of the law (an ideal yet often naive notion), bribes and wasta rattle their ethical core—but this is mostly because they're simply accustomed to a different kind of corruption.

So before one gets too self-righteous, it's important to recall the countless examples of Western atrocities committed in the name of the law. From the Christian Crusades, when soldiers competed to see how many Jewish babies they could fit on a sword, to the Global War on Terrorism, in which countless victims continue to suffer in the name of national security, the law has been used to justify unimaginable crimes against humanity. All too often the perpetrators' defense has been that they were "just following orders."

In the previous two sections, I shared a number of anecdotal accounts. At face value it may appear that I'm discrediting the other two worldviews, but far from it. My purpose is not to elevate any one worldview or to discredit the others—quite the contrary. My aim is rather to demonstrate just how easy it is to see perceived injustices in a foreign culture—particularly when one attempts to understand that culture via the cultural conditioning of another worldview—which we all do. As products of our cultural conditioning, we find it extremely difficult to do otherwise. It takes training and great effort. Given this obstacle, it's no wonder that the world is experiencing intractable conflict.

Assumptions vary from culture to culture. Definitions of right and wrong also vary as do a myriad of mores and values. Often these are so automatic and unconscious that they are rarely even contemplated much less articulated—until one of them is violated. Even then people are so programmed and indoctrinated by their own culture's mechanisms of social control that effective intercultural communication can be extremely difficult once conflict has occurred.

As an academic I like to demonstrate this concept to my students by a simple pedagogical device known as a card game. I split my students up into pairs and give each pair a sheet of paper with the rules to the card game. The students sit two pairs per table, and the pairs challenge each other in a game of cards. The winning pair gets to stay at the table, while the losing pair has to move to the next table (the tables are numbered). There are only two rules to this activity: (1) absolutely no talking or written communication is allowed, and (2) the students must obey the rules written on the sheet they received at the beginning of the activity.

It's usually not long before tempers start flaring, and students start throwing cards, accusing one another of cheating, and stomping out in anger. What the students don't know is that each pair has received a different set of rules. From who goes first to the order of play to which card is highest in value to what is allowed and what is not—every pair has a different set of rules. So the students have an opportunity to experience firsthand a little taste of what it's like to encounter another culture as an outsider.

What's interesting is that Western students almost invariably jump to the conclusion that the other students are cheating. They naturally assume that the rules are the same for everyone. My non-Western students rarely make that assumption. Usually, depending on their dominant worldview, they either defer to whoever has the highest social standing or to the one with the most power. According to the innocent/ guilt perspective, cheating is wrong and should not be tolerated by anyone. The other two perspectives are more concerned with either saving face (avoiding shame) or aligning with power.

Provisos

Now of course there are many exceptions to the generalizations made above, and there are at least a billion objections that I could raise. I'll consider a few of them now.

First, the colors of conflict lens is a theoretical model—an *intentional* oversimplification—employed to parse out one possible distinction between cultures. Reality is much more complicated, with most cultures celebrating a blend of all three colors. Individuals are even more complex, each possessing his or her own unique mix of the three colors—sort of like a fingerprint.

Second, even if the colors lens were able to present a more realistic snapshot of society, it's based primarily on observation rather than empirical evidence. As an American observing the world through my own cultural lens, I can hardly claim to be impartial. Nor can I pretend to understand the other two primary colors as intuitively as I do my own.

Third, perpetrators of terrorism and extremist violence don't necessarily share the same values as the general population they claim to represent. While they very well may, one should never assume that they do. Therefore, like the perception of the other lens, the colors of conflict lens is only a tool.

There are many limitations to the use of theoretical models, particularly when used in isolation. This is especially true in terrorism studies, where practitioners and gatekeepers alike tend to favor one model to the exclusion of all others. When used to complement a comprehensive analysis, however, theoretical models are indispensable to the research process.

Still, some will no doubt take exception to this approach. That's to be expected. In fact it's encouraged as intellectual dialogue is the main means of enlightenment and discovery in the social sciences. In the next section, I'll apply the model and see what it reveals.

The Heart of Conflict

In most cases of intractable conflict, those involved in the heart of the dispute are simply unable or unwilling to view the situation from the other's perspective. Rather than attempting to enforce an impartial peace (which usually doesn't last anyway), a more effective approach would be to search for points of convergence between the two positions.

It isn't uncommon to discover that the disputants are actually much more alike than they are different. Take the biblical story of Cain and Abel for example. The narrative doesn't disclose why Cain killed his brother Abel; it simply states that both brothers made an offering to God. Cain offered the fruit of the soil, while Abel offered fat from the firstborn of his flock. The account further informs us that God "looked with favor upon Abel and his offering, but on Cain and his offering he did not look with favor. So Cain was very angry, and his face was downcast."[9]

The written depiction of the first murder in history gives surprisingly little information concerning Cain's motive, not to mention what he was hoping to accomplish. Most people simply assume that Cain killed his brother Abel out of envy and write it off as a crime of passion.

I'm going to suggest that rather than envy, Cain reacted out of jealousy. What's the difference? Envy is something people feel when someone has something that they want. Jealousy is an emotion people experience when somebody acquires what used to be theirs.

When one looks a little closer, one discovers that the biblical tale of Cain and Abel reveals more than initially meets the eye. First of all, Cain was the elder brother. In the culture of the ancient Near East, the firstborn son was awarded special privileges. He was appointed as second in line to his father and exercised authority over his younger brothers and sisters. The firstborn son also received a double portion of his father's estate and assumed leadership of the family when his father died. As head of the family, he was also the spiritual leader of the household. He was expected to care for his mother for the remainder of her life and provide for his sisters until they married.[10]

Assuming these rights of the firstborn were in effect at the time, one can understand this to mean that Cain expected to take over as the head of the household and that he already exercised some level of authority over Abel. It was no doubt troubling to Cain that Abel received God's favor because spiritual leadership was directly tied to the inheritance and authority of the firstborn son.

Furthermore, the text states that Cain was a farmer and Abel was a shepherd. When one considers their occupations in light of the fact that Cain was the firstborn, one can infer that perhaps Cain had already assumed possession of his inheritance—if not in fact, at least in principle.

Rather than feeling envious that God looked on Abel's offering with favor, Cain quite possibly killed his brother to defend his primogeniture.

I can already hear some of you rolling your eyeballs. What does the story of Cain and Abel have to do with modern-day conflict? Absolutely nothing unless one is willing to recognize the fact that a land war has been raging in the Middle East since antiquity. Rather than simply dismiss the story because it's from the Bible, as so many are inclined to do, the wiser alternative would be to consider what it might teach us about the conflict the world is experiencing today.

Cain and Abel had a lot in common. They came from the same family. They served the same God. They shared a common culture, including the law of primogeniture. There are many areas where one could build bridges between their two respective positions. Sound familiar?

The age-old conflict between the Jews and the Palestinians is basically a dispute over who has the rightful claim to the land—a piece of real estate that all three monotheistic religions hold sacred. Since Jews, Christians, and Muslims all claim Abraham as their patriarch, one could view the violence in the Middle East as basically a disagreement over who possesses the right of the firstborn son.

The Jews obviously claim a legal right to the land. They enjoy international recognition as a state and membership in the United Nations. One can apply the guilt/innocence worldview to Israel. The Palestinians are a little more difficult to locate within this model, but still one can make a compelling argument that places them in the color of honor/shame. So much of the Palestinian opposition to Israel is centered in anger over the humiliation they've endured since 1948 and the atrocities committed against them. For the Palestinians honor is to remain in their homeland, while shame is to be dispossessed.

Still, many Israelis and Palestinians are reaching across the aisle, building bridges of peace, and engaging in dialogue with one another. They're neighbors, colleagues, coworkers, and friends. My favorite movies from the region are the ones in which "forbidden" love flourishes against all odds. These movies demonstrate to the world that the conflict can be resolved.

It isn't for me to say what the solution should be; that should be left to the people of the region to decide. However, it seems to me that rather than a one-state solution or a two-state solution, the answer lies in a no-state solution. The modern nation-state is still a relatively new construct in the region—and not a very successful one at that. Why limit the options? All three Abrahamic faiths claim Jerusalem as a sacred site, and all three have a vested interest in preserving it, so why not preserve it? Why not make it an international preserve, free from any claims of statehood?

The debate over whether Jerusalem is the capital of Israel or Palestine would be rendered irrelevant if Jews, Muslims, and Christians could simply agree that the Holy Land is holy and to stop desecrating it. No more fighting over land. No more killing in the name of God. No more violence at all. I know many Palestinians and Jews who would love to raise their children in peace.

The "uncivil" war in Syria is another example. At first glance the conflict in Syria appears extremely complex—and it is—but if one could parse out the various components, it would be considerably more manageable. At the heart of the conflict is President Bashar al-Assad and his Baʿath Party government on the one side and those who want to overthrow him on the other.

The Baʿath Party rose in popularity in Syria in the 1940s as an Arab socialist political movement committed to the promotion of secular Arab nationalism, Arab socialism, pan-Arabism, and militarism—but this is no longer an accurate description of Assad and his party in Damascus.[11]

The Syrian Baʿath Party was founded in Damascus in 1947. It rose to prominence in 1963 after a military coup established it as the only legal political party in Syria. Hafez al-Assad seized power in another military coup in 1970 and—other than constitutionally requiring the president to be a Muslim—he was successful in resisting pressure from the Muslim Brotherhood to declare Syria an Islamic republic.[12]

Bashar al-Assad dramatically changed course after the U.S. invaded Iraq in 2003. The Syrian government played down its secular status in favor of proclaiming itself a Muslim state. The Arab Spring reached Syria in 2011, but the popular uprising was crushed by the Syrian army when Assad ordered it to open fire on the protesters.[13] The violence quickly escalated into a full-scale civil war, and Assad has since been accused of committing horrific crimes against his own people.

Because Assad and most of his inner circle are Alawite (Shia) and the majority of the population in Syria are Sunni, the conflict attracted a number of armed militias from both sides of the Sunni/Shia divide, and it is now widely recognized as a proxy war between Saudi Arabia and Iran. Complicating the chaos is the involvement of the United States, Russia, and Turkey. The situation today is nearing total anarchy.

Obviously, there are no easy solutions to the ongoing violence in Syria. However, identifying the main elements of social control being employed would be more than a step in the right direction. Much like

Israel Assad is claiming a legal right to remain in power. However, a majority of those opposed to him are Sunni Muslims fighting for the honor of Islam.

Again, rather than attempting to enforce an unsustainable peace along sectarian lines (which has already failed several times in Syria), a more fruitful approach would be to try to find common ground in which the interests of the parties involved converge. Contrary to popular belief, Islam might not be the most logical place to start because this appears to be one of the most divisive issues in the conflict.

For example Sunni and Shia both believe that Syria will be the site of a great future battle between good and evil. Many Christians and Jews believe the same thing. In fact the Old Testament book of Isaiah predicts that Damascus "will become a heap of ruins."[14] While there is broad agreement across religious traditions regarding the location of the battle, the very definitions of "good" and "evil" are in dispute, with each faction claiming itself as good and its opponents as evil.

Hardcore believers insist that the destruction of Damascus is inevitable—even desirable—and that it will usher in a long-awaited era of peace and prosperity. Meanwhile, diehard skeptics argue that if anything, the conflict in Syria is a self-fulfilling prophecy spurred on by religious extremists and those who profit from the violence. Most everyone else just wants the suffering to end. Hasn't there been enough bloodshed?

Certainly the majority of Syrians—whether Sunni, Shia, or Christian— fall within this third category. Most don't want to see their homes and families and lives destroyed any further. Since Syria is a sovereign state, the decision should be left to the Syrian people—not the Americans, or the Russians, or the Turks, or anyone else. Still, foreigners are carrying out most of the fighting. In this case I would suggest the exact opposite solution to the one I propose for the Israeli/Palestinian dilemma.

Ba'athism originally emerged in opposition to European colonialism, and in a certain sense one could argue that the Syrian civil war is the product of neocolonialism. In my opinion the international community needs to respect the sovereignty of the Syrian state. This is only the first step, of course, but clearly the foreign troops and militias need to pull out before any lasting peace can be established in the country.

These are just two examples of how to apply the colors of conflict model. First, one needs to acknowledge that the parties to the conflict most likely cannot come to an agreement that's acceptable to all sides because they're speaking different cultural languages. Second, it's absolutely critical to find areas where the parties' interests convergence. Finally, there needs to be sufficient political will to begin building a bridge.

This brief introduction to the approach is just that, an introduction. By developing the colors of conflict lens further, I hope to expand Westerners' understanding of groups such as al-Qaeda and the Islamic State beyond a mere knowledge of *what* their strategic goals are and *how* they view others to include *why* this is so in the first place. While this knowledge may not produce easy or immediate solutions (to be certain, it most likely will not), it will provide a methodological starting point and a strategy with which to move forward. The rest is up to us.

CHAPTER TWELVE

THE DEFINITION OF INSANITY

Wisdom makes the wise man stronger than ten rulers of a city.

—Ecclesiastes 7:19

The Wisdom of Solomon

The quote from Ecclesiastes is credited to King Solomon, who is considered by many to have been the wisest man who ever lived. Even if the written accounts are only somewhat exaggerated, Solomon is said to have reigned over a vast empire in peace and prosperity.[1] Isn't that the sort of environment that most people want today?

While a fair share of violence has been committed in the name of religion, most people of all religions want peace. Most perhaps, but not all: There are—and have always been—those misguided few who believe that by killing people they're doing the will of God. Unfortunately, as long as some people don't want peace, the world will have to deal with the reality of violence. Still, one should minimize this violence as much as possible.

It should be no surprise that militant groups such as al-Qaeda and the Islamic State attack and kill civilians. As heinous as it might seem, this is exactly what most states do in armed conflict—not just "rogue" states but status quo states as well.

During World War I, for example, Britain made a clear distinction between its policy objectives concerning the German people (which it intended to liberate) and the German government (which it intended to overthrow). Yet Britain made little distinction between government and civilian targets in its urban bombing campaigns.

Still, David Lloyd George fully expected the German people to side with the Crown rather than with the kaiser even though British bombs were killing them. The November 1918 German revolution is often cited as evidence that the British achieved their goals. Again, in March 2003, the U.S. (backed by Britain) made the same play in Iraq with less measurable success. More recently hospitals have been intentionally (and repeatedly) bombed in Syria. Let's not forget that Winston Churchill was a staunch advocate for the use of aerial bombing and poisonous gas against civilian populations in the colonies.[2]

The war of us versus them has been raging since the world began, and it isn't likely to end any time soon. As critical thinkers and consumers of the news, the best people can do is to hold themselves accountable for the prepackaged information that they accept as true—and *never* listen to the loudest voices simply because they're the loudest.

As for Muslim extremist ideology, like all extremism it's also been around for a long time. In this book I've distinguished between three categories of Muslim extremist ideology (Islamist, jihadist, and takfiri), and I've examined how they borrow from the past.

I've demonstrated that only a tiny percentage of Muslims are Islamic extremists. The rest are just like everyone else. Most are hardworking people trying to provide for their families and give their children opportunities that they never had. "They" don't hate "us" any more than "we" hate "them." This notion is simply a lie that's been perpetrated by fearmongers since antiquity, and it's still prominent today.

I've further demonstrated that not all Islamists engage in terrorism. In fact most are nonviolent and prefer to contest in free and fair elections. Only a very small percentage employ violence to achieve their objectives, and of those that do, the majority are insurgents involved in civil conflicts—not "terrorists."

Therefore, the common practice of blaming every violent attack on Islamic extremists and concluding that "it must have been ISIS" is ridiculous at best. It's also foolish because it prevents people from facing the truth: *the media* is radicalizing our young people through the lure of international fame, and consumers of the media are allowing it to happen.

Celebrating sensational violence the way that the public currently does rewards the perpetrators of horrific violence and grants them instant celebrity status—naming massacres after them and providing them with a platform from which to spread their message and generate a following. In the case of perpetrators who die during violent attacks, the media spreads their message for them by distributing it through international news outlets, bombarding the world with their faces and names, and inspiring others to imitate them.

Again, the majority of Muslims are not violent. Islamic extremists account for only about one in every seventy-four thousand people in the world. However, since those who do employ violence tend to organize into groups, it only makes sense to study these groups and determine the threat that they actually pose rather than simply accept the distorted picture that the media presents.

For instance most jihadist organizations largely follow al-Banna's more conciliatory bottom-up approach. They believe that the ummah should be taught the true way of Islam from the ulama. Only a very small minority follows Qutb's authoritarian top-down approach. Those who do are takfiri groups that believe apostate Muslims should be killed—not as a means to an end but as an end in itself.

Furthermore, very few Islamist organizations engage in terrorism. After comparing and contrasting the ideological underpinnings of al-Qaeda and the Islamic State and by tracing the respective influences that each has borrowed from its predecessors, I've concluded that al-Qaeda is a jihadist organization that engages in terrorism and the Islamic State is a takfiri group that does not (contrary to popular belief, most of the violence committed by the Islamic State does not qualify as terrorism).

When Push Comes to Shove

It should be evident by now that terrorism is a tactic—a means to an end—and nothing more. Furthermore, terrorist violence is not an end in itself. Therefore, random acts of violence that serve no other purpose are not terrorism. In order to be analytically useful, however, the use of terrorist violence should be understood as a rational decision rather than either an immoral act or the result of some external cause.

On the one hand, defining terrorism as the result of a grievance, injustice, or inequality is problematic because these factors fall within the realm of motive, which is often difficult to establish and not necessarily very useful even when we can. On the other hand, the assumption that terrorism is immoral leads to efforts to prevent and punish it. The current Global War on Terrorism is a classic example. The political climate created by the GWOT has allowed political actors to abuse the concept, each labeling their enemies as terrorists and thus stripping the term of any true conceptual value. Both approaches subject the term to value-laden interpretations and eliminate any objective position from which to begin.

Nearly twenty years ago, Richard Betts suggested that strategic studies focus "on the essential Clausewitzian problem: how to make force a rational instrument of policy rather than mindless murder."[3] This is also the task of the terrorism scholar. Yet few consider how (or even if) violence serves the actor's strategic objective. Most focus entirely on either causes or motives, which leads to the overall impression among the general public that terrorism is either the result of a grievance or senseless and irrational.

When true acts of terrorism are conflated with other types of random attacks such as hate crimes and those perpetrated by copycats or disturbed individuals—and when these are all assumed to be somehow related to Islamic extremism (or racism, or whatever)—the belief that violence is senseless and irrational understandably generates fear. When push comes to shove, fear leads to toleration (if not demand) for policies that discriminate against and oppress targeted groups. Just look at many of the right-wing parties gaining popularity across Europe today as well as the white nationalist groups gaining traction in the United States.

I would remind anyone who believes that such discriminatory and oppressive polices could never be implemented in the civilized countries of the West (or by the hand of their governments) to recall the massive Auschwitz complex (and nearly a dozen others) in Poland; Bergen-Belsen, Buchenwald, and Dachau (to name just a few) in Germany; Janowska in Ukraine; Kaiserwald in Latvia; Mauthausen in Austria; Natzweiler-Struthof in France; Terezin in the Czech Republic; and Westerbork in the Netherlands.

Still not convinced? What about the 120,000 Japanese Americans who were rounded up and incarcerated in U.S. internment camps during

World War II? How about the 100,000 plus Iraqis who were dragged from their homes in the middle of the night and left to languish in Camp Bucca? And who can forget Abu Ghraib or the infamous Guantanamo?[4]

There are countless examples. A friend of mine was once a successful advertising executive in Uganda until the irrational tide of fear and hatred turned, and he found himself in the wrong place at the wrong time. He, his wife, and their two children (and thousands of others) lost everything as they fled for their lives across the border into Kenya. Unfortunately, their story is typical and not at all unusual.

The current migrant crisis is nothing new. It's simply found its way to the borders of Western Europe, so now the world is taking notice of it. The sad reality is that groups have been targeted for violence throughout history, and they continue to be to this day.

The Path Ahead

As I indicated in the preface, this book represents an ambitious attempt to connect what appears to be a number of unrelated dots in order to arrive at a much bigger picture than one is likely to get from the mainstream media. As I've analyzed disparate events throughout recent history, a truly disturbing reality has come into focus: all the great geopolitical conflicts since the beginning of the twentieth century have been waged over oil.[5]

Great Britain, France, Italy, and Russia signed a secret agreement to divide the Ottoman Empire among themselves, primarily in pursuit of its promising oil resources.[6] Up through the Cold War, realist brokers called the shots. Power politics was the name of the game. Since realism has neither friends nor enemies, only interests, the race for oil was framed in geopolitical terms as a battle for freedom and democracy.[7] After the Cold War, the neocons took power. The epic battle for oil is now framed as a quest for the Holy Grail—a war against evil. Both realists and neocons, however, have demonized the rightful owners of the world's oil supplies—all so that they could justify spilling the blood of the innocent in order to satisfy their neoliberal lust for profit.

A century after World War I, the great war for oil is still raging, with many of the same fronts as before and also a few new ones. Throughout it all—whether waged by realists, neoliberals, or neocons—war has been extremely good for business.

GLOSSARY

bid'a	Religious innovation
caliph	Deputy of the Prophet
caliphate	Islamic empire
Dar al-Harb	The house of war
Dar al-Islam	The house of peace
Dar al-Sulh	A third realm composed of non-Muslims living at peace with Islam
da'wa	Proselytizing and conversion
emir	Ruler, commander, or chief
fatwa	A ruling on a point of Islamic law given by a recognized authority
hadith	A saying attributed to the Prophet; plural, *ahadith*
hajj	Pilgrimage
ijtihad	The interpretation of Islamic scripture based on reason
imam	An Islamic leader or a position of leadership
Islamist	A Muslim who wants to see the establishment of the caliphate and sharia
jahiliya	Ignorance
jihad	Struggle, from the verb *jahada*, meaning to struggle or to exert

jihadist	One who struggles
kaafir	Infidel
Kharajites	Outsiders; seventh-century Muslims who opposed the Ummayad dynasty, claiming that they were not true Muslims
kufr	False worship
the Mahdi	Guided one
mujahid	One who fights in a jihad; plural, *mujahidin*
salaf	Pious forefathers (usually the first three generations after Muhammad)
Salafism	Movement that stresses a strict interpretation of the Quran
salat	Prayer
saum	Fasting
shahada	The profession of faith
sharia	Islamic law
shirk	Idolatry
Sufism	Movement that emphasizes inner spirituality rather than outward behavior
sunna	Religious practices established by the example of the Prophet
taghoot	A ruler who does not follow sharia
tajdid	Islamic revivalism
takfir	An accusation of apostasy
takfiri	Muslim who accuses another of apostasy
ulama	Muslim scholars
ummah	Muslim community
Wahhabis	Followers of Muhammad al-Wahhab
zakat	Alms

NOTES

PREFACE
1. Thomas Hobbes, *Leviathan* (1651). https://tinyurl.com/y7fxx3ht.

1. WHO'S THE ENEMY?
1. Arvanitopoulos, "Geopolitics of Oil."
2. Denber, "Glad to be Deceived."
3. Dunlop, *Russia Confronts Chechnya.*
4. Souleimanov, *Endless War.*
5. Brauer, "Chechens."
6. Al-Turabi et al., "Islamic State."
7. Mwangi, "Union of Islamic Courts."
8. Møller, *Somali Conflict.*
9. Kapteijns, "Test-Firing."
10. Samatar, "Open Letter to Uncle Sam."
11. Shinn, "Somalia's New Government"; Mingst and Karns, *United Nations.*
12. Sangvic, *Battle of Mogadishu.*
13. Brewer, *Yesterday and Tomorrow.*
14. Karabell, "Wrong Threat."
15. Scully, "10 Dangerous Beaches."
16. Walsh, "In the War."
17. Mosher and Gould, "How Likely?"
18. See, for example, Bergen, *Holy War, Inc.*; Kulwicki, "Practice of Honor Crimes"; Armanios, "Islamic Traditions"; Juergensmeyer, *Global Rebellion*; Juergensmeyer, *Terror in the Mind*; Stern, *Terror in the Name*; Kepel, *Jihad*; Kepel, *War for Muslim Minds*; Roy, *Globalized Islam*; Kalu et al., *Religion, History, and Politics in Nigeria*; McCormack, "African Vortex"; Bergen and Pandey, "Madrassa Myth"; Ahmed, *Jihad*; Ahmed, "Coexistence and/or Confrontation?"; Haynes, "Religious Fundamentalism and Politics"; Haynes,

"Religion and International Relations"; Haynes, *Religion and Development;* Haynes, "Conflict, Conflict Resolution and Peace-Building"; Venkatraman, "Religious Basis for Islamic Terrorism"; Pargeter, *New Frontiers of Jihad;* Selengut, *Sacred Fury;* Hegghammer, "Rise of Muslim Foreign Fighters"; Kean, *9/11 Commission Report;* Sageman, *Leaderless Jihad;* Olomojobi, *Frontiers of Jihad.*

19. Fukuyama, "Their Target." See also Ferrero, who concludes that radicalization may be an optimal reaction to perceived failure" ("Radicalization as a Reaction," 199).

20. See for example, Taylor, *Islamic Question in Middle East Politics.*

21. Ajami, "End of Pan-Arabism," offers an excellent discussion of secular nationalism and pan-Arabism in the wake of the Six Day War.

22. See, for example, Payne, *Why Nations Arm.*

23. Geaves, *Aspects of Islam.*

24. Byman, "Al-Qaeda as an Adversary."

25. Menkhaus, "Panel 2."

26. Al-Zawahiri, "Letter."

27. See, for example, Gerges, *Far Enemy.*

28. Gelvin, "Nationalism, Anarchism, Reform"; Hill, *Sufism in Northern Nigeria.*

29. Zakariya, "Concept of Islamic Education Curriculum," 102.

30. Moghadam and Fishman, *Fault Lines in Global Jihad.*

31. See, for example, Carroll, "Brussels Attack"; Watkins, "Losing Territory and Lashing Out."

32. Davis and Jenkins, *Deterrence and Influence in Counterterrorism.*

33. Clayer and Germain, *Islam in Interwar Europe.*

34. Pargeter, *New Frontiers of Jihad.*

35. Lasswell, *Politics.*

36. Schmid and Jongman, *Political Terrorism,* 3.

37. *Mujahidin* (sometimes transliterated as *mujahideen*) is plural for *mujahid,* meaning one who struggles.

38. Ahmad, *Terrorism.*

39. Dunkle, *Gladiators.*

40. Lickona, *Educating for Character.*

41. Bond, "Rio Olympics."

42. CNN, "Munich, Germany."

43. The McDonalds chosen by the Munich shooter was also located across the street from the Olympia Mall in Germany, which is located next to the stadium where Black September kidnapped and killed eleven Israeli athletes during the 1972 Olympics.

44. J. Burke, *Al-Qaeda;* Venhaus, "Why Youth Join Al-Qaeda."

45. Foucault, *History of Sexuality,* 1:31.

46. See, for example, 10News, "Sweden's Islamic Rape Epidemic." See also King, "Sweden's Rape Crisis."

47. NationMaster, "Crime > Rape Rate."
48. Rockguitarnow, "White Women Grabbed by Muslims."
49. NationMaster, "Crime > Rape Rate."
50. Lowery, "Analysis."
51. Carson, "Prisoners in 2013"; NAACP, "Criminal Justice Fact Sheet."
52. Lewis, "Why Turkey," 43.
53. Davis, *Between Jihad and Salaam.*
54. See, for example, Roy, *Failure of Political Islam.*
55. Moussalli, "Hasan al-Bannā's Islamist Discourse."
56. Bergen et al., *2014.*
57. Feldman, *Fall and Rise.*

2. THE FIRST ACT OF TERRORISM

1. Farr, "Diplomacy."
2. Angeles, "Development"; Campbell, "Leadership Succession in Early Islam."
3. Jaʿfari, *Origins.*
4. Regarding Shia Ali, see Lane, *Arabic-English Lexicon,* 1632.
5. C. M. Blanchard, *Islam.*
6. Kenney, "Rebellion."
7. Angeles, "Development of the Shia Concept."
8. Kenney, "Rebellion."
9. Angeles, "Development of the Shia Concept."
10. Furnish, "Bin Ladin."
11. Kudelin, Matrosov, and Chuprygin, "Practices of Islamic State."
12. Halm, *Shi'a Islam.*
13. Worth, "Blast Destroys Shrine in Iraq."
14. Napoleoni, *Insurgent Iraq.*
15. Roy, *Globalized Islam.*
16. Heck, *Charlemagne.*
17. Breton, *Political Extremism and Rationality.*
18. Carter and Simkins, "Market's Reaction."
19. Borgen Project, "15 World Hunger Statistics."
20. World Health Organization, "Violence against Women."
21. Global Slavery Index, "45.8 Million People Are Enslaved."

3. THE MEANING OF JIHAD

1. Gilles, *Jihad.*
2. Islam-Husain, "Mahjabeen's Musings."
3. Ali and Rehman, "Concept of Jihad."
4. Ali and Rehman, "Concept of Jihad," 331.
5. Kennedy, "Is One Person's Terrorist?"
6. Firestone, *Jihad.*
7. Guillaume, *Life of Muhammad*; Bukay, "Peace or Jihad?"

8. Makari, *Ibn Taymiyyah's Ethics.*
9. Pipes, "There Is No Moderate Islam."
10. Cook, *Understanding Jihad,* 2.
11. Zawātī, *Is Jihād a Just War?*
12. Schmid, *Routledge Handbook of Terrorism Research.*
13. Bush, "Remarks by the President."
14. Bostom, *Legacy of Jihad.*
15. Andrae, *Mohammed.*
16. Holt, Lambton, and Lewis, *Central Islamic Lands,* 44–63; Kirk, *Short History.*
17. Lappin, *Virtual Caliphate.*
18. The clans that Abu Bakr united were the Beni Asad, Beni Bakr, Beni Hanifa, Beni Kinana, Beni Saida, Beni Sulaym, and Beni Tamim.
19. See, for example, E. W. Brooks, "Arab Occupation of Crete"; Butler, *Arab Conquest of Egypt.*
20. Badr, "Islamic Law"; Badr, "Survey of Islamic International Law."
21. Al-Matroudi, *Hanbali School.*
22. Jansen, "Ibn Taymiyyah."
23. Abrahamov, "Ibn Taymiyya."
24. Firro, "Political Context."
25. Delong-Bas, *Wahhabi Islam.*
26. Farrar, "Islamism and Terror."
27. Al-Yassini, *Religion and State.*
28. C. M. Blanchard, "Islamic Traditions."
29. Algar, *Wahhabism.*
30. Maududi, *Jihad in Islam.*
31. Adams, "Mawdudi and the Islamic State"; Rahman, "Islam."
32. Nasr, "Mawdudi and the Jamaʿat-i Islami."
33. Adams, "Mawdudi and the Islamic State."
34. Nasr, "Mawdudi and the Jamaʿat-i Islami."
35. Botman, *Egypt from Independence to Revolution.*
36. Berger, *Hassan al-Banna.*
37. Krämer, *Hasan al-Banna.*
38. Farrar, "Islamism and Terror."
39. Investigative Project on Terrorism, "Muslim Brotherhood."
40. Haddad, "Sayyid Qutb."
41. Qutb, *Islam.*
42. Tripp, "Sayyid Qutb."
43. Henzel, "Origins of al Qaeda's Ideology"; Curtis, *Secret Affairs.*
44. Qutb, *Islam*; Berman, *Terror and Liberalism.*
45. Qutb, *Social Justice in Islam,* 315.
46. Musallam, "Sayyid Qutb and Social Justice."
47. Commins, "Hasan al-Banna."

48. Tripp, "Sayyid Qutb."
49. Ruthven, *Fundamentalism.*
50. Tripp, "Sayyid Qutb."
51. Kepel, *Jihad.*
52. Tripp, "Sayyid Qutb."
53. Qutb, *Social Justice in Islam*; Qutb, *Ma'alim fi-l-Tariq.*
54. Qutb, *Ma'alim fi-l-Tariq.*
55. Tripp, "Sayyid Qutb."
56. Al-Banna, *What Is Our Message?*
57. Al-Banna, *Toward the Light.*
58. Napoleoni, *Insurgent Iraq.*
59. Napoleoni, *Insurgent Iraq.*
60. Azzam, *Defence of the Muslim Lands.*
61. McGregor, "Jihad and the Rifle Alone."
62. Azzam, *Defence of the Muslim Lands. Mujahidin* (sometimes transliterated as *mujahideen*) is the plural of *mujahid*, meaning one who struggles.
63. Azzam, *Defence of the Muslim Lands.*
64. Bar, *Warrant for Terror.*
65. Azzam, *Defence of the Muslim Lands.*
66. Bergen, *Osama bin Laden I Know.*
67. Azzam, *Defence of the Muslim Lands.*
68. Sageman, *Understanding Terror Networks.*
69. Raphaeli, "Ayman Muhammad Rabi'Al-Zawahiri."
70. L. Wright, *Looming Tower.*
71. Faraj, "Neglected Duty."
72. Leiken and Brooke, "Moderate Muslim Brotherhood."
73. Zawahiri adapted the concept of *tattarus* (dressing up or shielding) to justify killing Muslims noncombatants in conflicts involving the enemies of Islam. He does not advocate killing fellow Muslims as an end in itself. See Al-Zawahiri, *Rule for Suicide-Martyr Operations*; Al-Zawahiri, *Knights under the Banner.*
74. Al-Zawahiri, *Knights under the Banner.*

4. THE CRIME OF THE CENTURY

1. MacIntyre, *Hegel.*
2. Marx, "Preface to Contribution," 328–29.
3. Marx, "Contribution to the Critique."
4. Marx, *Karl Marx, Friedrich Engels.*
5. Rolo, *Entente Cordiale.*
6. Toprani, "Oil and Grand Strategy."
7. Atwood, *Baghdad Railway.*
8. Newcombe and Greig, "Baghdad Railway."
9. McMurray, *Distant Ties.*

10. Oil reserves in the Caucasus are estimated to exceed 25 billion barrels, equivalent to those in Kuwait. See Baev, *Russia's Policies in the Caucasus*; Cohen, New "'Great Game'"; Forsythe, *Politics of Oil*.
11. Williams, "Strategic Background."
12. Hall, *Balkan Wars*.
13. White et al., "Convention respecting the Free Navigation."
14. Dahl, "Naval Innovation."
15. Corley, *History*.
16. G. Jones, "Persian Oil 1900–14"; Lambert, *Sir John Fisher's Naval Revolution*.
17. Farmanfarmaian, *Blood and Oil*.
18. Askari, "Oil-Discovery and Production."
19. Crinson, "Abadan."
20. Dahl, "Naval Innovation"; G. Jones, "Persian Oil 1900–14."
21. Stork, *Middle East Oil*; G. G. Jones, "British Government."
22. Kent, *Oil and Empire*.
23. Simon and Tejirian, *Creation of Iraq*.
24. Gökay, "Battle for Baku"; Gökay, *Politics of Caspian Oil*.
25. G. Jones, "Persian Oil 1900–14."
26. Safavi, "Nationalisation of Oil Industry."
27. Elm, *Oil, Power, and Principle*.
28. Caviggia, *British and German Logistics Support*.
29. Eichholtz, *War for Oil*.
30. Weinberg, *World at Arms*.
31. Arvanitopoulos, "Geopolitics of Oil."
32. Folly, "Soviet-German War 1942."
33. E. M. Wright, "Iran as a Gateway."
34. Tarbell, *History*.
35. Brown, *Oil, God, and Gold*.
36. Simmons, *Twilight in the Desert*.
37. Zabih, *Mossadegh Era*.
38. Cable, *Intervention at Abadan*.
39. Razwy, "Anglo-Iranian Oil Dispute."
40. Onslow, "'Battlelines for Suez.'"
41. Ebrahimi, "British Retaliation."
42. Zahrani, "Coup."
43. Gasiorowski, "1953 Coup d'État in Iran."
44. Longhurst, *Adventure in Oil*.
45. Thomas and Conant, *Trojan War*.
46. Steil, *Battle of Bretton Woods*.
47. Bialer, *Oil and the Arab-Israeli Conflict*.
48. Stoff, *Oil, War, and American Security*.
49. Fawcett, *International Relations*.
50. Savranskaya and Zubok, "Cold War in the Caucasus."

51. Powaski, *Cold War.*

52. Norman, *Oil Card.*

53. Lenin, *Imperialism.*

54. Gilpin, *Political Economy of International Relations.*

55. Harvey, *Brief History of Neoliberalism.*

56. Roberts, "New Keynesian Economics."

57. Santoni, "Employment Act of 1946."

58. Mikesell, *Bretton Woods Debates.*

59. Mundell, "Reconsideration of the Twentieth Century."

60. Aïssa and Jouini, "Structural Breaks."

61. Frieden and Lake, *International Political Economy.*

62. Irwin, "Nixon Shock after Forty Years."

63. Isard, "How Far Can We Push?"

64. Geisst, *Exchange Rate Chaos.*

65. Barsky and Kilian, "Oil and the Macroeconomy."

66. Mishkin, Gordon, and Hymans, "What Depressed the Consumer?"; Hamilton, "Historical Oil Shocks."

67. Bryan, *Great Inflation.*

68. Fisher, "I Discovered the Phillips Curve."

69. Phelps, "Phillips Curves."

70. Friedman, "Role of Monetary Policy."

71. Woolley, *Monetary Politics.*

72. Arestis and Sawyer, *Re-examining Monetary and Fiscal Policy.*

73. Arestis and Sawyer, *Re-examining Monetary and Fiscal Policy.*

74. Sowell, *Say's Law,* 4.

75. Feldstein, "Supply Side Economics."

76. Canto, Joines, and Laffer, *Foundations of Supply-Side Economics.*

77. Laffer, "Supply-Side Economics."

78. Laffer, "Laffer Curve."

79. Hemming and Kay, "Laffer Curve."

80. Knowles, "Laffer Curve Revisited."

81. Keynes, "Balance of Payments."

82. Frieden and Lake, *International Political Economy.*

83. Friedman, "Role of Monetary Policy."

84. Friedman, *Capitalism and Freedom.*

85. Friedman and Schwartz, *Monetary History.*

86. Friedman, "Monetarism."

87. O. J. Blanchard, "Reaganomics."

88. Mussa, Volcker, and Tobin, "Monetary Policy."

89. Evans and Novak, *Reagan Revolution*; Ackerman, *Reaganomics.*

90. Ellwood, "Congress Cuts the Budget."

91. Eissa, "Labor Supply."

92. Amadeo, "President Ronald Reagan's Economic Policies."

93. U.S. Department of the Treasury, "Historical Debt Outstanding."
94. Greenspan quoted in Andolfatto, "Conventional Macroeconomic Wisdom," 2.
95. Balkin, *Investing with Impact*.
96. Clinton, *Vision of Change for America*.
97. Ebert and Spielmann, "North American Free Trade Agreement."
98. Strachan, "U.S. Economy."
99. Barber, *Jihad vs. McWorld*.
100. Gingrich et al., *Contract with America*.
101. Haskins, *Work over Welfare*.
102. Woodward, *Maestro*.
103. Fleckenstein and Sheehan, *Greenspan's Bubbles*.
104. Greenspan, "Fed Didn't Cause"; S. Johnson, "Quiet Coup."
105. Duca, Muellbauer, and Murphy, "Housing Markets."
106. Mishkin, "Over the Cliff."
107. Coates, "Dire Consequences."
108. Ensign, "Banks Start Announcing Earnings"; Persinos, "3 Toxic Bank Stocks."
109. Greenspan quoted in D. Brooks, "Behavioral Revolution."

5. THE ROAD TO PERDITION
1. Parsons, *Birth of Modern Politics*.
2. Zakaria, "Rise of Illiberal Democracy."
3. Tomasi, *Free Market Fairness*.
4. Milkis, *President and the Parties*.
5. Brinkley, "Democratic Enlargement."
6. Boot, "Neocons."
7. Wolfson, "Conservatives and Neoconservatives."
8. Mayer, *Republican Party*.
9. Kissinger, *Diplomacy*.
10. U.S. Department of State, "Secretary's Meeting with Foreign Minister."
11. Kissinger quoted in Nagourney, "In Tapes, Nixon Rails."
12. Preston, "Reagan's 'New Beginning.'"
13. Cram, "'Peace, Yes.'"
14. The phrase was most likely coined by Pentagon analysts in the late 1970s. See, for example, R. H. Johnson, "Reconsiderations."
15. S. Diamond, *Roads to Dominion*.
16. Reagan, "First Inaugural Address."
17. U.S. Department of the Treasury, "Historical Debt Outstanding."
18. Carothers, "Promoting Democracy and Fighting Terror."
19. Bush, *National Security Strategy* (2002), 6, 15, 29.
20. Zakaria, "Beyond Bush," 22.
21. See, for example, Kagan, "Power and Weakness"; Leffler, "Response."
22. Offner, "Rogue President, Rogue Nation."
23. Finkelstein, "Rule of Law."

24. Liu, "Current U.S.-China Relations."
25. Huntington, "Lonely Superpower."
26. Krauthammer, "New Unilateralism."
27. Mieder, *"Yes We Can."*
28. Bush, *National Security Strategy* (2006), 23.
29. Gaddis, "Grand Strategy."
30. Reiter, "Exploring the Bargaining Model."
31. Falk, "New Bush Doctrine."
32. R. G. Carter, "Leadership at Risk."
33. D. Shah, "Conundrums of Emerging Virtuous War."
34. G. Miller, "Under Obama, an Emerging Global Apparatus."
35. Hambling, "Send in the Drones?"
36. D. Shah, "Conundrums of Emerging Virtuous War."
37. Hendrickson and Tucker, "Test of Power."
38. Akturk, "Military History"; Owen, "Democracy, Realistically."
39. Krauthammer, "Unipolar Moment."
40. Committee on the Budget, *Budgeting for War Costs.*
41. Wooley, "Bill Clinton."
42. A. Shah, "Landmines."
43. R. Paul, "Congress' Latest Billion-Dollar Boondoggle"; Office of Management and Budget, *Budget of the U.S. Government*; Blakely, "Trump Administration's FY 2018 Defense Budget."
44. Desjardins, *U.S. Military Personnel Deployments.*
45. J. Miller, "God Has Ninety-Nine Names"; Bellah, "Righteous Empire."
46. Wilhelmsen and Flikke, "Evidence of Russia's Bush Doctrine."
47. Lind, "Beyond American Hegemony."
48. Buzan, "'Global War on Terrorism'?"
49. Schanzer, "Ansar al-Islam," 41.
50. J. Stern, "Fearing Evil."
51. Etzioni, *How Patriotic Is the Patriot Act?*
52. See, for example, Thayer, "In Defense of Primacy."
53. R. G. Carter, "Leadership at Risk."
54. R. Jackson, "Security, Democracy," 150.
55. Lynch, "Volunteers Swell."
56. Thomas, "U.S. Regional Security Policy."
57. Freeman, "Democracy."
58. Falk, "New Bush Doctrine."
59. Posen, "Command of the Commons."
60. Einstein, *Ultimate Quotable Einstein*, 281.

6. THE IRAQ WARS

Epigraph: Bush quoted in C. Johnson, "Transcript."

1. Klein, "Downsizing in Disguise."

2. Kristol et al., Letter to President Bush.

3. Miller and Mylroie, *Saddam Hussein*. See also Mylroie, *Study of Revenge*; Perle, "U.S. Must Strike"; Isikoff and Corn, *Hubris*.

4. Danner, "Secret Way to War"; Risen, *State of War*.

5. Mearsheimer and Walt, "Can Saddam Be Contained?"

6. Mearsheimer and Walt, "Can Saddam Be Contained?"

7. Mearsheimer and Walt, "Can Saddam Be Contained?"

8. Stone and Hunt, *Bush Crime Family*.

9. Beaty and Gwynne, *Outlaw Bank*, 275.

10. Hershey, "President Abolishes Last Price Controls."

11. Weist, "Hinckley."

12. Phillips, *American Dynasty*.

13. Swansbrough, *Test by Fire*.

14. Phillips, *American Dynasty*.

15. Fitzgerald, "Invasion of Kuwait."

16. Yetiv, *Persian Gulf Crisis*.

17. Murdico, *Gulf War*.

18. Swansbrough, *Test by Fire*.

19. Yetiv, *Persian Gulf Crisis*.

20. Duncan, *Bush and Cheney's War*.

21. Tyler, "U.S. Strategy Plan," 8.

22. Hartung, "Military-Industrial Complex Revisited."

23. Tabb, "Mr. Bush and Neo-Liberalism."

24. Duncan, *Bush and Cheney's War*.

25. Duncan, *Bush and Cheney's War*.

26. D. Cheney, R. B. Cheney, and L. Cheney, *In My Time*.

27. R. Cheney, "Speech to Institute of Petroleum."

28. D. Cheney, R. B. Cheney, and L. Cheney, *In My Time*.

29. Morse and Jaffe, *Strategic Energy Policy*, 56, 146.

30. Purdum, *Time of Our Choosing*, 11.

31. Rice, "Campaign 2000," 48.

32. Rice, "Campaign 2000," 47.

33. Woodward, *Plan of Attack*.

34. Purdum, *Time of Our Choosing*.

35. Purdum, *Time of Our Choosing*.

36. Witkopf and Jones, *American Foreign Policy*.

37. Woodward, *Plan of Attack*.

38. Woodward, *Plan of Attack*.

39. Witkopf and Jones, *American Foreign Policy*.

40. McGeary, "Odd Man Out."

41. Purdum, *Time of Our Choosing*.

42. McGeary, "Odd Man Out."

43. Woodward, *Plan of Attack*.

44. Woodward, *Plan of Attack*.
45. J. P. Burke, "Neutral/Honest Broker Role," 236.
46. Woodward, *Plan of Attack*.
47. Renshon, "Assessing the Personality," 393.
48. Tenet and Harlow, *At the Center*.
49. Woodward, *Plan of Attack*, 25.
50. Ikenberry, "America's Imperial Ambition," 49.
51. Lobe, "Triumph of Unilateralism."
52. Woodward, *Plan of Attack*, 9, 129.
53. Dean, *Worse than Watergate*.
54. Woodward, *Plan of Attack*.
55. Woodward, *Plan of Attack*, 411.
56. Ricks, *Fiasco*.
57. Ricks, *Fiasco*.
58. Cheney, *Meet the Press*.
59. Select Committee on Intelligence, *Current and Projected National Security Threats*.
60. Woodward, *Plan of Attack*, 122.
61. Ricks, *Fiasco*, 46–7.
62. Ricks, *Fiasco*, 49–50.
63. Bush, President George Bush Discusses Iraq.
64. Purdum, *Time of Our Choosing*.
65. Woodward, *Plan of Attack*.
66. Woodward, *Plan of Attack*, 129.
67. Pelley, "George Tenet."
68. Pelley, "George Tenet."
69. Powell, "Remarks," 6.
70. Bush, *State of the Union Address*.
71. Ricks, *Fiasco*, 70.
72. Mandela quoted in Kuang and Bonk, "Preemptive War," 160.
73. See, for example, Betts, "Soft Underbelly of American Primacy."
74. Feith, *War and Decision*.
75. Bush, *National Security Strategy* 2002.
76. R. G. Carter, "Leadership at Risk," 17.
77. Hasegawa, *Racing the Enemy*.
78. Bina, "American Tragedy."
79. National Energy Policy Development Group, *Energy for America's Future*.
80. International Energy Agency, *World Energy Outlook*.
81. Arvedlund, "Iraq and Roll?"
82. Duncan and Chand, "Economics"; C. Johnson, "America's Empire of Bases."
83. Cha, "Who Benefits?"
84. Baker, "Breaking Windows"; R. J. King, "Big, Easy Money."
85. Makinson, "Outsourcing the Pentagon."

86. Tabb, "Mr. Bush and Neo-Liberalism."
87. J. Mayer, "What Did the Vice-President Do?"
88. D. Cheney, R. B. Cheney, and L. Cheney, *In My Time*.
89. Blackwill, "India Imperative," 9.
90. Merritt, "Use of War to Profit."
91. Cooling, "Military-Industrial Complex."
92. Obama quoted in Goldberg, "Obama Doctrine," 53.
93. Biden, "Iraq," 1.
94. Bush, *National Security Strategy* (2006).
95. Truman, "Radio Address."
96. Bergen and Cruickshank, "Al-Qaeda."
97. Bar and Minzili, "Zawahiri Letter"
98. Cha, "Who Benefits?"

7. FROM BIN LADEN TO BAGHDADI

1. Gerges, *Far Enemy*.
2. Sageman, *Understanding Terror Networks*.
3. McCants, *ISIS Apocalypse*.
4. Al-Zawahiri, *Knights under the Banner*.
5. Cullison, "Inside Al-Qaeda's Hard Drive."
6. Bush, "Address to a Joint Session."
7. Frum and Perle, *End to Evil*.
8. Posen, "Struggle against Terrorism."
9. Bin Laden, "Letter to America."
10. Anonymous, "Washington's Approach to Terrorism."
11. Carter, Deutch, and Zelikow, "Catastrophic Terrorism."
12. Cullison, "Inside Al-Qaeda's Hard Drive."
13. Cordesman and Burke, "Islamic Extremism."
14. C. Miller, "Saudi Arabia."
15. Atwan, *Secret History of Al Qaeda*.
16. It does fit the Islamic State's strategy, however, as the group's frequent targeting of Muslims demonstrates (see next section).
17. Quiggin, "Understanding al-Qaeda's Ideology."
18. Kilcullen, *Accidental Guerrilla*.
19. Kepel, *War for Muslim Minds*; L. Wright, *Looming Tower*.
20. Teslik, "Profile."
21. L. Smith, "Timeline."
22. Napoleoni, *Insurgent Iraq*.
23. Fishman, "After Zarqawi."
24. Shia Muslims observe practices that are considered *bid'a* (innovation); therefore, Zarqawi considered them all to be apostates.
25. It is also possible that Zarqawi and bin Laden first met in Kandahar. See Fishman, "After Zarqawi"; Teslik, "Profile."

26. Fishman, "After Zarqawi."
27. Bradley, *Saudi Arabia Exposed*. See also Fishman ("After Zarqawi"), who refers to Abu Hamzah al-Baghdadi, chief of Zarqawi's sharia committee, and the book he posted online reiterating Zarqawi's views, "Why Do We Fight, and Whom Do We Fight?"
28. Allawi, *Occupation of Iraq*.
29. Kaplan, *Insurgents*, 77.
30. M. Lynch, "Explaining the Awakening."
31. Weiss and Hassan, *ISIS*.
32. Gunter, "Iraq, Syria, ISIS."
33. For example, the group released video footage of the beheading of Americans Jack Hensley and Eugene Armstrong and a British citizen, Ken Bigley.
34. Al-Zawahiri, Letter from al-Zawahiri to al-Zarqawi.
35. Caldwell, "U.S. Identifies Successor to Zarqawi."
36. Fishman, "After Zarqawi."
37. Gunter, "Iraq, Syria, ISIS."
38. Al-Zawahiri, *General Guidelines for Jihad*.
39. McCants, *ISIS Apocalypse*.
40. Gunter, "Iraq, Syria, ISIS."
41. Chulov, "ISIS."
42. Furnish, "Beheading."
43. Gambhir, "Dabiq."
44. McCants, *ISIS Apocalypse*.
45. Al-Iʿtisam of the Koran and Sunnah [Sudan]-1 Aug. 2014, Abu Sayyaf Group [Philippines]-25 Jun. 2014, Ansar al-Khilafah [Philippines]-14 Aug. 2014, Ansar al-Tawhid in India [India]-4 Oct. 2014, Bangsamoro Islamic Freedom Fighters (BIFF) [Philippines]-13 Aug. 2014, Bangsmoro Justice Movement (BJM) [Philippines]-11 Sep. 2014, Jemaah Islamiyah [Philippines] 27 Apr. 2015, al-Huda Battalion in Maghreb of Islam [Algeria]-30 Jun. 2014, The Soldiers of the Caliphate in Algeria [Algeria]-30 Sep. 2014, al-Ghurabaa [Algeria]-7 Jul. 2015, Djamaat Houmat ad-Daʿwa as-Salafiya (DHDS) [Algeria] 19 Sep. 2015, al-Ansar Battalion [Algeria] 4 Sep. 2015, Jundullah [Pakistan]-17 Nov. 2014, Islamic Movement of Uzbekistan (IMU) [Pakistan/Uzbekistan]-31 Jul. 2015, Tehreek-e-Khilafat [Pakistan]-9 Jul. 2014, Leaders of the Mujahid in Khorasan [Pakistan]-10 Jan. 2015, Islamic Youth Shura Council [Libya]-22 Jun. 2014, Jaish al-Sahabah in the Levant [Syria]-1 Jul. 2014, Martyrs of al-Yarmouk Brigade [Syria]-Dec. 2014, Faction of Katibat al-Imam Bukhari [Syria]-29 Oct. 2014, Jamaat Ansar Bait al-Maqdis [Egypt]-30 Jun. 2014, Jund al-Khilafah in Egypt [Egypt]-23 Sep. 2014, Liwa Ahrar al-Sunna in Baalbek [Lebanon]-30 Jun. 2014, Islamic State Libya (Darnah) [Libya]-9 Nov. 2014, Lions of Libya [Libya]-24 Sep. 2014, Shura Council of Shabab al-Islam Darnah [Libya]-6 Oct. 2014, Jemaah Anshorut Tauhid (JAT) [Indonesia]-Aug. 2014, Mujahidin Indonesia Timor (MIT) [Indonesia]-1 Jul. 2014, Mujahidin

Shura Council in the Environs of Jerusalem (MSCJ) [Egypt]-1 Oct. 2014, Okba Ibn Nafaa Battalion [Tunisia]-20 Sep. 2014, Jund al-Khilafah in Tunisia [Tunisia]-31 Mar. 2015, Central Sector of Kabardino-Balakria of the Caucasus Emirate (CE) [Russia]-26 Apr. 2015, Mujahidin of Tunisia of Kairouan [Tunisia] 18 May 2015, Mujahidin of Yemen [Yemen]-10 Nov. 2014, Supporters for the Islamic State in Yemen [Yemen]-4 Sep. 2014, al-Tawheed Brigade in Khorasan [Afghanistan]-23 Sep. 2014, Heroes of Islam Brigade in Khorasan [Afghanistan]-30 Sep. 2014, Supporters of the Islamic State in the Land of the Two Holy Mosques [Saudi Arabia]-2 Dec. 2014, Ansar al-Islam [Iraq]-8 Jan. 2015, Boko Haram [Nigeria]-7 Mar. 2015, The Nokhchico Wilayat of the Caucasus Emirate (CE) [Russia]-15 Jun. 2015, al-Ansar Battalion [Algeria]-4 Sep. 2015, al-Shabaab Jubba Region Cell Bashir Abu Numan [Somalia]-7 Dec. 2015. IntelCenter, "Islamic State's 43 Global Affiliates."

46. Kadercan, "Making Sense."

8. UTTER CONFUSION

1. Disaster Center, "New York Crime Rates."
2. Fromkin, "Strategy of Terrorism," 697.
3. Aron, "Evolution of Modern Strategic Thought," 25.
4. Centers for Disease Control and Prevention, "2014–2016 Ebola Outbreak."
5. Parpia et al., "Effects of Response."
6. Lombardo, "How Many People Die."
7. Brady Campaign to Prevent Gun Violence, "Key Gun Violence Statistics."
8. IntelCenter, "Islamic State's 43 Global Affiliates."
9. Attackers killed a priest in Saint-Étienne-du-Rouvray, France, on July 26, 2016.
10. See, for example, McCants, "Why Did ISIS Attack Paris?"
11. Chaliand and Blin, *History of Terrorism*.

9. NAVIGATING THE DELUGE

1. Tzu, *Art of War*, 73.
2. Waltz, *Theory of International Relations*.
3. Liddell Hart, *Strategy*, 366.
4. Dandeker and Gow, "Future of Peace Support Operations."
5. Etzioni, "COIN."
6. Stockman, "Obama, U.S. Viewed Less Favorably."
7. See, for example, Beg, "Ideological Battle."
8. Bush, "Address to a Joint Session."
9. Sorkin, "Donald Trump."
10. Donald Trump, "There's Nothing Wrong with America's Foreign Defense Policy That a Little Backbone Can't Cure," advertisement in the *New York Times*, September 2, 1987.
11. A. Smith, "Donald Trump Mocks Hillary Clinton."
12. Trump, "Donald J. Trump Statement."

13. Kemp, "Donald Trump Gets Tough."
14. NAACP, "Criminal Justice Fact Sheet."
15. Pianin, "Obama Administration."
16. Kliff, "Trump."
17. Drutman, "Kochs Are Retreating."
18. Cordesman and Hashim, *Iran*.
19. Lewis, "Time for Toppling."
20. Metzl, Review, 565.

10. A CULTURAL COMPASS

1. Turner, "On Structure and Entropy."
2. Gibbs, "Norms."
3. Benhabib, *Claims of Culture*.
4. P. V. Paul, "Mythical Average."

11. THE COLORS OF CONFLICT

1. See, for example, Creighton, "Revisiting Shame and Guilt Cultures"; Liem, "Shame and Guilt"; Fung, "Becoming a Moral Child."
2. Müller, *Honor and Shame*.
3. Flanagan, "Hierarchy in Simple "Egalitarian" Societies."
4. Jaʿfari, *Origins and Early Development*.
5. S. M. Stern, "ʿAbd Al-Jabbār's Account."
6. M. Gaddis, *There Is No Crime*.
7. Ferguson, "Tertullian"; Witte, *Reformation of Rights*.
8. Murphy, *Rhetoric in the Middle Ages*.
9. Genesis 4:4–5.
10. Davies, "Inheritance of the First-Born."
11. Gelfand, *Syria*.
12. Picard, "Arab Military in Politics."
13. Wieland, *Syria*.
14. Isaiah 17:1.

12. THE DEFINITION OF INSANITY

1. See, for example, 1 Kings 5:4.
2. Catherwood, *Churchill's Folly*.
3. Betts, "Should Strategic Studies Survive?," 8.
4. Anderson, "What to Do."
5. Eland, *No War for Oil*.
6. Catherwood, *Churchill's Folly*.
7. Engler, *Politics of Oil*.

BIBLIOGRAPHY

Abrahamov, B. "Ibn Taymiyya on the Agreement of Reason with Tradition1." *Muslim World* 82, no. 3–4 (1992): 256–72.

Ackerman, F. *Reaganomics: Rhetoric vs. Reality*. Boston: South End Press, 1982.

Adams, C. J. "Mawdudi and the Islamic State." In *Voices of Resurgent Islam*, edited by John L. Esposito, 99–133. New York: Oxford University Press, 1983.

Ahmad, E. *Terrorism: Theirs and Ours*. New York: Seven Stories Press. 2011.

Ahmed, H. "Coexistence and/or Confrontation? Towards a Reappraisal of Christian-Muslim Encounter in Contemporary Ethiopia." *Journal of Religion in Africa* 36, no. 1 (2006): 4–22.

Aïssa, M. S. B., and J. Jouini. "Structural Breaks in the US inflation Process." *Applied Economics Letters* 10, no. 10 (2003): 633–36.

Ajami, F. "The End of Pan-Arabism." *Foreign Affairs* 57, no. 2 (Winter 1978–79): 355–73. https://www.foreignaffairs.com/articles/yemen/1978-12-01/end-pan-arabism.

Akturk, S. "A Military History of the New World Order and the Emergence of the U.S. Hegemony." *Alternatives: Turkish Journal of International Relations* 5, no. 1–2 (2006): 65–72.

Al-Banna, H. *Toward the Light: The Five Tracts of Hassan al-Banna*. Cambridge: Cambridge University Press, 1978.

——— . *What Is Our Message?* Oneonta NY: Islamic Publications. 1974.

Algar, H. *Wahhabism: A Critical Essay*. Oneonta NY: Islamic Publications, 2002.

Ali, S. S., and J. Rehman. "The Concept of Jihad in Islamic International Law." *Journal of Conflict and Security Law* 10, no. 3 (2005): 321–43.

Allawi, A.A. *The Occupation of Iraq: Winning the War, Losing the Peace*. New Haven CT: Yale University Press. 2008.

Al-Matroudi, A. H. I. *The Hanbali School of Law and Ibn Taymiyyah: Conflict or Conciliation*. New York: Routledge. 2006.

Al-Turabi, H., Z. Sardar, M. Jamal, and M. Zuber. "The Islamic State." In *Voices of Resurgent Islam*, edited by John L. Esposito, 241–51. New York: Oxford University Press, 1983.

Al-Yassini, A. *Religion and State in the Kingdom of Saudi Arabia*. Boulder CO: Westview Press. 1985.

Al-Zawahiri, A. *General Guidelines for Jihad*. Intelligence Group. 2013. http://www.talibeilm.net/uploads/4/7/1/3/4713847/general_guidelines_for_jihad.pdf .

———. *Knights under the Banner of the Prophet*. London: Al-Sharq al-Awsat, 2001. https://azelin.files.wordpress.com/2010/11/6759609-knights-under-the-prophet-banner.pdf.

———. "Knights under the Prophet's Banner." In *The Theory and Practice of Islamic Terrorism: An Anthology*, edited by Marvin Perry and Howard E. Negrin, 49–57. New York: Palgrave Macmillan. 2008.

———. Letter from al-Zawahiri to al-Zarqawi. 2005. https://ctc.usma.edu/posts/zawahiris-letter-to-zarqawi-english-translation-2.

———. *Statement of Ayman al-Zawahiri to the American People*. BBC News, "Profile: Ayman al-Zawahiri," August 13, 2015. http://www.bbc.com/news/world-middle-east-13789286.

Amadeo, K. "President Ronald Reagan's Economic Policies: How Reagan Ended the 1980s Recession." The Balance. May 10, 2017. https://www.thebalance.com/president-ronald-reagan-s-economic-policies-3305568.

Amanat, A. "Empowered through Violence: The Reinventing of Islamic Extremism." In *The Age of Terror: America and the World after September 11*, edited by Strobe Talbott and Nayan Chanda, 23–52. New York: Basic Books; New Haven CT: Yale Center for the Study of Globalization, 2001.

Anderson, K. "What to Do with Bin Laden and Al Qaeda Terrorists: A Qualified Defense of Military Commissions and United States Policy on Detainees at Guantanamo Bay Naval Base." *Harvard Journal of Law and Public Policy* 25, no. 2 (Spring 2002): 593–634.

Andolfatto, D. "Conventional Macroeconomic Wisdom: A Caveat." 2005. http://www.sfu.ca/~dandolfa/wisdom.pdf.

Andrae, T. *Mohammed: The Man and His Faith*. Mineola NY: Dover, 2000.

Angeles, V. S. "The Development of the Shia Concept of the Imamate." *Asian Studies* 21 (1983): 145–60.

Anonymous. "Washington's Approach to Terrorism and Weapons of Mass Destruction: An Evaluation of U.S. Foreign Policy and Its Implications." December, 5, 2003. http://web.stanford.edu/class/e297a/Washington's%20Approach%20to%20Terrorism%20and%20Weapons%20of%20Mass%20Destruction.doc.

Arestis, P., and M. Sawyer. *Re-examining Monetary and Fiscal Policy for the 21st Century*. Northampton MA: Edward Elgar, 2004.

Armanios, F. "The Islamic Traditions of Wahhabism and Salafiyya." CRS Report for Congress. December 22, 2003. https://digital.library.unt.edu/ark:/67531/metacrs5273/m1/1/high_res_d/RS21695_2003Dec22.pdf.

Aron, R. "The Evolution of Modern Strategic Thought." In *Problems of Modern Strategy*, 25. London: Institute of Strategic Studies by Praeger, 1970.

Arvanitopoulos, C. "The Geopolitics of Oil in Central Asia." *Journal of Modern Hellenism* 15 (1998): 67–90.

Arvedlund, E. "Iraq and Roll? Lukoil's Disputed Contract Could Be a Cheap Call on Post-Saddam Oil Business." *Barron's*, June 9, 2003. https://www.barrons .com/articles/SB105494444326665900. June 9, 2003.

Askari, H. "Oil-Discovery and Production in the Persian Gulf (1900–1945)." In *Collaborative Colonialism: The Political Economy of Oil in the Persian Gulf*, 27–55. New York: Palgrave Macmillan, 2013.

Atwan, A. B. *The Secret History of al Qaeda*. Berkeley: University of California Press. 2006.

Atwood, V. H. "The Baghdad Railway." Master's thesis, University of Texas at Austin, 2013. http://hdl.handle.net/2152/22585.

Azzam, S. A. *Defence of the Muslim Lands*. Allentown PA: Maktabah, 2002.

Badr, G. M. "Islamic Law: Its Relation to Other Legal Systems." *American Journal of Comparative Law* 26 (1977): 187.

——— . "A Survey of Islamic International Law." In *Proceedings of the Annual Meeting American Society of International Law* 76 (1982 annual): 56–61.

Baev, P. *Russia's Policies in the Caucasus*. Washington DC: Brookings Institution Press, 1997.

Baker, R. W. "Breaking Windows: In the Neighborhood and in Iraq." *International Journal of Contemporary Iraqi Studies* 9, no. 2 (2015): 83–104.

Balkin, J. *Investing with Impact: Why Finance Is a Force for Good*. New York: Routledge, 2016.

Bar, S. *Warrant for Terror: The Fatwas of Radical Islam and the Duty to Jihad*. Lanham MD: Rowman & Littlefield, 2006.

Bar, S., and Y. Minzili. "The Zawahiri Letter and the Strategy of Al-Qaeda." *Current Trends in Islamist Ideology* 3, no. 38 (2006): 38–51.

Barber, B. R. *Jihad vs. McWorld*. New York: Random House. 1996.

Barsky, R. B., and L. Kilian. "Oil and the Macroeconomy since the 1970s." *Journal of Economic Perspectives* 18, no. 4 (2004): 115–34.

Beaty, J., and S. C. Gwynne. *The Outlaw Bank: A Wild Ride into the Secret Heart of BCCI*. Philadelphia: Beard Books. 2004.

Beg, S. "The Ideological Battle: Insight from Pakistan." *Perspectives on Terrorism* 2, no. 10 (2010). http://www.terrorismanalysts.com/pt/index.php/pot /article/view/52/html.

Bellah, R. N. "Righteous Empire: Imperialism, American-Style." *Christian Century* 120, no. 5 (March 8, 2003): 20–25.

Benhabib, S. *The Claims of Culture: Equality and Diversity in the Global Era*. Princeton NJ: Princeton University Press. 2002.

Bergen, P. *Holy War, Inc.: Inside the Secret World of Osama bin Laden*. New York: Simon & Schuster. 2002.

———. *The Osama bin Laden I Know: An Oral History of al Qaeda's Leader.* New York: Simon & Schuster. 2006.

Bergen, P., and P. Cruickshank. "Al-Qaeda: Self-Fulfilling Prophecy." *Mother Jones,* October 18, 2007. http://www.motherjones.com/politics/2007/10/al-qaeda-self-fulfilling-prophecy/.

Bergen, P., and S. Pandey. "The Madrassa Myth." *New York Times,* June 14, 2005. http://www.nytimes.com/2005/06/14/opinion/14bergen.html.

Bergen, P., E. Schneider, D. Sterman, B. Cahall, and T. Maurer. *2014: Jihadist Terrorism and Other Unconventional Threats.* Bipartisan Policy Center. September 2014. http://bipartisanpolicy.org/wp-content/uploads/sites/default/files/BPC%20HSP%202014%20Jihadist%20Terrorism%20and%20Other%20Unconventional%20Threats%20September%202014.pdf.

Berger, L. G. "Hassan al-Banna." In *Cultural Sociology of the Middle East,* edited by A. Stanton, vol. 1 of *Cultural Sociology of the Middle East, Asia, & Africa: An Encyclopedia,* edited by A. Stanton, E. Ramsamy, and P. Seybolt. Thousand Oaks CA: Sage, 2012. http://eprints.whiterose.ac.uk/76395/.

Berman, P. *Terror and Liberalism.* New York: W. W. Norton. 2003.

Betts, R. K. "Should Strategic Studies Survive?" *World Politics* 50, no. 1 (1997): 7–33.

———. "The Soft Underbelly of American Primacy: Tactical Advantages of Terror." In *Terrorism and Counterterrorism: Understanding the New Security Environment,* 2nd ed., edited by Russell D. Howard and Reid L. Sawyer, 386–401. Dubuque IA: McGraw-Hill, 2006.

Bialer, U. *Oil and the Arab-Israeli Conflict, 1948–63.* London: Palgrave Macmillan. 1999.

Biden, J. "Iraq: A Way Forward." May 1, 2006. http://www.timothyhorrigan.com/documents/iraq_a_way_forward.pdf.

Bina, C. "The American Tragedy: The Quagmire of War, Rhetoric of Oil, and the Conundrum of Hegemony." *Journal of Iranian Research and Analysis* 20, no. 2 (2004): 7–22.

Bin Laden, O. "Bin Laden's Letter to America." *The Guardian,* November 24, 2002. https://www.theguardian.com/world/2002/nov/24/theobserver.

———. "Text of Fatwa Urging Jihad against Americans." February 23, 1998. https://www.investigativeproject.org/documents/case_docs/Boyd_Ex47.pdf.

Blackwill, R. D. "The India Imperative: A Conversation with Robert D. Blackwill." *National Interest,* no. 80 (Summer 2005): 9–17.

Blakeley, K. "The Trump Administration's FY 2018 Defense Budget in Context." Center for Strategic and Budgetary Assessments. August 3, 2017. http://csbaonline.org/reports/the-trump-administrations-fy-2018-defense-budget-in-context.

Blanchard, C. M. "Islam: Sunnis and Shiites." Congressional Research Service. January 28, 2009. https://fas.org/irp/crs/RS21745.pdf.

———. "The Islamic Traditions of Wahhabism and Salafiyya." CRS Report for Congress. January 24, 2007. https://fas.org/sgp/crs/misc/RS21695.pdf.

Blanchard, O. J. "Reaganomics." *Economic Policy* 2, no. 5 (1987): 15–56.

Boot, M. "Neocons." *Foreign Policy* (2004): 20–28.

Bond, A. "Rio Olympics: ISIS Terror Cell Arrested over Plot to Launch Large Scale Attack at Games." *The Mirror*, July 21, 2016. http://www.mirror.co .uk/news/world-news/rio-olympics-isis-terror-cell-8465656.

The Borgen Project. "15 World Hunger Statistics." 2017. https://borgenproject .org/15-world-hunger-statistics/.

Bostom, A. G., ed. *The Legacy of Jihad: Islamic Holy War and the Fate of Non-Muslims.* Amherst NY: Prometheus Books, 2005.

Botman, S. *Egypt from Independence to Revolution, 1919–1952.* Syracuse NY: Syracuse University Press, 1991.

Bradley, J. R. *Saudi Arabia Exposed: Inside a Kingdom in Crisis.* New York: Palgrave Macmillan, 2005.

Brady Campaign to Prevent Gun Violence. "Key Gun Violence Statistics." https:// www.bradycampaign.org/key-gun-violence-statistics.

Brauer, B. "Chechens and the Survival of Their Cultural Identity in Exile." *Journal of Genocide Research* 4, no. 3 (2002): 387–400.

Breton, A., ed., *Political Extremism and Rationality.* New York: Cambridge University Press, 2002.

Brewer, W. D. "Yesterday and Tomorrow in the Persian Gulf." *Middle East Journal* 23, no. 2 (1969): 149–58.

Brinkley, D. "Democratic Enlargement: The Clinton Doctrine." *Foreign Policy*, no. 106 (1997): 111–27.

Brooks, D. "The Behavioral Revolution." *New York Times*, October 27, 2008, A23.

Brooks, E. W. "The Arab Occupation of Crete." *English Historical Review* 28, no. 111 (1913): 431–43.

Brown, A. C. *Oil, God, and Gold: The Story of Aramco and the Saudi Kings.* New York: Houghton Mifflin, 1999.

Bryan, M. *The Great Inflation 1965–1982.* November 22, 2013. https://www .federalreservehistory.org/essays/great_inflation.

Bukay, D. "Peace or Jihad? Abrogation in Islam." *Middle East Quarterly* (Fall 2007): 3–11.

Burke, J. *Al-Qaeda: The True Story of Radical Islam.* New York: IB Tauris, 2004.

Burke, J. P. "The Neutral/Honest Broker Role in Foreign Policy Decision Making: A Reassessment." *Presidential Studies Quarterly* 35, no. 2 (2005): 229–58.

Bush, G. W. "Address to a Joint Session of Congress and the American People." *Harvard. Journal of Law and Public Policy*, no. 25 (2001): xviii.

———. *The National Security Strategy of the United States of America, September 2002.* Washington DC: Executive Office of the President, 2002. https://www .state.gov/documents/organization/63562.pdf.

———. *The National Security Strategy of the United States of America, March 2006.* Washington DC: Executive Office of the President, 2006. http:// goodbadstrategy.com/wp-content/downloads/NSS2006.pdf.

————. President George Bush Discusses Iraq in National Press Conference. March 6, 2003. https://georgewbush-whitehouse.archives.gov/news/releases/2003/03/20030306-8.html.

————. President's Remarks at National Day of Prayer and Remembrance. September 14, 2001.https://georgewbush-whitehouse.archives.gov/news/releases/2001/09/20010914-2.html.

————. "Remarks by the President in Photo Opportunity with the National Security Team." September 12, 2001. https://2001-2009.state.gov/coalition/cr/rm/2001/5042.htm.

————. *State of the Union Address.* January 28, 2003. https://georgewbush-whitehouse.archives.gov/news/releases/2002/01/20020129-11.html.

Butler, A. J. *The Arab Conquest of Egypt and the Last Thirty Years of the Roman Dominion.* Oxford: Clarendon Press, 1902.

Buzan, B. "Will the 'Global War on Terrorism' Be the New Cold War?" *International Affairs* 82, no. 6 (2006): 1101–18.

Byman, D. L. "Al-Qaeda as an Adversary: Do We Understand Our Enemy?" *World Politics* 56, no. 1 (2003): 139–63.

Cable, J. *Intervention at Abadan: Plan Buccaneer.* New York: St. Martin's Press, 1991.

Caldwell, W. "U.S. Identifies Successor to Zarqawi." *New York Times,* June 15, 2006.

Campbell, R. A. "Leadership Succession in Early Islam: Exploring the Nature and Role of Historical Precedents." *Leadership Quarterly* 19, no. 4 (2008): 426–38.

Canto, V. A., D. H. Joines, and A. B. Laffer. *Foundations of Supply-Side Economics: Theory and Evidence.* New York: Academic Press, 2014.

Carothers, T. "Promoting Democracy and Fighting Terror," *Foreign Affairs* 82, no. 1 (January/February 2003): 84–97. https://www.foreignaffairs.com/articles/2003-01-01/promoting-democracy-and-fighting-terror.

Carroll, J. "Brussels Attack: Islamic State Is Moving the Battle and Australia Must Be Prepared." March 23, 2016. http://www.abc.net.au/news/2016–03–23/carroll-australia-must-prepare-itself-for-brussels-style-attacks/7269440.

Carson, E. A. "Prisoners in 2013." U.S. Department of Justice. September 30, 2014. https://www.bjs.gov/content/pub/pdf/p13.pdf.

Carter, A., J. Deutch, and P. Zelikow. "Catastrophic Terrorism: Tackling the New Danger." *Foreign Affairs* 77, no. 6 (November/December 1998): 80–94. https://www.foreignaffairs.com/articles/united-states/1998-11-01/catastrophic-terrorism-tackling-new-danger.

Carter, D. A., and B. J. Simkins. "The Market's Reaction to Unexpected, Catastrophic Events: The Case of Airline Stock Returns and the September 11th Attacks." *Quarterly Review of Economics and Finance* 44, no. 4 (2004): 539–58.

Carter, R. G. "Leadership at Risk: The Perils of Unilateralism." *PS: Political Science & Politics* 36, no. 1 (2003): 17–22.

Catherwood, C. *Churchill's Folly: How Winston Churchill Created Modern Iraq.* New York: Basic Books, 2005.

Caviggia, J. D. *British and German Logistics Support during the World War 2 North African Campaign*. Carlisle Barracks PA: Army War College 1990. http://www.dtic.mil/dtic/tr/fulltext/u2/a220715.pdf.

Centers for Disease Control and Prevention. "2014–2016 Ebola Outbreak in West Africa." 2016. https://www.cdc.gov/vhf/ebola/outbreaks/2014-west-africa/index.html.

Cha, A. E. "Who Benefits? $1.9 Billion of Iraq's Money Goes to US Contractor." *Washington Post*, national weekly ed., August 9–15, 2004.

Chaliand, G., and A. Blin. *The History of Terrorism: From Antiquity to al Qaeda*. Berkeley: University of California Press, 2007.

Cheney, D. "Meet the Press." *NBC*, September 14, 2002. https://www.nbcnews.com/id/3080244/ns/meet_the_press/t/transcript-sept/#/Wmm6WKiWblU.

Cheney, D., R. B. Cheney, and L. Cheney. *In My Time: A Personal and Political Memoir*. New York: Simon & Schuster, 2011.

Cheney, R. "Speech to Institute of Petroleum." London Institute of Petroleum, 1999. http://www.resilience.org/stories/2004-06-08/full-text-dick-cheneys-speech-institute-petroleum-autumn-lunch-1999/.

Chulov, M. "ISIS: The Inside Story." *The Guardian*, December 11, 2014. https://www.theguardian.com/world/2014/dec/11/-sp-isis-the-inside-story.

Clayer, N., and E. Germain, eds. *Islam in Interwar Europe*. New York: Columbia University Press, 2008.

Clinton, W. J. *A Vision of Change for America*. Washington DC: Executive Office of the President, Office of Management and Budget, 1993.

CNN. "Munich, Germany: Allahu Akbar Gunman Shoots Several People Dead (Situation Ongoing)." *CNN*. July 22, 2016. https://www.youtube.com/watch?v=r_mtoB-DdSY.

Coates, D. "Dire Consequences: The Conservative Recapture of America's Political Narrative?" *Cambridge Journal of Economics* 36, no. 1 (2012): 145–53.

Cohen, A. "The New 'Great Game': Oil Politics in the Caucasus and Central Asia." Heritage Foundation. 1996. http://www.heritage.org/europe/report/the-new-great-game-oil-politics-the-caucasus-and-central-asia.

Commins, D. "Hasan al-Banna (1906–1949)." In *Pioneers of Islamic Revival*, edited by Ali Rahnema, 125–53. London: Zed Books, 2008.

Committee on the Budget. *Budgeting for War Costs: Hearing before the Committee on the Budget*. House of Representatives, 110th Congress, First Session, January 18, 2007. Washington DC: US Government Printing Office. 2007

Cook, D. *Understanding Jihad*. Berkeley: University of California Press, 2015.

Cooling, B. F. "The Military-Industrial Complex." In *A Companion to American Military History*, edited by James C. Bradford, 2:966–89. Oxford: Wiley-Blackwell, 2010.

Cordesman, A. H., and A. A. Burke. "Islamic Extremism in Saudi Arabia and the Attack on Al Khobar." Washington DC: Center for Strategic and International

Studies, June 2001. https://csis-prod.s3.amazonaws.com/s3fs-public/legacy _files/files/media/csis/pubs/saudi_alkhobar.pdf.

Cordesman, A. H., and A. Hashim. *Iran: Dilemmas of Dual Containment*. Boulder CO: Westview Press, 1997.

Corley, T. A. B. *A History of the Burmah Oil Company: 1924–66*. Vol. 2. London: Heinemann, 1988.

Cram, T. J. "'Peace, Yes, but World Freedom as Well': Principle, Pragmatism, and the End of the Cold War." *Western Journal of Communication* 79, no. 3 (2015): 367–86.

Creighton, M. R. "Revisiting Shame and Guilt Cultures: A Forty-Year Pilgrimage." *Ethos* 18, no. 3 (1990): 279–307.

Crinson, M. "Abadan: Planning and Architecture under the Anglo-Iranian Oil Company." *Planning Perspectives* 12, no. 3 (1997): 341–59.

Cullison, A. "Inside Al-Qaeda's Hard Drive." *Atlantic Monthly* 294, no. 2 (2004): 55–65.

Curtis, M. *Secret Affairs: Britain's Collusion with Radical Islam*. London: Serpent's Tail, 2010.

Dahl, E. J. "Naval Innovation: From Coal to Oil." *JFQ: Joint Force Quarterly* 27 (Winter 2000-2001): 50–56.

Dandeker, C., and J. Gow. "The Future of Peace Support Operations: Strategic Peacekeeping and Success." *Armed Forces & Society* 23, no. 3 (1997): 327–47.

Danner, M. "The Secret Way to War." *New York Review of Books* 52, no. 10 (2005): 9.

Davis, J. *Between Jihad and Salaam: Profiles in Islam*. New York: St. Martin's Press, 1997.

Davis, P. K., and B. M. Jenkins. *Deterrence and Influence in Counterterrorism: A Component in the War on al Qaeda*. Santa Monica: Rand Corporation, 2002.

Davies, E. W. "The Inheritance of the First-Born in Israel and the Ancient Near East." *Journal of Semitic Studies* 38, no. 2 (1993): 175.

Dean, J. W. *Worse than Watergate: The Secret Presidency of George W. Bush*. New York: Little, Brown, 2004.

Delong-Bas, N. J. *Wahhabi Islam: From Revival and Reform to Global Jihad*. New York: Oxford University Press, 2008.

Denber, R. "'Glad to Be Deceived': The International Community and Chechnya." Human Rights Watch World Report, 2004. http://pantheon.hrw.org/legacy /wr2k4/7.htm.

Desjardins, J. *U.S. Military Personnel Deployments by Country*. March 18, 2017. http://www.visualcapitalist.com/u-s-military-personnel-deployments -country/.

Diamond, L. J., M. F. Plattner, and D. Brumberg, eds. *Islam and Democracy in the Middle East*. Baltimore: Johns Hopkins University Press, 2003.

Diamond, S. *Roads to Dominion: Right-Wing Movements and Political Power in the United States*. New York: Guilford Press, 1995.

Disaster Center. "New York Crime Rates 1960–2015." 2015. http://www .disastercenter.com/crime/nycrime.htm.

Drutman, L. "The Kochs Are Retreating from National Elections: Here's What We Should Learn." Vox. May 16, 2016. https://www.vox.com/polyarchy/2016/5/16/11685584/koch-brothers-election-money.

Duca, J. V., J. Muellbauer, and A. Murphy. "Housing Markets and the Financial Crisis of 2007–2009: Lessons for the Future." *Journal of Financial Stability* 6, no. 4 (2010): 203–17.

Duncan, H. *Bush and Cheney's War: A War without Justification.* Victoria BC: Trafford, 2006.

Duncan, R., and S. Chand. "The Economics of the 'Arc of Instability.'" *Asian-Pacific Economic Literature* 16, no. 1 (2002): 1–9.

Dunkle, R. *Gladiators: Violence and Spectacle in Ancient Rome.* New York: Routledge, 2013.

Dunlop, J. B. *Russia Confronts Chechnya: Roots of a Separatist Conflict.* New York: Cambridge University Press, 1998.

Ebert, M., and S. B. Spielmann. "The North American Free Trade Agreement (NAFTA): A Summary of Its Major Provisions." *European Business Journal* 6, no. 1 (1994): 25.

Ebrahimi, M. "British Retaliation after the Nationalisation of Iran's Oil." In *The British Role in Iranian Domestic Politics (1951–1953)*, 15–34. New York: Springer International, 2016.

Eichholtz, D. *War for Oil: The Nazi Quest for an Oil Empire.* Washington DC: Potomac Books, 2012.

Einstein, A. *The Ultimate Quotable Einstein.* Princeton NJ: Princeton University Press, 2010.

Eissa, N. "Labor Supply and the Economic Recovery Tax Act of 1981." In *Empirical Foundations of Household Taxation*, edited by Martin Feldstein and James M. Poterba, 5–38. Chicago: University of Chicago Press, 1996.

Eland, I. *No War for Oil: US Dependency and the Middle East.* Oakland CA: Independent Institute, 2011.

Elm, M. *Oil, Power, and Principle: Iran's Oil Nationalization and Its Aftermath.* Syracuse NY: Syracuse University Press, 1994.

Ellwood, J. W. "Congress Cuts the Budget: The Omnibus Reconciliation Act of 1981." *Public Budgeting & Finance* 2, no. 1 (1982): 50–64.

Engler, R. *The Politics of Oil: A Study of Private Power and Democratic Directions.* Chicago: University of Chicago Press, 1967.

Ensign, R. L. "Banks Start Announcing Earnings on Wednesday, and a Big Focus Will Be on Little-Known but Massive Unfunded Loans." *Wall Street Journal*, April 12, 2016. https://www.wsj.com/articles/banks-face-massive-new-headache-on-oil-loans-1460453401.

Etzioni, A. "COIN: A Study of Strategic Illusion." *Small Wars & Insurgencies* 26, no. 3 (2015): 345–76.

——— . *How Patriotic Is the Patriot Act? Freedom versus Security in the Age of Terrorism.* New York: Routledge, 2005.

Evans, R., and R. D. Novak. *The Reagan Revolution*. New York: Dutton Adult, 1981.

Falk, R. "The New Bush Doctrine." *The Nation*, June 27, 2002. https://www.thenation.com/article/new-bush-doctrine/.

Faraj, M. A. S. "Jihad, the Absent Obligation." In *Voices of Terror: Manifestos, Writings, and Manuals of Al Qaeda, Hamas, and Other Terrorists from around the World and throughout the Ages*, edited by Walter Laqueur, 401–3. New York: Reed Press, 2004.

Farmanfarmaian, R. *Blood and Oil: Memoirs of a Persian Prince*. New York: Random House, 1997.

Farr, T. F. "Diplomacy in an Age of Faith: Religious Freedom and National Security." *Foreign Affairs* 87, no. 2 (March/April 2008): 110–24. https://www.foreignaffairs.com/articles/2008-03-02/diplomacy-age-faith.

Farrar, M. "Islamism and Terror: A Western Way of Doing Politics." In *Islam in the West: Key Issues in Multiculturalism*, edited by Max Farrar, Simon Robinson, Yasmin Valli, and Paul Wetherly, 216–38. New York: Palgrave Macmillan UK, 2012.

Fawcett, L. *International Relations of the Middle East*. 4th ed. New York: Oxford University Press, 2016.

Feith, D. J. *War and Decision: Inside the Pentagon at the Dawn of the War on Terrorism*. New York: Harper, 2008.

Feldman, N. *The Fall and Rise of the Islamic State*. Princeton NJ: Princeton University Press, 2008.

Feldstein, M. S. "Supply Side Economics: Old Truths and New Claims." *American Economic Review* 76, no. 2 (May 1986): 26–30.

Ferguson, E. "Tertullian." *Expository Times* 120, no. 7 (2009): 313–21.

Ferrero, M. "Radicalization as a Reaction to Failure: An Economic Model of Islamic Extremism." *Public Choice* 122, no. 1–2 (2005): 199–220.

Finkelstein, L. S. "The Rule of Law, the United States, and the United Nations: An Ambiguous Record." *American Foreign Policy Interests* 28, no. 4 (2006): 297–303.

Firestone, R. *Jihad: The Origin of Holy War in Islam*. New York: Oxford University Press, 1999.

Firro, T. K. "The Political Context of Early Wahhabi Discourse of Takfir." *Middle Eastern Studies* 49, no. 5 (2013): 770–89.

Fisher, I. "I Discovered the Phillips Curve: 'A Statistical Relation between Unemployment and Price Changes.'" *Journal of Political Economy* 81, no. 2, part 1 (1973): 496–502.

Fishman, B. "After Zarqawi: The Dilemmas and Future of al Qaeda in Iraq." *Washington Quarterly* 29, no. 4 (2006): 19–32.

Fitzgerald, P. "The Invasion of Kuwait." The Finer Times. 2008. http://www.thefinertimes.com/War-in-The-Middle-East/the-invasion-of-kuwait.html.

Flanagan, J. G. "Hierarchy in Simple 'Egalitarian' Societies." *Annual Review of Anthropology* 18, no. 1 (1989): 245–66.

Fleckenstein, W. A., and F. Sheehan. *Greenspan's Bubbles: The Age of Ignorance at the Federal Reserve*. New York: McGraw-Hill, 2008.

Folly, M. H. "The Soviet-German War 1942." In *The Palgrave Concise Historical Atlas of the Second World War*, 41–42. London: Palgrave Macmillan UK, 2004.

Foucault, M. *The History of Sexuality*. Vol. 1, *An Introduction*. Translated by Robert Hurley. New York: Vintage, 1990.

Forsythe, R. *The Politics of Oil in the Caucasus and Central Asia*. Oxford: Oxford University Press, 1996.

Freeman, M. "Democracy, Al Qaeda, and the Causes of Terrorism: A Strategic Analysis of U.S. Policy." *Studies in Conflict & Terrorism* 31, no. 1 (2008): 40–59.

Frieden, J. A., and D. A. Lake. *International Political Economy: Perspectives on Global Power and Wealth*. 4th ed. Boston: Bedford/St. Martin's, 2000.

Friedman, M. *Capitalism and Freedom*. Chicago: University of Chicago Press, 2009.

———. "Monetarism in Rhetoric and in Practice." *Bank of Japan Monetary and Economic Studies* 1, no. 2 (1983): 1–14.

———. "The Role of Monetary Policy." *American Economic Review* 58, no. 1 (1968): 1–17.

Friedman, M., and A. J. Schwartz. *A Monetary History of the United States, 1867–1960*. Princeton NJ: Princeton University Press, 2008.

Fromkin, D. "The Strategy of Terrorism." *Foreign Affairs* 53, no. 4 (July 1975): 683–98. https://www.foreignaffairs.com/articles/1975-07-01/strategy-terrorism.

Frum, D., and R. N. Perle. *An End to Evil: How to Win the War on Terror*. New York: Random House Digital, 2004.

Fukuyama, F. "Their Target: The Modern World." *Newsweek*, December 17, 2001, 14–24.

Fung, H. "Becoming a Moral Child: The Socialization of Shame among Young Chinese Children." *Ethos* 27, no. 2 (1999): 180–209.

Furnish, T. R. "Beheading in the Name of Islam." *Middle East Quarterly* 12, no. 2 (2005): 51–57.

———. "Bin Ladin: The Man Who Would Be Mahdi. *Middle East Quarterly* 9, no. 2 (2002): 53–59.

Gaddis, J. L. "Grand Strategy in the Second Term." *Foreign Affairs* 84, no. 1 (January/February 2005): 2–15. https://www.foreignaffairs.com/articles/2005-01-01/grand-strategy-second-term.

Gaddis, M. *There Is No Crime for Those Who Have Christ: Religious Violence in the Christian Roman Empire*. Berkeley: University of California Press, 2005.

Gambhir, H. K. "Dabiq: The Strategic Messaging of the Islamic State." Institute for the Study of War. August 15, 2014. http://www.understandingwar.org/sites/default/files/Dabiq%20Backgrounder_Harleen%20Final.pdf.

Gasiorowski, M. J. "The 1953 Coup d'État in Iran." *International Journal of Middle East Studies* 19, no. 3 (1987): 261–86.

Geaves, R. *Aspects of Islam*. Washington DC: Georgetown University Press, 2005.

Geisst, C. R. *Exchange Rate Chaos: 25 Years of Finance and Consumer Democracy.* New York: Routledge, 2002.

Gelfand, D. E. *Syria.* Minneapolis: ABDO, 2013.

Gelvin, J. L. "Nationalism, Anarchism, Reform: Political Islam from the Inside Out." *Middle East Policy* 17, no. 3 (2010): 118–33.

Gerges, F. A. *The Far Enemy: Why Jihad Went Global.* New York: Cambridge University Press, 2005.

Gibbs, J. P. "Norms: The Problem of Definition and Classification." *American Journal of Sociology* 70, no. 5 (1965): 586–94.

Gilles, K. *Jihad: The Trail of Political Islam.* London: IB Tauris, 2002.

Gilpin, R. *The Political Economy of International Relations.* Princeton NJ: Princeton University Press, 2016.

Gingrich, N., R. K. Armey, E. Gillespie, and B. Schellhas, eds. *Contract with America: The Bold Plan by Rep. Newt Gingrich, Rep. Dick Armey and the House Republicans to Change the Nation.* New York: Times Books, 1994.

Global Slavery Index. "45.8 Million People Are Enslaved in the World Today." 2016. https://www.globalslaveryindex.org/.

Gökay, B. "The Battle for Baku (May–September 1918): A Peculiar Episode in the History of the Caucasus." *Middle Eastern Studies* 34, no. 1 (1998): 30–50.

——— . *The Politics of Caspian Oil.* New York: Macmillan, 2001.

Goldberg, J. "The Obama Doctrine." *The Atlantic,* April 2016, 50–80.

Greenspan, A. "The Fed Didn't Cause the Housing Bubble." *Wall Street Journal,* March 11, 2009.

Guillaume, A. *The Life of Muhammad.* New York: Oxford University Press, 1955.

Gunter, M. M. "Iraq, Syria, ISIS and the Kurds: Geostrategic Concerns for the US and Turkey." *Middle East Policy* 22, no. 1 (2015): 102–11.

Haddad, Y. "Sayyid Qutb: Ideologue of Islamic Revival." In *Voices of Resurgent Islam,* edited by John L. Esposito, 20–30. New York: Oxford University Press, 1983.

Hall, R. C. *Balkan Wars, 1912–1913.* Oxford: Blackwell, 2000.

Halm, H. *Shiʿa Islam: From Religion to Revolution.* Translated from German by Allison Brown. Princeton NJ: Markus Wiener, 1997.

Hambling, D. "Send in the Drones?" *New Scientist* 230, no. 3069 (2016): 18–19.

Hamilton, J. D. "Historical Oil Shocks." NBER Working Paper no. 16790. National Bureau of Economic Research, Cambridge MA, February 2011. https://doi.org/10.3386/w16790.

Hartung, W. D. "The Military-Industrial Complex Revisited: Shifting Patterns of Military Contracting in the Post-9/11 Period." Costs of War, Watson Institute for International and Public Affairs. 2012. http://watson.brown.edu/costsofwar/files/cow/imce/papers/2011/The%20Military-Industrial%20Complex%20Revisited.pdf.

Harvey, D. *A Brief History of Neoliberalism.* New York: Oxford University Press, 2007.

Hasegawa, T. *Racing the Enemy: Stalin, Truman and the Surrender of Japan.* Cambridge MA: Harvard University Press, 2006.

Haskins, R. *Work over Welfare: The Inside Story of the 1996 Welfare Reform Law.* Washington DC: Brookings Institution Press, 2007.

Haynes, J. "Conflict, Conflict Resolution and Peace-Building: The Role of Religion in Mozambique, Nigeria and Cambodia." *Commonwealth & Comparative Politics*, 47, no.1, (2009): 52–75.

———. *Religion and Development.* New York: Palgrave Macmillan, 2007.

———. "Religion and International Relations after '9/11.'" *Democratization* 12, no. 3 (2005): 398–413.

———. "Religious Fundamentalism and Politics." In *Major World Religions: From their Origins to the Present,* edited by L. Ridgeon, 324–75. London: RoutledgeCurzon, 2003.

Heck, G. W. *Charlemagne, Muhammad, and the Arab Roots of Capitalism.* New York: Walter de Gruyter, 2006.

Hegghammer, T. "The Rise of Muslim Foreign Fighters: Islam and the Globalization of Jihad." *International Security* 35, no. 3 (2010): 53–94.

Heintz, M. "St. Augustine's Dilemma: Grace and Eternal Law in the Major Works of Augustine of Hippo." *Journal of Early Christian Studies* 6, no. 2 (1998): 324–25.

Hemming, R., and J. A. Kay. "The Laffer Curve." *Fiscal Studies* 1, no. 2 (March 1980): 83–90. https://doi.org/10.1111/j.1475-5890.1980.tb00554.x.

Hendrickson, D.C., and R. W. Tucker. "A Test of Power: U.S. Policy and Iran." *National Interest* 85 (September/October 2006): 49–56.

Henzel, C. "The Origins of al Qaeda's Ideology: Implications for U.S. Strategy." *Parameters: The U.S. Army War College Quarterly* (Spring 2005): 69–80. http://ssi.armywarcollege.edu/pubs/parameters/articles/05spring/henzel.htm.

Hershey, R. D., Jr. "President Abolishes Last Price Controls on U.S.-Produced Oil." *New York Times,* January 29, 1981. http://www.nytimes.com/1981/01/29/us/president-abolishes-last-price-controls-on-us-produced-oil.html.

Hill, J. N. C. *Sufism in Northern Nigeria: Force for Counter-Radicalization?* Carlisle PA: Strategic Studies Institute, U.S. War College, 2010. https://ssi.armywarcollege.edu/pubs/display.cfm?pubID=989.

Holt, P. M., A. K. S. Lambton, and B. Lewis. *The Central Islamic Lands from Pre-Islamic Times to the First World War.* Vol. 1A of *The Cambridge History of Islam.* Cambridge: Cambridge University Press, 1977.

Huntington, S. P. "The Lonely Superpower." *Foreign Affairs* 78, no. 2 (March/April 1999): 35–49. https://www.foreignaffairs.com/articles/united-states/1999-03-01/lonely-superpower.

Hussain, N. "The 'Islamic State' and Its Implications for the World Peace." *Journal of Political Studies* 23, no. 1 (Summer 2016): 1–16.

Ikenberry, G. J. "America's Imperial Ambition." *Foreign Affairs* 81, no. 5 (September/October 2002), 44–60. https://www.foreignaffairs.com/articles/united-states/2002-09-01/americas-imperial-ambition.

IntelCenter. "Islamic State's 43 Global Affiliates Interactive World Map." 2016. https://intelcenter.com/maps/is-affiliates-map.html#gs.0_ICd6M.

International Energy Agency. *World Energy Outlook: Assessing Today's Supplies to Fuel Tomorrow's Growth; 2001 Insights*. https://www.iea.org/media /weowebsite/2008-1994/weo2001.pdf.

Investigative Project on Terrorism. "The Muslim Brotherhood." May 25, 2005. http://www.discoverthenetworks.org/Articles/Muslim%20Brotherhood.pdf.

Irwin, D. A. "The Nixon Shock after Forty Years: The Import Surcharge Revisited." *World Trade Review* 12, no. 1 (January 2013), 29–56. https://doi.org /10.1017/S1474745612000444.

Isard, P. "How Far Can We Push the Law of One Price?" *American Economic Review* 67, no. 5 (December 1977): 942–48.

Isikoff, M., and D. Corn. *Hubris: The Inside Story of Spin, Scandal, and the Selling of the Iraq War*. New York: Broadway Books. 2006.

Islam-Husain, M. "Mahjabeen's Musings: A Muslim-American Traveler along the American Way; In Islam, Jihad and Terrorism Are Opposites." *Washington Report on Middle East Affairs* 12, no. 7 (November 1998): 117–20.

Jackson, R. "Constructing Enemies: 'Islamic Terrorism' in Political and Academic Discourse." *Government and Opposition* 42, no. 3 (Summer 2007): 394–426. https://doi.org/ 10.1111/j.1477-7053.2007.00229.x.

———. "Security, Democracy, and the Rhetoric of Counter-Terrorism." *Democracy and Security* 1, no. 2 (2005): 147–71. https://doi.org/10.1080 /17419160500322517.

Jackson, S. A. "Ibn Taymiyyah on Trial in Damascus." *Journal of Semitic Studies* 39, no. 1 (Spring 1994): 41–85. https://doi.org/10.1093/jss/XXXIX.1.41.

Ja'fari, S. H. M. *The Origins and Early Development of Shia Islam*. Oxford: Oxford University Press, 2000.

Jansen, J. J. G. "Ibn Taymiyyah and the Thirteenth Century: A Formative Period of Modern Muslim Radicalism." *Quaderni di Studi Arabi* 5–6 (1987): 391–96.

Johnson, C. "America's Empire of Bases." Global Policy Forum, January 2004. https://www.globalpolicy.org/component/content/article/153/26119.html.

———. "Transcript: President Bush, Part 2." CBS News. September 6, 2004. https://www.cbsnews.com/news/transcript-president-bush-part-2/.

Johnson, R. H. "Reconsiderations: Periods of Peril; The Window of Vulnerability and Other Myths." *Foreign Affairs* 61, no. 4 (Spring 1983): 950–70. https:// www.foreignaffairs.com/articles/united-states/1983-03-01/reconsiderations -periods-peril-window-vulnerability-and-other.

Johnson, S. "The Quiet Coup." *The Atlantic*, May 2009. https://www.theatlantic .com/magazine/archive/2009/05/the-quiet-coup/307364/.

Jones, G. "Persian Oil 1900–14." In *The State and the Emergence of the British Oil Industry*, 128–59. London: Palgrave Macmillan UK, 1981.

Jones, G. G. "The British Government and the Oil Companies 1912–1924: The Search for an Oil Policy." *Historical Journal* 20, no. 3 (September 1977): 647–72. https://doi.org/10.1017/S0018246X00011286.

Juergensmeyer, M. *Global Rebellion: Religious Challenges to the Secular State, from Christian Militias to al Qaeda.* Comparative Studies in Religion and Society 16. Berkeley: University of California Press. 2008.

——. *Terror in the Mind of God: The Global Rise of Religious Violence.* Comparative Studies in Religion and Society 13. Berkeley: University of California Press. 2003.

Kadercan, B. "Making Sense of the Islamic State: Four Frameworks." War on the Rocks. December 31, 2015. http://warontherocks.com/2015/12/making-sense-of-the-islamic-state-four-frameworks/.

Kagan, R. "Power and Weakness." *Policy Review* 113, no. 3 (June/July 2002): 3–28.

Kalu, O., O. Nnaemeka, C. J. Korieh, and G. U. Nwokeji. *Religion, History, and Politics in Nigeria: Essays in Honor of Ogbu U. Kalu.* Lanham MD: University Press of America, 2005.

Kaplan, F. *The Insurgents: David Petraeus and the Plot to Change the American Way of War.* New York: Simon & Schuster. 2014.

Kapteijns, L. "Test-Firing the 'New World Order' in Somalia: The US/UN Military Humanitarian Intervention of 1992–1995." *Journal of Genocide Research* 15, no. 4 (2013): 421–42. https://doi.org/10.1080/14623528.2013.856085.

Karabell, Z. "The Wrong Threat: The United States and Islamic Fundamentalism." *World Policy Journal* 12, no. 2 (Summer 1995): 37–48.

Kean, T. *The 9/11 Commission Report: Final Report of the National Commission on Terrorist Attacks upon the United States.* Washington DC: Government Printing Office, 2011. https://govinfo.library.unt.edu/911/report/911Report.pdf.

Kemp, T. "Donald Trump Gets Tough on China by Borrowing a Little from Beijing's Playbook." CNBC. December 6, 2016. https://www.cnbc.com/2016/12/06/donald-trump-gets-tough-on-china-by-borrowing-from-beijings-playbook.html.

Kennedy, R. "Is One Person's Terrorist Another's Freedom Fighter? Western and Islamic Approaches to 'Just War' Compared." *Terrorism and Political Violence* 11, no. 1 (1999): 1–21. https://doi.org/10.1080/09546559908427493.

Kent, M. *Oil and Empire: British Policy and Mesopotamian Oil, 1900–1920.* London: Macmillan. 1976.

Kepel, G. *Jihad: The Trail of Political Islam.* London: IB Tauris. 2006.

——. *The War for Muslim Minds: Islam and the West.* Translated by Pascale Ghazaleh. Cambridge MA: Belknap Press of Harvard University Press, 2004.

Keynes, J. M. "The Balance of Payments of the United States." *Economic Journal* 56, no. 222 (June 1946): 172–87.

Kilcullen, D. *The Accidental Guerrilla: Fighting Small Wars in the Midst of a Big One.* New York: Oxford University Press, 2011.

King, C. "Sweden's Rape Crisis: Is Migration to Blame?" *Caltimes*, February 23, 2017. https://www.caltimes.org/3159/showcase/swedens-rape-crisis-is-migration-to-blame/.

King, R. J. "Big, Easy Money: Disaster Profiteering on the American Gulf Coast." Corpwatch. August 17, 2006. http://www.corpwatch.org/article.php?id=14023.

Kirk, G. E. *A Short History of the Middle East: From the Rise of Islam to Modern Times*. New York: Routledge. 2016.

Kissinger, H. *Diplomacy*. New York: Simon & Schuster, 1994.

Klein, N. "Downsizing in Disguise." *The Nation*, June 5, 2003. https://www.thenation.com/article/downsizing-disguise/.

Kliff, S. "Trump Is Slashing Obamacare's Advertising Budget by 90%." Vox. August 31, 2017. https://www.vox.com/2017/8/31/16236280/trump-obamacare-outreach-ads.

Knowles, M. "Laffer Curve Revisited." *Yale Economic Review* 6, no. 1 (2010): 8.

Krämer, G. *Hasan al-Banna*. New York: Oneworld, 2014.

Krauthammer, C. "The New Unilateralism." *Washington Post*, June 8, 2001, A29. https://www.washingtonpost.com/archive/opinions/2001/06/08/the-new-unilateralism/20dcb60e-e8af-4a87-837c-e4cf85e96756/?utm_term=.81a6d5a81e80.

———. "The Unipolar Moment." *Foreign Affairs* 70, no. 1:22–33.

Kristol, W., R. Allen, and G. Bauer. Letter to President Bush on the War on Terrorism. *Project for the New American Century*, September 20, 2001. http://www.agriculturedefensecoalition.org/sites/default/files/file/constitution_1/1Z_2008_PNAC_Project_for_the_New_American_Century_2008_Wikipedia.pdf.

Kuang, X., and J. Bonk. "Preemptive War and a World out of Control." *Positions: East Asia Cultures Critique* 13, no. 1 (2005): 157–67.

Kudelin, A. A., V. A. Matrosov, and A. V. Chuprygin. "Practices of Islamic State (ISIS) in the Context of Islamic Eschatology." *RUDN Journal of World History* 3 (2016): 19–31.

Kulwicki, A. D. "The Practice of Honor Crimes: A Glimpse of Domestic Violence in the Arab World." *Issues in Mental Health Nursing* 23, no. 1 (2002): 77–87.

Laffer, A. B. "The Laffer Curve: Past, Present, and Future." *Heritage Foundation Backgrounder* 1765 (2004): 1176–96.

———. "Supply-Side Economics." *Financial Analysts Journal* 37, no. 5 (1981): 29–43.

Lambert, N. A. *Sir John Fisher's Naval Revolution*. Columbia: University of South Carolina Press, 2002.

Lane, E. W. *An Arabic-English Lexicon*. 8 vols. London: Williams & Norgate, 1863.

Lappin, Y. *Virtual Caliphate: Exposing the Islamist State on the Internet*. Dulles VA: Potomac Books, 2010.

Lasswell, H. D. *Politics: Who Gets What, When, How*. Cleveland: Meridian Books, 1936.

Leffler, M. P. "Response." *Diplomatic History* 29, no. 3 (2005): 441–44.

Leiken, R. S., and S. Brooke. "The Moderate Muslim Brotherhood." *Foreign Affairs* 8, no. 2 (March/April 2007): 107–21. https://www.foreignaffairs.com/articles /2007-03-01/moderate-muslim-brotherhood.

Lenin, V. I. *Imperialism: The State and Revolution*. New York: Vanguard Press. 1927.

Lewis, B. "Time for Toppling." *Wall Street Journal*, September 27, 2002, A 14.

———. "Why Turkey Is the Only Muslim Democracy." *Middle East Quarterly* 1, no. 1 (March 1994): 41–49.

Lickona, T. *Educating for Character: How Our Schools Can Teach Respect and Responsibility*. New York: Bantam, 2009.

Liddell Hart, B. H. *Strategy: The Indirect Approach*. 4th ed. London: Faber, 1967.

Liem, R. "Shame and Guilt among First- and Second-Generation Asian Americans and European Americans." *Journal of Cross-Cultural Psychology* 28, no. 4 (1997): 365–92.

Lind, M. "Beyond American Hegemony." *National Interest*, May/June 2007. http:// nationalinterest.org/article/beyond-american-hegemony-1558.

Liu, C. K. "Current U.S.-China Relations." *Asia Times Online*, June 2006. http:// www.henryckliu.com/page77.html.

Lobe, J. "US and the Triumph of Unilateralism." *Asia Times Online*, September 2002. http://www.atimes.com/atimes/Middle_East/DI10Ak03.html.

Lombardo, C. "How Many People Die from Malnutrition Each Year." VisionLaunch. April 3, 2017. http://visionlaunch.com/many-people-die-malnutrition-year/.

Longhurst, H. *Adventure in Oil: The Story of British Petroleum*. London: Sidgwick & Jackson, 1959.

Lowery, W. "Analysis: More Whites Killed by Police, but Blacks 2.5 Times More Likely To Be Killed." *Chicago Tribune*, July 11, 2016. http://www .chicagotribune.com/news/nationworld/ct-police-shootings-race-20160711 -story.html.

Lynch, C. "Volunteers Swell a Reviving Qaeda, UN Warns." *International Herald Tribune*, December 19, 2002, 3.

Lynch, M. "Explaining the Awakening: Engagement, Publicity, and the Transformation of Iraqi Sunni Political Attitudes." *Security Studies* 20, no. 1 (2011): 36–72.

MacIntyre, A. C., ed. *Hegel: A Collection of Critical Essays*. Notre Dame IN: University of Notre Dame Press, 1976.

Makari, V. E. *Ibn Taymiyyah's Ethics*. Vol. 34. Chico CA: Scholars Press, 1983.

Makinson, L. "Outsourcing the Pentagon: Who Benefits from the Politics and Economics of National Security?" Center for Public Integrity. September 29, 2004. https://www.publicintegrity.org/2004/09/29/6620/outsourcing -pentagon.

Marx, K. "Contribution to the Critique of Hegel's Philosophy of Right." *Deutsch-Französische Jahrbücher* 7 & 10 (1844). https://www.marxists.org/archive /marx/works/1843/critique-hpr/intro.htm.

———. "A Preface to Contribution to the Critique of Political Economy." In *Marx and Engels Selected Works*, 361–65. London: Lawrence & Wishart, 1859.

Marx, K. *Karl Marx, Friedrich Engels*. Berlin: Dietz Verlag, 1963.

Maududi, A. *Jihad in Islam*. Beirut: Holy Koran Publishing House, 1980.

Mayer, G. H. *The Republican Party, 1854–1964*. New York: Oxford University Press, 1964.

Mayer, J. "What Did the Vice-President Do for Halliburton?" *New Yorker*, February 2004. http://www.playtime.rlbunn.com/Politics_and_Policy/Content_Text /Dubya/HlpMeUnd/The%20New%20Yorker_%20HalliCheney.pdf.

McCants, W. *The ISIS Apocalypse: The History, Strategy, and Doomsday Vision of the Islamic State*. New York: St. Martin's Press, 2015.

——— . "Why Did ISIS Attack Paris?" *The Atlantic*, November 2015. https:// www.theatlantic.com/international/archive/2015/11/isis-paris-attack -why/416277/.

McCormack, D. "An African Vortex: Islamism in Sub-Saharan Africa." Center for Security Policy Occasional Papers Series 4, no. 4 (January 2005).

McGeary, J. "Odd Man Out." *Time*, September 10, 2001, 24–32.

McGregor, A. "Jihad and the Rifle Alone": 'Abdullah' Azzam and the Islamist Revolution. *Journal of Conflict Studies* 23, no. 2 (Fall 2003). https://journals .lib.unb.ca/index.php/jcs/article/view/219/377.

McMurray, J. S. *Distant Ties: Germany, the Ottoman Empire, and the Construction of the Baghdad Railway*. Westport CT: Greenwood, 2001.

Mearsheimer, J. J., and S. M. Walt. "Can Saddam Be Contained? History Says Yes." *Foreign Policy Bulletin* 14, no. 1 (Winter 2003): 219–24. https://doi.org /10.1017/S1052703600006109.

Menkhaus, K. "Panel 2: Somalia Case Study (al Shabaab)." *Foreign Policy Research Institute*. March 18, 2016. https://www.youtube.com/watch?v= A4jAHNA6k58.

Merritt, W. "The Use of War to Profit." *Justice Policy Journal* 9, no. 1 (Spring 2012): 1–30.

Metzl, J. F. Review of *Jihad vs. McWorld* by Benjamin Barber. *Harvard Journal of Law and Technology* 9, no. 2 (Winter 1996): 565–77.

Mieder, W. *"Yes We Can": Barack Obama's Proverbial Rhetoric*. New York: Peter Lang. 2009.

Milkis, S. M. *The President and the Parties: The Transformation of the American Party System since the New Deal*. New York: Oxford University Press, USA, 1993.

Mikesell, R. F. *The Bretton Woods Debates: A Memoir*. Essays in International Finance 192. Princeton NJ: International Finance Section, Department of Economics, Princeton University, 1994.

Miller, C. "Saudi Arabia: In al-Qaeda's Sights." *Council on Foreign Relations*, November 11. 2003.

Miller, G. "Under Obama, an Emerging Global Apparatus for Drone Killing." *Washington Post*, December 27, 2011.

Miller, J. "God Has Ninety-Nine Names: Reporting from a Militant Middle East." *Human Rights Quarterly* 18, no. 3 (August 1996): 703.

Miller, J., and L. Mylroie. *Saddam Hussein and the Crisis in the Gulf*. New York: Three Rivers Press. 1990.

Mingst, K. A., and M. P. Karns. *The United Nations in the 21st Century*. Boulder CO: Westview Press. 2011.

Mishkin, F. S. "Over the Cliff: From the Subprime to the Global Financial Crisis." *Journal of Economic Perspectives* 25, no. 1 (Winter 2011): 49–70.

Mishkin, F. S., R. J. Gordon, and S. H. Hymans. "What Depressed the Consumer? The Household Balance Sheet and the 1973–75 Recession." *Brookings Papers on Economic Activity*, no. 1 (1977): 123–74.

Moghadam, A., and B. Fishman, eds. *Fault Lines in Global Jihad: Organizational, Strategic, and Ideological Fissures*. New York: Routledge, 2011.

Møller, B. *The Somali Conflict: The Role of External Actors*. Copenhagen: DIIS Reports/Danish Institute for International Studies, 2009. https://www.econstor.eu/bitstream/10419/59871/1/592906116.pdf.

Morse, E. L., and A. M. Jaffe. *Strategic Energy Policy: Challenges for the 21st. Century*. Council on Foreign Relations and James A. Baker III Institute for Public Policy Rice University, April 12, 2001. https://www.cfr.org/report/strategic-energy-policy-challenges-21st-century.

Mosher, D., and S. Gould. "How Likely Are Foreign Terrorists to Kill Americans? The Odds May Surprise You." *Business Insider*, January 31, 2017. http://www.businessinsider.com/death-risk-statistics-terrorism-disease-accidents-2017-1.

Moussalli, A. S. "Hasan al-Bannā's Islamist Discourse on Constitutional Rule and Islamic State." *Journal of Islamic Studies* 4, no. 2 (July 1993): 161–74.

Müller, R. *Honor and Shame: Unlocking the Door*. Bloomington IN: Xlibris, 2000.

Mundell, R. A. "A Reconsideration of the Twentieth Century." *American Economic Review* 90, no. 3 (June 2000): 327–40.

Murdico, S. J. *The Gulf War*. New York: Rosen, 2003.

Murphy, J. J. *Rhetoric in the Middle Ages: A History of Rhetorical Theory from Saint Augustine to the Renaissance*. Berkeley: University of California Press, 1974.

Mussa, M. L., P. A. Volcker, and J. Tobin. "Monetary Policy." In *American Economic Policy in the 1980s*, edited and with an introduction by Martin Feldstein, 81–164. Chicago: University of Chicago Press, 1994.

Musallam, A. A. "Sayyid Qutb and Social Justice, 1945–1948." *Journal of Islamic Studies* 4, no. 1 (January 1993): 52–70.

Mwangi, O. G. "The Union of Islamic Courts and Security Governance in Somalia." *African Security Review* 19, no. 1 (2010): 88–94.

Mylroie, L. *Study of Revenge: The First World Trade Center Attack and Saddam Hussein's War Against America*. Washington DC: American Enterprise Institute. 2001.

NAACP. "Criminal Justice Fact Sheet." 2017. http://www.naacp.org/criminal-justice-fact-sheet/.

Nagourney, A. "In Tapes, Nixon Rails about Jews and Blacks." *New York Times*, December 10, 2010. http://www.nytimes.com/2010/12/11/us/politics/11nixon.html?_r=0.

Napoleoni, L. *Insurgent Iraq: Al Zarqawi and the New Generation*. New York: Seven Stories Press, 2011.

Nasr, S. "Mawdudi and the Jama'at-i Islami: The Origins, Theory and Practice of Islamic Revivalism." In *Pioneers of Islamic Revival*, edited by Ali Rahnema, 98–124. London: Zed Books, 2008.

National Energy Policy Development Group. *Reliable, Affordable, and Environmentally Sound Energy for America's Future: Report of the National Energy Policy Development Group*. Washington DC: Government Printing Office, 2001. https://www.wtrg.com/EnergyReport/National-Energy-Policy.pdf.

NationMaster. "Crime > Rape Rate: Countries Compared." 2017. http://www.nationmaster.com/country-info/stats/Crime/Rape-rate.

Newcombe, S. F., and J. P. S. Greig. "The Baghdad Railway." *Geographical Journal* 44, no. 6 (December 1914): 577–80.

Norman, J. R. N. *The Oil Card: Global Economic Warfare in the 21st Century*. Walterville OR: Trine Day, 2008.

Office of Management and Budget. *Budget of the U.S. Government: A New Foundation for American Greatness, Fiscal Year 2018*. 2017. https://www.whitehouse.gov/sites/whitehouse.gov/files/omb/budget/fy2018/budget.pdf.

Offner, A. A. "Rogue President, Rogue Nation: Bush and US National Security." *Diplomatic History* 29, no. 3 (June 2005): 433–35.

Olomojobi, Y. *Frontiers of Jihad: Radical Islam in Africa*. Ibadan: Safari Books, 2015.

Onslow, S. "'Battlelines for Suez': The Abadan Crisis of 1951 and the Formation of the Suez Group." *Contemporary British History* 17, no. 2 (2003): 1–28. https://doi.org/10.1080/13619460308565441.

Owen, J. M. "Democracy, Realistically." *National Interest* 83 (Spring 2006): 35–42.

Oxford Islamic Studies Online. "Rebellion," by Jeffrey T. Kenney. 2017. http://www.oxfordislamicstudies.com/article/opr/t342/e0025.

Pargeter, A. *The New Frontiers of Jihad: Radical Islam in Europe*. Philadelphia: University of Pennsylvania Press. 2008.

Parpia, A. S., M. L. Ndeffo-Mbah, N. S. Wenzel, and A. P. Galvani. "Effects of Response to 2014–2015 Ebola Outbreak on Deaths from Malaria, HIV/AIDS, and Tuberculosis, West Africa." *Emerging Infectious Diseases* 22, no. 3 (March 2016): 433–41.

Parsons, L. H. *The Birth of Modern Politics: Andrew Jackson, John Quincy Adams, and the Election of 1828*. New York: Oxford University Press. 2009.

Paul, P. V. "The Mythical Average in an Age of Individual Complexity." *American Annals of the Deaf* 162, no. 3 (Summer 2017): 239–42. https://doi.org/10.1353/aad.2017.0027.

Paul, R. "What Congress' Latest Billion-Dollar Boondoggle Means for America." *The Crux*. http://thecrux.com/ron-paul-what-congress-latest-billion-dollar-boondoggle-means-for-america/.

Payne, J. L. *Why Nations Arm*. New York: Blackwell. 1989.

Pelley, S. "George Tenet: At the Center of the Storm." *60 Minutes*. April 25, 2007. http://www.cbsnews.com/news/george-tenet-at-the-center-of-the -storm/3.

Pelling, H. *Winston Churchill.* New York: Springer. 1989.

Peristiany, J. G. *Honour and Shame: The Values of Mediterranean Society.* London: Weidenfeld & Nicolson, 1965.

Perle, R. "The U.S. Must Strike at Saddam Hussein." *New York Times,* December 28, 2001. http://www.nytimes.com/2001/12/28/opinion/the-us-must-strike -at-saddam-hussein.html.

Persinos, J. "3 Toxic Bank Stocks with Energy Sector Overexposure." *The Street,* March 19, 2016. https://www.thestreet.com/story/13493535/1/get-ready-for -bankmegeddon-3-toxic-bank-stocks-with-energy-sector-overexposure.html.

Phelps, E. S. "Phillips Curves, Expectations of Inflation and Optimal Unemployment over Time." *Economica* 34, no. 135 (August 1967): 254–81.

Phillips, K. *American Dynasty: Aristocracy, Fortune, and the Politics of Deceit in the House of Bush.* New York: Penguin. 2004.

Pianin, E. "Obama Administration Spent Billions on Image Advertising." *Fiscal Times,* October 9, 2015. http://www.thefiscaltimes.com/2015/10/09/Obama -Administration-Spent-Billions-Image-Advertising.

Picard, E. "Arab Military in Politics: From Revolutionary Plot to Authoritarian State." In *The Arab State,* edited by Giacomo Luciani, 189–219. Berkeley: University of California Press, 1990.

Pipes, D. "There Is No Moderate Islam—Only a Figment of Imagination and Pipe Dream!!!" September 8, 2010. http://www.danielpipes.org/comments /177892.

Posen, B. R. "Command of the Commons: The Military Foundation of U.S. Hegemony." *International Security* 28, no. 1 (2003): 5–46. http://www .mitpressjournals.org/doi/pdf/10.1162/016228803322427965.

———. "The Struggle against Terrorism: Grand Strategy, Strategy, and Tactics." *International Security* 26, no. 3 (Winter 2001/02): 39–55. https://www .belfercenter.org/publication/struggle-against-terrorism-grand-strategy -strategy-and-tactics.

Powaski, R. E. *The Cold War: The United States and the Soviet Union, 1917–1991.* New York: Oxford University Press. 1997.

Powell, C. L. "Remarks to the United Nations Security Council." U.S. Department of State, February 5. 2003. https://2001-2009.state.gov/secretary/former /powell/remarks/2003/17300.htm.

Preston, C. T., Jr. "Reagan's 'New Beginning': Is It the 'New Deal' of the Eighties?" *Southern Journal of Communication* 49, no. 2 (1984): 198–211. https://doi .org/10.1080/10417948409372600.

Purdum, T. S. *A Time of Our Choosing: America's War in Iraq.* New York: Times Books. 2003.

Quiggin, T. "Understanding al-Qaeda's Ideology for Counter-Narrative Work." *Perspectives on Terrorism* 3, no. 2 (2009). http://www.terrorismanalysts.com/pt/index.php/pot/article/view/67.

Qutb, S. *In the Shadow of the Qur'an.* 10th ed. Beirut: Dar al-Shuruq, 1982.

——. *Islam: The Misunderstood Religion.* Kuwait: Al. Darul Bayan Bookshop, 1964.

——. *Ma'alim fi-l-Tariq* [Milestones]. Cairo: Dar al-Shuruq, 1964.

——. *Social Justice in Islam.* Oneonta NY: American Council of Learned Societies, 1953.

Rahman, F. "Islam and the Constitutional Problem of Pakistan." *Studia Islamica* 32, no. 4 (1970): 275–87.

Raphaeli, N. "Ayman Muhammad Rabi'Al-Zawahiri: The Making of an Arch-Terrorist." *Terrorism and Political Violence* 14, no. 4 (2002), 1–22. https://doi.org/10.1080/714005636.

Rashid, A. *Descent into Chaos: How the War against Islamic Extremism Is Being Lost in Pakistan, Afghanistan and Central Asia.* London: Penguin UK, 2012.

——. *Jihad: The Rise of Militant Islam in Central Asia.* New York: Penguin. 2002.

Razwy, A. A. The Anglo-Iranian Oil Dispute. *Pakistan Horizon* 6, no. 2 (June 1953): 75–85.

Reagan, R., 1981. "First Inaugural Address of Ronald Reagan." January 20, 1980. http://avalon.law.yale.edu/20th_century/reagan1.asp.

Record, J. *Dark Victory: America's Second War against Iraq.* Annapolis MD: Naval Institute Press. 2004.

Reiter, D. "Exploring the Bargaining Model of War." *Perspectives on Politics* 1, no. 1 (March 2003): 27–43. https://doi.org/10.1017/S1537592703000033.

Renshon, S. A. "Assessing the Personality of George W. Bush." In *The Domestic Sources of American Foreign Policy: Insights and Evidence*, 5th ed., edited by Eugene R. Wittkopf and James M. McCormick, 385–98. Lanham MD: Rowman & Littlefield, 2008.

Rice, C. "Campaign 2000: Promoting the National Interest." *Foreign Affairs* 79, no. 1 (January/February 2000). https://www.foreignaffairs.com/articles/2000-01-01/campaign-2000-promoting-national-interest.

Ricks, T. E. *Fiasco: The American Military Adventure in Iraq.* New York: Penguin, 2006.

Risen, J. *State of War: The Secret History of the CIA and the Bush Administration.* New York: Simon & Schuster, 2008.

Roberts, J. M. "New Keynesian Economics and the Phillips Curve." *Journal of Money, Credit and Banking* 27, no. 4 (1995): 975–84.

Rockguitarnow. "White Women Grabbed by Muslims and Raped." January 13, 2016. https://www.youtube.com/watch?v=Sr64n_Ri3qg.

Rolo, P. J. V. *Entente Cordiale: The Origins and Negotiation of the Anglo-French Agreements of 8 April 1904.* New York: Macmillan, 1969.

Roosevelt, K. *Countercoup, the Struggle for the Control of Iran.* New York: McGraw-Hill, 1979.

Roy, O. *The Failure of Political Islam.* Cambridge MA: Harvard University Press. 1994.

———. *Globalized Islam: The Search for a New Ummah.* New York: Columbia University Press. 2004.

Ruthven, M. *Fundamentalism: The Search for Meaning.* Oxford: Oxford University Press. 2004.

Safavi, M. "Nationalisation of Oil Industry in Iran." *Pakistan Horizon* 4, no. 2 (June 1951): 93–101.

Sageman, M. *Leaderless Jihad: Terror Networks in the Twenty-First Century.* Philadelphia: University of Pennsylvania Press. 2011.

———. *Understanding Terror Networks.* Philadelphia: University of Pennsylvania Press. 2004.

Saikal, A. "Islam and the West: Where to from Here?" In *Beyond the Iraq War: The Promises, Pitfalls and Perils of External Interventionism,* edited by Michael Heazle and Iyanatul Islam, 111–19. Cheltenham UK: Edward Elgar, 2003.

Samatar, S. S. "An Open Letter to Uncle Sam: America, Pray Leave Somalia to Its Own Devices." *Journal of Contemporary African Studies* 28, no. 3 (2010): 313–23.

Sangvic, R. N. *Battle of Mogadishu: Anatomy of a Failure.* DTIC report. 1998. http://webcache.googleusercontent.com/search?q=cache:Y3-H12b3HfoJ: www.dtic.mil/get-tr-doc/pdf%3FAD%3DADA366316+&cd=1&hl=en&ct =clnk&gl=ae.

Santoni, G. J. "The Employment Act of 1946: Some History Notes." *Federal Reserve Bank of St. Louis Review* 68 (1986): 5–16.

Savranskaya, S., and V. Zubok. "Cold War in the Caucasus: Notes and Documents from a Conference." *Cold War International History Project (CWIHP) Bulletin* 14/15 (Winter 2003/Spring 2004): 399–451.

Schanzer, J. "Ansar al-Islam: Back in Iraq." *Middle East Quarterly* 11, no. 1 (Winter 2004): 41–50.

Schmid, A. P., ed. *The Routledge Handbook of Terrorism Research.* New York: Taylor & Francis, 2011.

Schmid, A. P., and A. J. Jongman. *Political Terrorism: A New Guide to Actors, Authors, Concepts, Data Bases, Theories, and Literature.* New York: Transaction, 1988.

Scully, S. "10 Dangerous Beaches of the World" (photos). The Weather Channel. June 30, 2015. https://weather.com/travel/news/most-dangerous-beaches.

Select Committee on Intelligence. *Current and Projected National Security Threats to the United States. Hearing before the Select Committee on Intelligence.* United States Senate, 109th Congress, Second Session, February 2. Washington DC: US Government Printing Office, 2006.

Selengut, C. *Sacred Fury: Understanding Religious Violence.* Lanham MD: Rowman & Littlefield, 2008.

Shah, A. "Landmines." *Global Issues,* November 27, 2009. http://www.globalissues .org/article/79/landmines.

Shah, D. "The Conundrums of Emerging Virtuous War." IndraStra Global. March 17, 2017. http://www.indrastra.com/2017/03/OPINION-Conundrums-of -Emerging-Virtuous-War-003-03-2017-0056.html.

Shinn, D. "Somalia's New Government and the Challenge of al Shabaab." *CTC Sentinel* 2, no. 3 (March 2009): 1–5. https://ctc.usma.edu/wp-content/uploads /2010/06/Vol2Iss3-Art1.pdf.

Simmons, M. R. *Twilight in the Desert: The Coming Saudi Oil Shock and the World Economy*. Hoboken NJ: John Wiley & Sons. 2006.

Simon, R. S., and E. H. Tejirian, eds. *The Creation of Iraq, 1914–1921*. New York: Columbia University Press, 2004.

Smith, A. "Donald Trump Mocks Hillary Clinton for Health Episode: 'She Can't Even Make It to Her Car.'" *Business Insider*, September 28. 2016. http:// www.businessinsider.com/donald-trump-hillary-clinton-health-2016-9.

Smith, L. "Timeline: Abu Musab al-Zarqawi." *The Guardian*, June 8. 2006. https:// www.theguardian.com/world/2006/jun/08/iraq.alqaida1.

Sorkin, A. "Donald Trump, a Failed Bully in His Debate with Clinton." *New Yorker*, September 27, 2016. http://www.newyorker.com/news/amy-davidson/donald -trump-a-failed-bully-in-his-debate-with-clinton.

Souleimanov, E. *An Endless War: The Russian-Chechen Conflict in Perspective*. Frankfurt am Main: Peter Lang. 2007.

Sowell, T. *Say's Law: An Historical Analysis*. Princeton NJ: Princeton University Press, 2015.

Stamp, L. D. "The Geology of the Oil Fields of Burma." *AAPG Bulletin* 11, no. 6 (June 1927): 557–79.

Steil, B. *The Battle of Bretton Woods: John Maynard Keynes, Harry Dexter White, and the Making of a New World Order*. Princeton NJ: Princeton University Press. 2013.

Stern, J. "Fearing Evil." *Social Research* 71, no. 4 (Winter 2004): 1111–26.

—— . "Pakistan's Jihad Culture." *Foreign Affairs* 79, no. 6 (November/December 2000): 115–26. https://www.foreignaffairs.com/articles/asia/2000-11 -01/pakistans-jihad-culture.

—— . *Terror in the Name of God: Why Religious Militants Kill*. New York: Ecco. 2003.

Stern, S. M. "'Abd Al-Jabbār's Account of How Christ's Religion Was Falsified by the Adoption of Roman Customs." *Journal of Theological Studies* 19 (1968): 128–85.

Stockman, Farah. "Obama, U.S. Viewed Less Favorably in Arab World." *Boston Globe*, July 13, 2011.

Stoff, M. B. *Oil, War, and American Security: The Search for a National Policy on Foreign Oil, 1941–1947*. New Haven CT: Yale University Press, 1980.

Stone, R., and S. J. Hunt. *The Bush Crime Family: The Inside Story of an American Dynasty*. New York: Skyhorse, 2017.

Stork, J. *Middle East Oil and the Energy Crisis*. New York: Monthly Review Press, 1975.

Strachan, M. "U.S. Economy Lost Nearly 700,000 Jobs because of NAFTA, EPI Says." Huffington Post. May 12, 2011. http://www.huffingtonpost.com/2011/05/12/nafta-job-loss-trade-deficit-epi_n_859983.html.

Swansbrough, R. *Test by Fire: The War Presidency of George W. Bush*. New York: Springer, 2008.

Tabb, W. K. "Mr. Bush and Neo-Liberalism." In *The Neo-Liberal Revolution: Forging the Market State*, edited by Richard Robison, 173–94. Basingstoke: Palgrave Macmillan UK, 2006.

Tarbell, I. M. *The History of the Standard Oil Company*. New York: Cosimo. 2009. First published 1904 by McClure, Phillips.

Taylor, A. R. *The Islamic Question in Middle East Politics*. Boulder CO: Westview Press, 1988.

Tenet, G., and B. Harlow. *At the Center of the Storm*. New York: HarperCollins. 2007.

10News. "Sweden's Islamic Rape Epidemic: Almost Half of Victims Are Children." July 8, 2017. https://www.10news.one/swedens-islamic-rape-epidemy-almost-half-of-victims-are-children/.

Teslik, L. H. "Profile: Abu Musab al-Zarqawi." Council on Foreign Relations. June 8, 2006.

Thayer, B. A. "In Defense of Primacy." *National Interest* 86 (November/December 2006): 32–37.

Thomas, C. G., and C. Conant. *The Trojan War*. Westport CT: Greenwood, 2005.

Thomas, R. G. C. "U.S. Regional Security Policy in South Asia." In *Strategy for Empire: U.S. Regional Security Policy in the Post-Cold War Era*, edited by Brian Loveman, 203–27. Lanham MD: Rowman & Littlefield, 2004.

Tomasi, J. *Free Market Fairness*. Princeton NJ: Princeton University Press, 2012.

Toprani, A. "Oil and Grand Strategy: Great Britain and Germany, 1918–1941." Belfeer Center for Science and International Affairs. December 6, 2012. https://www.belfercenter.org/publication/oil-and-grand-strategy-great-britain-and-germany-1918-1941.

Tripp, C. "Sayyid Qutb: The Political Vision." In *Pioneers of Islamic Revival*, edited by Ali Rahnema, 154–83. London: Zed Books. 2008.

Truman, H. "Radio Address to the American People after the Signing of the Terms of Unconditional Surrender by Japan." American Presidency Project. September 1, 1945. http://www.presidency.ucsb.edu/ws/index.php?pid=12366.

Trump, D. "Donald J. Trump Statement regarding Tragic Terrorist Attack in Orlando, Florida." Facebook, June 12, 2016. https://www.facebook.com/DonaldTrump/posts/10157160462435725.

Turner, T. "On Structure and Entropy: Theoretical Pastiche and the Contradictions of" Structuralism." *Current Anthropology* 31, no. 5 (December 1990): 563–68.

Tyler, P. E. "U.S. Strategy Plan Calls for Insuring No Rivals Develop a One-Superpower World." *New York Times*, March 8, 1992. http://www.nytimes.com/1992/03/08/world/us-strategy-plan-calls-for-insuring-no-rivals-develop.html?pagewanted=all.

Tzu, S. *The Art of War*. Translated by S. B. Griffith. New York: Oxford University Press, 1963.

U.S. Department of State. "Secretary's Meeting with Foreign Minister Chatchai of Thailand." Department of State. December 11, 1975. http://nsarchive2 .gwu.edu/NSAEBB/NSAEBB193/HAK-11-26-75.pdf.

U.S. Department of the Treasury. "Historical Debt Outstanding: Annual 1950– 1999." Treasury Direct. May 5, 2013. https://www.treasurydirect.gov/govt /reports/pd/histdebt/histdebt_histo4.htm.

Venhaus, J. M. "Why Youth Join al-Qaeda." United States Institute of Peace. May 4, 2010. https://www.usip.org/publications/2010/05/why-youth-join -al-qaeda.

Venkatraman, A. "Religious Basis for Islamic Terrorism: The *Quran* and Its Interpretations." *Studies in Conflict & Terrorism* 30, no. 3 (2007): 229–48.

Walsh, B. "In the War between Sharks and People, Humans Are Killing It." *Time*, December 3, 2013. http://science.time.com/2013/12/03/in-the-war-between -sharks-and-people-humans-are-killing-it/.

Waltz, K. *Theory of International Relations*. Reading MA: Addison-Webley, 1979.

Watkins, A. "Losing Territory and Lashing Out: The Islamic State and International Terror." *CTC Sentinel* 9, no. 3 (March 2016): 14–18. https://ctc .usma.edu/posts/losing-territory-and-lashing-out-the-islamic-state-and -international-terror.

Weinberg, G. L. *A World at Arms: A Global History of World War II*. New York: Cambridge University Press. 1995.

Weiss, M., and H. Hassan. *ISIS: Inside the Army of Terror*. New York: Simon & Schuster, 2015.

Weist, V. "Hinckley—Bush Family Friend—Nears Release." Rense.com. November 28, 2003. http://www.rense.com/general45/hink.htm.

White, W. A., M. Florez y Garcia, G. de Montebello, A. Blanc, G. Keun, and M. Saïd. "Convention Respecting the Free Navigation of the Suez Maritime Canal. Signed at Constantinople, October 29, 1888." *American Journal of International Law* 3, no. 2, supplement (April 1909): 123–27.

Wieland, C. *Syria—A Decade of Lost Chances: Repression and Revolution from Damascus Spring to Arab Spring*. Seattle: Cune Press, 2012.

Wijsen, F. "'There Are Radical Muslims and Normal Muslims': An Analysis of the Discourse on Islamic Extremism." *Religion* 43, no. 1 (2013): 70–88.

Wilhelmsen, J., and G. Flikke. "Evidence of Russia's Bush Doctrine in the CIS." *European Security* 14, no. 3 (2005): 387–417.

Williams, B. J. "VI. The Strategic Background to the Anglo-Russian Entente of August 1907." *Historical Journal* 9, no. 3 (1966): 360–73.

Witkopf, E. R., and C. M. Jones. *American Foreign Policy: Pattern and Process*. Belmont CA: Thomson Wadsworth. 2008.

Witte, J. *The Reformation of Rights: Law, Religion and Human Rights in Early Modern Calvinism*. New York: Cambridge University Press, 2007.

Wolfson, A. "Conservatives and Neoconservatives." *Public Interest* 33 (2004): 32–48.

Woodward, B. *Maestro: Greenspan's Fed and the American Boom.* New York: Simon & Schuster, 2001.

——— . *Plan of Attack.* New York: Simon & Schuster, 2004.

Wooley, L. "Bill Clinton and the Decline of the Military." *Human Events,* December 21, 2006. http://humanevents.com/2006/12/21/bill-clinton-and-the-decline-of-the-military/.

Woolley, J. T. *Monetary Politics: The Federal Reserve and the Politics of Monetary Policy.* New York: Cambridge University Press, 1985.

World Health Organization. "Violence against Women: Intimate Partner and Sexual Violence against Women." November 2017. http://www.who.int/mediacentre/factsheets/fs239/en/.

Worth, R. F. "Blast Destroys Shrine in Iraq, Setting off Sectarian Fury." *New York Times,* February 22, 2006.

Wright, E. M. "Iran as a Gateway to Russia." *Foreign Affairs* 20, no. 2 (January 1942): 367. https://www.foreignaffairs.com/articles/russian-federation/1942-01-01/iran-gateway-russia.

Wright, L. *The Looming Tower: Al-Qaeda's Road to 9/11.* London: Penguin, 2007.

Yetiv, S. A. *The Persian Gulf Crisis.* Westport CT: Greenwood, 1997.

Zabih, S. *The Mossadegh Era: Roots of the Iranian Revolution.* Chicago: Lakeview Press, 1982.

Zahrani, M. T. "The Coup That Changed the Middle East: Mossadeq v. the CIA in Retrospect." *World Policy Journal* 19, no. 2 (Summer 2002): 93–99.

Zakaria, F. "Beyond Bush: What the World Needs Is an Open, Confident America." *Newsweek,* June 11, 2007, 22–29.

——— . "The Rise of Illiberal Democracy." *Foreign Affairs* 76, no. 6 (November/December 1997): 22–43. https://www.foreignaffairs.com/articles/1997-11-01/rise-illiberal-democracy.

Zakariya, D. M. "The Concept of Islamic Education Curriculum: The Study of Tawhid in Al-Islam Pesantren Lamongan Indonesia." *Journal of Social Sciences and Humanities* 1, no. 2 (2015): 98–104.

Zawātī, Ḥ. *Is Jihād a Just War? War, Peace, and Human Rights under Islamic and Public International Law.* Studies in Religion and Society 53. Lewiston NY: Edwin Mellen Press, 2001.

INDEX

31901063805206